❀ KAMAKURA ❀

鎌倉

Rutland, Vermont & Tokyo, Japan

KAMAKURA
Fact & Legend

Iso Mutsu

With a Foreword by Lady Bouchier

CHARLES E. TUTTLE COMPANY

Cover. Statue of Buddha at Tokei-ji.
Photo by Fumio Sekiguchi.

Frontispiece. Incorporates "On the road to Enoshima."
Woodblock print by Hiroshige.

The symbols used on pages 8, 54, etc., are signatures
of Minamoto no Yoritomo.

*Published by the Charles E. Tuttle Company, Inc.
of Rutland, Vermont & Tokyo, Japan
with editorial offices at
2-6 Suido 1-chome, Bunkyo-ku, Tokyo 112*

First published by Tokyo News Service, Ltd., 1918
© 1995 by Charles E. Tuttle Publishing Co., Inc.

LCC Card No. 94-61007
ISBN 0-8048-1968-8

First Tuttle edition, 1995

Printed in Japan

❀ Contents ❀

Foreword *by* Lady Bouchier   11

Preface *by* Ian Mutsu   15

Historical Sketch   19

Kamakura:
  1 Egara Tenjin   43
  2 Sugimoto-dera   48
  3 Hōkoku-ji   55
  4 Jōmyō-ji   60
  5 Kōsoku-ji (Jūniso)   66
  6 Zuisen-ji   72
  7 Kamakura Shrine   78
  8 Kakuon-ji   82
  9 The Tomb of Yoritomo   91
 10 Tsurugaoka Hachiman Shrine   94
 11 Kenchō-ji   107
 12 Arai no Enmadō (Ennō-ji)   123

{ 5 }

CONTENTS

13 Tōkei-ji   127

14 Engaku-ji   131

15 Meigetsu-in   163

16 Jōchi-ji   168

17 The Fudo Temple and Lake of Imaizumi   169

18 Jufuku-ji   172

19 Eishō-ji   179

20 The Tomb of Tamesuke   181

21 Kuzuharagaoka Jinja   187

22 Kaizō-ji   190

23 The Daibutsu, Sasuke-Inari, and Zeni-arai Benten   203

24 Yugyō-ji (Fujisawa)   210

25 Amanawa Jinja   222

26 Kōsoku-ji   223

27 Hase Kannon   225

28 Gongorō Jinja   234

29 The Road to Enoshima   236

30 Gokuraku-ji   240

31 Inamuragasaki   247

32 Ryūkō-ji (Katase)   253

33 Nichiren Shōnin   258

34 Myōhon-ji   272

35 Hongaku-ji and Myōryū-ji   277

36 Hōkai-ji   279

37 Enmei-ji   281

38 Fudaraku-ji   283

39 Nichiren Temples (Ankokuron-ji, Myōhō-ji, and
    Chōshō-ji)   287

40 Kōmyō-ji   293

41	Jinmu-ji and Kanazawa	309
42	The Cave of Taya (Taya no Dōkutsu)	313
43	Enoshima	316
	Index	331

Area map of Kamakura

Macrons, signifying long vowels in romanized Japanese, have been re-tained only in the Table of Contents, chapter headings, and Japanese words within the text.

❈ List of Illustrations ❈

Asterisks indicate color plates.

Frontispiece. Incorporates "On the road to Enoshima." Woodblock
print by Hiroshige.

  1. Egara Tenjin   44

  2. Statue of Yoritomo, founder of Kamakura shogunate   93

  3. First *torii* leading to Tsurugaoka Hachiman Shrine   98

  4. Interior of Shariden at Engaku-ji   141

 *5. Enma at Enno-ji   145

 *6. "Samurai on horseback." Scroll, Kamakura period   146–47

 *7. *Mokugyo* block at Jufuku-ji   148

 *8. Shariden gate at Engaku-ji   148

 *9. Statue of Kannon at Hase-dera   149

*10. Temple bell at Engaku-ji   150

*11. Temple gate of Kencho-ji   151

*12. Statue of Nichiren at Ryuko-ji, Katase   152

*13. Approach to Jochi-ji   153

*14. View from the grounds of Komyo-ji temple near Yuiga-
hama   154–55

*15. Bamboo grove at Hokoku-ji   156

*16. Early spring in Tokei-ji   156

*17. Tsurugaoka Hachiman Shrine   157

*18. Sunset at Sagami Bay   158–59

*19. Statue of Buddha surrounded by autumn flowers   160

20. Wooden statue of Myoan Eisai (1141–1215)   173

21. Wooden statue of Jizo Bosatsu at Jufuku-ji   175

22. Giant wooden statue of one of the pair of Nio guardian deities at Jufuku-ji   176

23. Stone Buddha at Jokomyo-ji   185

*24. Daibutsu, the Great Buddha at Kotoku-in   193

*25. Enoshima island   194–95

*26. Tomb of Minamoto no Yoritomo   196

*27. Mutsu family grave at Jufuku-ji   196

*28. Nio, guardian deity at Sugimoto-dera   197

*29. Zen priests meditating at Engaku-ji   198

*30. Zen priests leaving Engaku-ji   199

*31. Snow on Jizo statues at Sugimoto-dera   200

32. Rear view of Daibutsu at Kotoku-in   207

33. Cave at Zeni-arai Benten   209

34. Nichiren Shonin Tsujiseppo-ato   260

❀ Foreword ❀

by Lady Bouchier
(Dorothy Britton)

I T GIVES me great joy that this, one of my favorite books, has at long last been reissued after having been out of print for nearly forty years. A generous grant from the prestigious Tokyo Club has made possible this new and revised edition, which has been brightened with new photographs—this time in color—carefully selected by the author's son Ian, a talented producer of many prize-winning cultural films on Japan.

My own beloved copy—the Second & Enlarged 1930 edition is worn from constant use, for it has been our family's vade mecum on the historic city of Kamakura for as long as I can remember. We lived in Yokohama, where I was born, and my father built a summer villa in Hayama, only a few miles from Kamakura, which my mother and I made our home on returning to Japan soon after World War II. Whenever there was time she and I would drive to Kamakura and visit temples and historic spots, clutching our *Kamakura: Fact and Legend* and letting the late Countess Mutsu be our enthralling guide.

And what a wonderful guide she continues to be, in spite of the inevitable changes that time has wrought, for her beautifully written book is the product of a lively, inquiring mind and is based on a foundation of deep scholarship.

She would spend hours with the abbots and high priests of the various temples and shrines, amassing information with which to "unseal for the Western world," as the *Japan Times* put it, "much of the secret of Kamakura's magnificent past." The newspaper, reporting her funeral of June 10, 1930, also recorded the unheard-of participation of a Buddhist priest at the Christian service in Kamakura's Methodist church when the vice abbot of the important Zen temple Engaku-ji, resplendent in gold and scarlet brocade, ascended the pulpit to deliver a special eulogy and chant a sutra for the solace of the departed soul.

I was too young, alas, to remember her, but my mother spoke often of the delightful teas she and mutual friend Maya Lindley Poole enjoyed with the lovely Countess Iso Mutsu in Kamakura in the twenties, talking about their shared interest in music and the colorful history of the ancient city they loved to explore.

Young Hirokichi Mutsu, born in 1869, followed in the footsteps of his famous parent Munemitsu, the "father of Japanese diplomacy." While preparing for his diplomatic career and studying law at Cambridge in 1888, Hirokichi fell in love with the beautiful and talented Gertrude Ethel Passingham. It was seventeen long years, however, before they were able to marry, following which they spent four years at the Japanese Embassy in London where, as First Secretary and then Counselor, Count Mutsu, who had by then succeeded to the title, helped to organize the highly successful Japan-British Exhibition that ran for six months at London's White City.

The Count retired after their return from London to spend the rest of his life administering a foundation he had created, aimed at social improvements mainly in education and the position of women, while the Countess set about delving into the history of the twelfth-century shogunal capital, Kamakura, where they decided to live, and devoted her considerable literary ability to writing this definitive in-depth work.

They settled near the sea with its peerless view of Mount Fuji across Sagami Bay, particularly lovely in dark relief as the sun goes down, leaving the sea aflame in roseate gold. When she became a Japanese subject on her marriage, Ethel took the name Isoko, "Beach Child," suggested by her husband because she so loved the seashore. She was bathing there when the Great Kanto Earthquake of 1923 struck, and a vivid description is included in the 1930 edition of this book. Seven years later, "How beautiful! The sunset!" were the last whispered words of this lady who so loved the history and the beauty of Kamakura. Much of that beauty still remains. And what is sadly gone lives on in the pages of this remarkable book.

Hayama, August 1994

We should never write save that which we love. Forgetfulness and silence are the penalties we should inflict upon all that we find ugly or commonplace in our journey through life.

—ERNEST RENAN

❀ Preface ❀

ISO MUTSU, an Englishwoman long married to a Japanese diplomat and philanthropist, lay dying. My father sat at her bedside in our home in Kamakura. Her last words softly spoken to him were: "How beautiful! The sunset." Soon afterward she lapsed into final sleep.

My father observed that from her reclining position in bed, with her back to the wall and facing an eastern window, it had been impossible for her to admire the sunset—as she had been wont to do—except in her own mind's eye.

At the time I was in England. Years later, in Japan, I heard my father recount the episode. He thought the last self-created vision most fitting for one who all her life had been deeply devoted to the beauties of Kamakura. One of the sights she loved most was that of the sun setting beyond the bay, in a symphony of changing colors, into the low, pale-blue ridges of the Izu mountains outlined far away in the West.

Kamakura: Fact and Legend is a product of the attachment this Englishwoman, an intense lover of poetry, painting, and music, had for an old Japanese seaside town, where she preferred to live more than in any other place.

During my boyhood days spent in Kamakura, I was frequently a rather bored companion of my mother on her numerous trips to the city's temples and shrines. She would visit them over and over again for the gentle pleasure they gave her and to gather material for her forthcoming book. I was then far too young to share in the quiet enjoyment. Yet I can remember vividly several minor incidents: my mother stopping for several minutes on a winding path, halted by the music of the wind in a thicket of bamboo trees; her pauses on the stone steps of a temple to listen to a group of Buddhist priests chanting a sutra to the accompaniment of poundings on their drum. Often she would tell me stories about the strange legends and exciting events of the remote past attached to these places, and she presented them so well that I still remember them.

The remains of Iso Mutsu repose in our family grave at the temple of Jufuku-ji, which is one of the oldest in Kamakura. The same cavelike sepulcher contains the ashes of her husband, Hirokichi Mutsu, and those of her father-in-law, Count Munemitsu Mutsu, a distinguished Japanese statesman of the Restoration era. Not far away, also in a little cave, stands the ancient tomb of Masako Yoritomo, founder of Jufuku-ji temple. Masako was the consort of Minamoto no Yoritomo, the man who established and ruled Kamakura as the capital of feudal Japan about seven centuries ago.

The death of Iso Mutsu occurred in 1930, during the forenoon of May 12, another reason why she could not have actually seen the sunset. My father wrote in English in his diary: "A peaceful end came at last to the placid life of Iso, at 9:10 A.M., with no suffering in the presence of Death."

The Kamakura temples and environs have changed little to this day and shed the same tranquil charm for those who wish to go to the trouble of visiting them. Kamakura city itself escaped any direct attack in the last war, and subsequently its population has considerably grown. Due to the development of transportation, the city today is far more heavily thronged by sightseers and holiday-makers, particularly during the summer, compared to the times when this book was written. But fortunately most of the places mentioned in it, with the exception of one or two very famous temples, continue to remain off the regular path of the multitudes. Kamakura's physical features are about the same except for the construction of a highway along the northern edge of Yuigahama Beach, the erection of a steel observation tower which rather mars the distant appearance of picturesque Enoshima island and the opening of a somewhat modernistic art gallery on the grounds of Tsurugaoka Hachiman Shrine. This establishment, along with the Tokyo National Museum, now houses many relics and treasures of art which footnote the history of Kamakura.

Considerable devastation was wrought by the great earthquake of 1923, and some of the geographical changes affect this book. For example, the "Hundred Kannon of Enkaku-ji" are no longer located in caves above the temple, but are now to be found on the temple's grounds. Where changes are considerable, this revised edition has footnoted them for the reader's benefit.

The thrilling history and romantic legends surrounding this ancient feudal capital come alive for the visitor to Kamukura who knows of them. I am pleased to see that yet another generation of readers will enjoy this wondrous experience.

—IAN MUTSU

Tokyo

You doors and ascending steps! you arches!
You grey stones of interminable pavements!
  you trodden crossings!

From all that has touch'd you I believe
you have imparted to yourselves,
  and now would impart the same secretly to me,

From the living and the dead
you have peopled your impassive surfaces,
and the spirits thereof would be evident
  and amicable with me.

—WALT WHITMAN

❋ Historical Sketch ❋

I
N THE PRESENT tranquil days it seems almost incredible to
recall that the plain of Kamakura—with its green valleys
intersecting the enclosing hills, was once the theater of a vast
and densely populated city, thickly intersected with busy streets;
studded with the splendid mansions of officials and retainers of
the ruler; abounding in rich architecture and beautiful temples—
in fact the most important city of the realm, the military capital of
Japan.

Yet it is a fact that some seven centuries ago this peaceful spot
witnessed some of the most thrilling events in the feudal history
of the nation: for, partly owing to the value of its strategic
position—being entirely surrounded by mountains on three
sides, with the ocean on the south—an important consideration
in those bellicose days, it was selected by the great Yoritomo as the
base of his operations, and in the year 1192, the first shogun of
the Minamoto family was established at Kamakura.

This part moreover had long been specially connected with
the house of Minamoto. Here Yoritomo's father Yoshitomo had
resided; also his famous ancestors Yoriyoshi and his son Yoshiie—
governors of this district, had exercised great influence and had
played a most effective role in their military capacity.

To the former valiant warrior the temple of Hachiman owes its existence, Yoriyoshi having originally caused it to be established in Kamakura in the hope that invocations at the shrine would propitiate the war god and secure success for his exploits upon the field of battle.

As the achievements of Yoritomo are so inseparably associated with the history of Kamakura it may be of interest to recount a brief sketch of this strange and dominant personality, whose name shines out with such luster as one of the giants of medieval times; the magician whose wand caused the obscure little fishing hamlet to blossom into the most famous city of the day.

For many years Japan had been torn by the civil wars of the rival factions Taira and Minamoto, but toward the latter half of the twelfth century the country lay practically beneath the sway of the Taira. Its chief, Kiyomori—a man of dauntless courage and brilliant military capacity—had succeeded in crushing the enemy and establishing the supremacy of his party. This despot ruled with a rod of iron. All the important posts of the government were occupied by prominent members of his great family; indeed their power was so absolute that a common saying of the time was to the effect that not to be of the Taira was to be deemed unworthy of belonging to the human race. So soaring was Kiyomori's ambition that even the cloistered Son of Heaven, the emperor himself, declared that his own position was not secure.

Yoshitomo, head of the rival faction, had been cruelly trapped and butchered by his enemies (1160); his adherents were scattered in flight and practically without a leader. His two elder sons had also fallen victims and shared the fate of their parent, but the third son Yoritomo had managed to escape with his life. From his exceptional sagacity this boy had always been his father's favorite, and although so young—only thirteen years of age—he is said to have advised Yoshitomo to take the initiative in this battle instead of waiting for the Taira's attack. However fate was against them: while escaping on horseback from their pursuers the over-wearied lad fell asleep in the saddle, and thus was left behind by his father and brothers. As he was passing through Moriyama (Omi province), the villagers recognized and attempted to seize the young Yoritomo, but the boy showed such unexpected spirit—cutting down two of his would-be captors with his sword—that the rest fell back and Yoritomo was able to continue his way unmolested, shortly afterward falling in with the retainer who had been sent to search for him, and thus was enabled to rejoin his party in safety.

But later, on account of a heavy snowstorm, the fugitives were compelled to dismount and walk through the blinding sleet, this effort causing such distress to the fatigued and exhausted boy that again he fell behind. This time he was rescued by a sympathizer who lived in that district named Sadayasu, and by him was concealed, first in a temple and later in the house of his preserver. Meanwhile his father Yoshitomo and his two elder brothers had all perished.

Soon afterward Yoritomo, leaving his temporary abode, went to the province of Mino, and from thence attempted to make his way to the Kanto plain. But the boy was unable to elude the vigilance of the enemy, and fell into the hands of Munekiyo, the Taira commander, who bore off his prey in triumph to Kyoto. By order of Kiyomori he was entrusted to the care of Munekiyo until his ultimate fate should be decided.

At this crisis the noble bearing of the young captive stood him in good stead. The lad's calm self-possession and fearless demeanor in the face of almost certain death softened the heart of his captor: when asked if he were ready for his fate, the young Yoritomo tactfully replied that he would prefer to live, since he alone was left to pray for the souls of his relatives.

Through the intervention of Kiyomori's stepmother, the boy's life was spared. At Munekiyo's suggestion she detected in him a resemblance to her own son who had died in early youth, so with tears and prayers she passionately besought that the child's doom might be averted. Her supplications at last met with success. Kiyomori consented that the boy's sentence should be banishment, and he was entrusted to the guardianship of two Taira adherents whose estates lay beyond Hakone, at Hirugashima in the province of Izu.

This act of benevolence was deplored as a lack of sagacity and sign of weakness by Kiyomori's entourage—a criticism to be amply justified by later events.

The lady to whom he owed his life sagely counseled the boy to spend his time in the study of the Scriptures and to refrain from shooting or the practice of any warlike sports lest he might incur suspicion: the retainers of Yoshitomo, moreover, on hearing the joyful news that their young lord was to be spared, suggested to him that the best way of ensuring his safety was to enter the priesthood. But as he was starting upon his journey into banishment, one Moriyasu Hanabusa secretly whispered into Yoritomo's ear to the effect that as the young master was saved, surely it must be the will of the Almighty that he should not become a priest, but the future hope of his party. This hint was not lost upon the shrewd boy, he nodded his assent in silence: the populace who witnessed his departure unanimously agreed that the young exile was quite apart from ordinary mortals, and to send him away thus was "letting loose a tiger-cub in the wilds."

The two guardians to whose safe custody the young exile was confided were Ito Sukechika of the Fujiwara family, and Hojo Tokimasa, who later was to become the famous head of the Hojo clan—to whose never-failing assistance and advice much of the success of Yoritomo's career has been attributed, and whose counsels exercised so much influence upon the early history of Kamakura.

The boy first found a home in the establishment of Sukechika. Later on, during the absence of her parent his daughter succumbed to the fascinations of the youthful Minamoto scion; tender relations were established, which flourished for a time in secret, until the birth of a son to the amorous pair brought discovery and retribution in its wake. The girl's stepmother betrayed this state of affairs to Sukechika, who promptly shattered the little drama with the bolt of his paternal ire. The unfortunate babe was cast into the water and drowned; his erring daughter was promptly united in marriage to another aspirant, and thus accorded the protection of a lawful lord and master. Vengeance was about to descend upon the head of the delinquent Yoritomo, but before his doom could be compassed he managed to flee from the scene, and escaped successfully to the domain of his other guardian, Tokimasa.

Although ostensibly a loyal supporter of the Taira clan, from various causes Tokimasa's partisanship for his faction had become secretly weakened and alienated: moreover a man of his acute penetration doubtless divined the impending downfall of the Taira ascendancy. By degrees the entire confidence and devotion of the older man was gained by his protégé, and their relations underwent a change, Tokimasa becoming the counselor, supporter, and prime minister of his illustrious son-in-law— a state of things that lasted unchanged until the day of Yoritomo's death.

Now Tokimasa had two daughters. The elder, Masako—who at this time was twenty-one years of age—was not only beautiful, but had inherited her father's sagacity and high order of intelligence. The younger one, the child of a second wife, was reputed of more ordinary capacity, and somewhat plain of feature to boot.

The young Yoritomo desired to strengthen his position with his guardian by espousing one of his daughters, and from motives of policy deemed it expedient to pay his addresses to the less attractive of the pair. Hence he composed a love-letter, and instructed his messenger to deliver it secretly to the younger of the two maidens. Coming events would seem to have cast their shadows before. According to the well-known tradition, the slumbers of the prospective recipient had been visited by a strange dream, in which she had beheld herself toiling up a mountainside with the sun and moon shining from her long sleeves, and holding on high an orange-bough laden with ripe fruit (*tachibana*). The shrewd Masako was well versed in legendary lore, signs, bodings, and portents. At once deeming this incident of an auspicious nature she coveted it for herself, and worked upon the credulity of the younger girl by pronouncing it an evil omen: moreover should a dream of good luck be related before seven years, or one of sinister portent before seven days had elapsed, the good results would be neutralized and the evil intensified.

To her alarmed sister Masako proposed a solution of the difficulty—she would buy the dream herself. "But how can one buy or sell what can neither be seen nor handled?" inquired the reluctant possessor of the dream. Masako fixed her sister with a searching gaze and overruled her objections as to the ill effects of such a transaction upon the purchaser: "I will buy it!" she proclaimed. As the price of her intangible bargain she paid to the younger girl a set of silken robes and a silver mirror. It is recorded that the latter was a valuable family heirloom which Tokimasa had given into the keeping of his eldest child owing to his affection and admiration for the character of Masako.

This strange barter seems to have exercised some occult influence upon its purchaser, for the same night Masako dreamed that a white dove* approached her, offering a golden box

* It will be remembered that Hachiman was the special protector and tutelary deity of the Minamoto family. The messengers of the god were supposed to be the sacred doves that, even at the present day, are always in evidence at the shrines dedicated to Hachiman. Amongst other instances, at the battle of Ishibashi-yama the life of Yoritomo was saved by two woodpigeons: later on, during the battle of Dan no Ura, at a crucial moment a pair of doves alighted upon the flagstaff of Yoshitsune's vessel, inspiring the hard-pressed warriors to further feats of courage and heroism.

containing a letter. The next morning this prophetic omen was realized, and Yoritomo's message was delivered: from that time it was not long before relations of a romantic and illicit nature were established.

Meanwhile Tokimasa was absent, being engaged in the execution of his duties as guard in Kyoto. He returned from the distant capital in company with Taira no Kanetaka, a relative of Kiyomori and governor of the province of Izu, and moreover to whom Tokimasa promised the hand of his eldest daughter in marriage.

But after his arrival, when tidings of this liaison that had flourished during his absence reached his ears, he was placed in a difficult position, and one that required delicate handling. However exalted might be his opinion of Yoritomo's talents and probabilities of a brilliant future, he hardly cared to risk incurring the odium of the whole Taira faction—including Kanetaka, the governor and prospective bridegroom—by uniting his daughter with their deadly enemy, the exiled scion of the hated Minamoto!

But the crafty Tokimasa proved equal of the occasion. Ostensibly ignoring the amour, he caused all preparations to be made for the celebration of the marriage with the governor, according to the original arrangement, but meanwhile there is no doubt that he was secretly conniving at his daughter's disappearance with her lover.

The nuptial festivities were celebrated with all due ceremony. But the same evening, under cover of the darkness and a convenient storm of wind and rain, the bride disappeared into the mountains, in which congenial retreat she was joined by the partner of her affection—the pair lying concealed until the father's pardon was accorded, and which was not long withheld.

From this time, assisted by Tokimasa, Yoritomo began to communicate in secret with the clansmen round about, and the military families in sympathy with his part. Meanwhile, a rising against the Taira was gathering strength in the south, under the auspices of Prince Mochihito, second son of the Emperor Go-Shirakawa. An order from this prince was dispatched to Yoritomo, requesting him to call to arms the Minamoto adherents, and to deliver the imperial family, as well as the country at large, from the selfish arrogance and tyrannous misrule of the Taira. This appeal was delivered to Yoritomo in the late spring of 1180; but while engaged in his preparations to comply, the fatal news arrived announcing the defeat and death of the prince in the battle on the Uji. Elated with this victory, the Taira were plotting to follow it up by exterminating the whole remainder of the Minamoto faction.

Yoritomo, being warned of this prospect, determined to take the field without loss of time, and as an initial attempt the stronghold of the governor Kanetaka—his former rival in the arts of love—was attacked. The fort was stormed, set on fire, and the unfortunate governor was beheaded.

This preliminary success decided the wavering adherents of the districts to rally around their new leader with contributions of men and arms, and war was soon declared. Supported by his little force of three hundred warriors, and bearing the prince's mandate attached to his standard, Yoritomo marched upon the foe at the historic hill of Ishibashi—a wooded eminence on the northern outskirts of the Hakone mountains. However, this valiant but premature attempt was doomed to failure. Woefully outnumbered by the enemy—who were encamped three thousand strong, and who attacked simultaneously from the front and from the rear—the Minamoto band suffered a crushing defeat and were almost annihilated, their leader only escaping from death by a hair's-breadth.

When Yoritomo was able to take cover in a grove of trees, his supporters had dwindled to the sorry remnant of six men. Acting upon their leader's advice these took refuge in flight: Yoritomo, with a single attendant, concealed himself in the hollow trunk of a tree. In this predicament signal service was rendered by

Kajiwara Kagetoki—a secret sympathizer with the Minamoto cause—who indicated to the pursuers that their quarry had taken an opposite route. However the Taira commander, Oba Kagechika, in riding past the hollow tree thrust his spear into the aperture, according to some accounts actually grazing the sleeve of Yoritomo's armor! At this dramatic moment the god Hachiman did not desert his protégé: two woodpigeons fluttered out from the tree—deluding the enemy into the assumption that no human being could be sheltering within—and the life of the fugitive was saved.

After this complete defeat at Ishibashi-yama Yoritomo became almost a solitary figure, leading a precarious existence concealed in the forests of that mountainous district. After some time he reached the seacoast, where he boarded a ship at Manazurugasaki and crossed over into the province of Awa. Here the tide of fortune speedily turned. Undaunted by the late fiasco, he was met and welcomed with utmost enthusiasm by crowds of followers, both old and new rallying to the white banner of their chief. The latter included the Taira clansman Hirotsune, who offered his allegiance to Yoritomo with an army of twenty thousand troops.

Before the arrival of the Minamoto scion, Hirotsune had been in a state of indecision whether to join forces with the newcomer, or whether to oppose and seize him. But again the force of Yoritomo's magnetic personality rescued him in the crucial hour. The Taira commander succumbed to the spell of the young hero, placing his forces at his disposal and becoming himself one of Yoritomo's loyal and important retainers. Throughout the eight provinces of the Kanto region manifestoes were circulated, to which the Minamoto adherents responded with alacrity, flocking to the standard in such large numbers that before long their chief found himself at the head of a mighty army. For strategic as well as political reasons he was advised to decide on establishing his military headquarters at Kamakura, and there he lost no time in propitiating the guardian deity of his ancestors by the erection of an imposing shrine to the war god Hachiman.

Naturally these demonstrations had not escaped the notice of Kiyomori. By this time, from his advancing age and the condition of his health, the crafty old Taira chief was unable to conduct an expedition in person to quell the foe; however, his nearest relatives were appointed for the undertaking, and they proved anything but efficient substitutes. On October 20, 1180, a body of fifty thousand troops was dispatched from Kyoto under the leadership of Tadamori, Kiyomori's youngest brother, and his grandson Koremori, to attack the upstart Yoritomo, scatter his followers, and dislodge him from Kamakura, his newly established stronghold. Yoritomo, at the head of a vast army two hundred thousand strong, went forth to meet the foe, whom early in November they confronted, encamped upon the southern bank of the Fujikawa—the broad and rapidly flowing torrent that rushes down to the sea from the slopes of the great mountain, and whose crossing presented so many obstacles in ancient times.

Now the Taira generals, in addition to being ill fitted for the campaign by their effete and luxurious manner of living in Kyoto, were alarmed and thrown into a state of consternation by the sudden notoriety of the newly arisen champion of the Minamoto cause; moreover, the unexpectedly imposing scale of the host that was drawn up upon the opposite bank of the river was ill calculated to allay their apprehensions. Yoritomo decided to attack by night. As the detachments of soldiers silently crossed the dark flood, landing in the swamp below the enemy's encampment, their appearance disturbed the multitudes of waterfowl that were roosting in the reeds. To the enemy the loud whirring of the birds' wings sounded like galloping hordes of war steeds rushing upon their prey; the ominous sound working such havoc upon the over-strained nerves of the Taira that the entire force was soon in full flight at precipitate haste, without the exchange of a single arrow! Yoritomo's first impulse was to hurl himself upon the foe and chase the fugitive army to Kyoto, but he was dissuaded from the project by the advice of his generals. It was held dangerous to withdraw the protection of so large a body of troops from the Kanto region while it was not yet clear of the enemy, thus leaving the military base open to attack; moreover, the Minamoto force was hardly equipped for a lengthy campaign against an adversary who were retiring to their own stronghold. So in the interests of caution the chief consented to waive vengeance for the present and withdraw.

During this retirement, and while the troops were encamped upon the banks of the Kisogawa, a dramatic incident occurred. A youthful samurai of dignified and noble mien suddenly appeared in the camp and requested an interview with Yoritomo. The new arrival proved to be the famous Yoshitsune, ninth son of Yoshitomo, and under these circumstances Yoritomo beheld for the first time the face of his youngest brother.

This most popular hero of medieval times—around whose name tradition has interwoven such countless thrilling and romantic incidents—was the son of Yoshitomo by his beautiful mistress Tokiwa Gozen. When her lord was slain, Tokiwa with her three children—Yoshitsune being a babe in arms—took flight from the vengeance of the enemy. On a bitter winter's night she escaped from the luxurious life at the palace into the storm without, enduring cruel hardships in the snowy mountains until shelter was found in a little hamlet of that remote region, where she and the three little ones were enabled to lie low and successfully evade detection.

But the agents of Kiyomori—determined to exterminate the whole brood of Yoshitomo, and foiled in their attempts to fathom her place of concealment—seized her mother as a hostage, threatening to inflict upon the unfortunate parent a cruel death, unless her daughter Tokiwa gave herself up. This ruse proved effective. When the fugitive—so beautiful and so forlorn—

appeared before Kiyomori, her fascinations made such a strong appeal to the fierce old warrior that he vowed her life should be spared, as well as her three children, if she would consent to transfer her allegiance from her dead lord to himself and submit to the blandishments of her sworn enemy! Poor Tokiwa was brought to bay: she held out for a time, but such merciless pressure was brought to bear upon her, in the doom that threatened her defenseless family, that loyalty became impossible and submission was the only course.

Thus the fate was averted that menaced her mother and her little sons; but with a view to rendering their future careers as innocuous as possible, the latter were deposited in monasteries, vowed to celibacy, and educated for the priesthood.

Possessed of great physical strength and almost superhuman activity, the fiery temperament of the young Yoshitsune was soon made manifest. At the age of fifteen (1174), he determined to elude the vigilance of his pious guardians, and with the assistance of a friendly merchant succeeded in effecting an escape to the province of Mutsu in the far north, a district too remote and too difficult of access to warrant pursuit. Here he was hospitably received, and lived for some years under the protection of Hidehira, governor of the whole province. The boy had inherited his father's spirit: passionately desirous of avenging his murder and espousing the family cause, he spent his day in equipping himself to that end, practicing warlike arts and acquiring a wide reputation for his feats of skill and valor. When the stirring news penetrated to those northern regions that the Minamoto were in arms and had taken the field against the Taira, Yoshitsune deemed the hour was ripe for action. So with a little band of twenty loyal and trusted followers—including the faithful giant Benkei, hero of a thousand tales of wild adventure—he started for the south, and thus the historic meeting came about.

This valuable recruit became a general in his brother's new army, where his brilliant exploits resulted in defeat after defeat of the enemy, culminating in the final destruction and annihilation of the Taira in the famous and oft-sung battle of Dan no Ura (1185).

Meanwhile the Taira chief Kiyomori had died in 1181; his last request upon his deathbed being that before any prayers or religious rites were performed for the repose of his soul, the head of his bitter foe Yoritomo should be placed upon his tomb. However, since the advent of the new Minamoto leader upon the horizon the star of the Taira had considerably waned, and no aspirant was bold enough to pacify the spirit of the departed with the longed-for trophy.

For the next few years Yoritomo remained at his base in Kamakura, gradually building it up into the great capital it later became, while his armies were adding laurel after laurel to his prestige: the decisive victory of Dan no Ura—when the sea was dyed red with blood, and even the infant emperor perished beneath the waves—leaving the Minamoto chief complete master of the situation.

However this tragic struggle proved the undoing of the conqueror as well as the conquered; for in spite of his brilliant achievements and the valuable aid he had rendered to the cause, Yoshitsune became the object of Yoritomo's jealousy and suspicion.

After evading various attempts upon his life, the former managed to escape to his old refuge and sanctuary in the north; but there an army followed him at the command of his pitiless brother. Further retreat being impossible, and his devoted band of comrades having all perished in the cause of loyalty, the trapped hero put an end to his wife and children and then died upon his own sword, his head being sent to Yoritomo as proof · that the fallen victor was no more. Yoritomo utilized this occasion to dispatch more armies to the north, thus adding vast and rich additions to his conquered territory; and from the year 1189 practically the whole of Japan lay at his feet.

Now that his supremacy was established upon a firm basis, and Yoritomo was virtual ruler of the country, his first efforts were to restore peace and prosperity to the war-devastated land. Justice was dispensed by a good and sound administrative system, and the judicious encouragement of agriculture, industry, and trade were potent factors in transforming "men's misery into happiness."

Kamakura became the finest and most flourishing city of the empire, presenting in every respect the strongest contrast to the effete and luxurious condition of society that prevailed in Kyoto, the imperial capital. Simplicity and frugality were Yoritomo's watchwords, the greatest encouragement being given to the sports that promoted manliness and physical vigor. Great hunting parties were organized—indeed proficiency in archery, swordsmanship, feats on horseback etc., were so highly estimated that instances are recorded of even criminals being occasionally granted a pardon on this account.

In the year 1192 Yoritomo was at the pinnacle of his fame. The title of *sei-i-tai-shōgun* (literally barbarian-subduing generalissimo) was conferred upon him by the emperor; thus the dual system of government was established by which the emperor's authority was completely overshadowed, and which lasted for almost seven centuries, until the restoration of imperial power in 1868. But now that the zenith of his ambition was attained, the first shogun only wielded the scepter for a brief seven years, his death occurring in the spring of 1199. No records regarding the mode of his demise have been preserved, the actual facts concerning the passing of this illustrious man being clouded in the mists of obscurity. But tradition credits him with a dramatic exit from the scene of his triumphs. The legend states that toward evening, as Yoritomo was returning from the function of opening a new bridge across the Sagami River—whither he had repaired with all pomp and ceremony, and attended by a regal retinue—suddenly the pallid specters of his murdered relatives appeared before him. The shogun passed this disconcerting apparition, but as his cortège was approaching Inamuragasaki, the figure of a young child arose from the sea. This phantom proclaimed itself the departed spirit of the emperor Antoku, in search of his enemy and slayer. The procession passed on, but the ghostly throng had fanned their destroyer with their shadowy wings; a few days later the great Yoritomo was dead.

This event took place January 13, 1199. He was succeeded in turn by his two sons, both meeting with violent deaths, but with the assassination of Sanetomo upon the steps of the Hachiman Shrine in Kamakura, the direct line of the Minamoto shoguns—that its illustrious founder hoped would last for all time—came to an end in the year 1219, a brief twenty years after the death of Yoritomo. Regarding his personal characteristics, Yoritomo's head is said to have been specially large in proportion to his height, his demeanor calm and suave. Profoundly penetrating, shrewd and cautious, he possessed the magnetic power of influencing others to an extraordinary degree, and was invariably magnanimous to those who served him loyally.

Many instances prove his gratitude to those who had helped him in the hour of need, but to the members of his own family falling under the ban of his suspicion and displeasure he proved merciless, and exterminated them without compunction. There is no doubt that Yoritomo was of a sincerely religious nature. It is recorded that upon the field of battle he carried a small statue of Kannon (the goddess of mercy) below his helmet, inserted in his *mage*, or topknot of hair, while his rosary invariably encircled his wrist. At the battle of Ishibashi-yama this latter pious emblem became detached and was lost, greatly to its owner's concern, but the beads were ultimately discovered and restored by his retainer. To his veneration for things spiritual he attributed his many triumphs, regarding the downfall of his enemies as mainly due to their disregard and contempt for the powers above, a condition specially manifested in their sacrilegious treatment of shrines and monasteries. To this attitude Kamakura owed the large number of beautiful and important temples that were erected and restored after the establishment of the military capital. Moreover, throughout the whole country Yoritomo exerted his influence as the patron of temples and shrines, thus incidentally affording a strong impetus to the development of many forms of art—painting, architecture, sculpture, etc.—a condition invariably attendant upon a religious awakening.

When the line of Yoritomo became extinct, the power was usurped by the family of his wife, the next chapter of history being known as the Hojo period. These rulers continued to reside in Kamakura, but although exercising absolute power, none of them assumed the title of shogun—they were known as the *shikken*, (literally power-holders) or regents.

An important event occurred under the regime of Yoshitoki, the second *shikken*, and son of Tokimasa. Owing to various causes the *bakufu* had become on strained terms with Kyoto. The emperor Go-Toba availed himself of disturbances in the military government to attempt to overthrow the usurpers and reinstate the imperial power: to that end he issued a decree denouncing the Hojo as traitors, and assembled an army with the object to destroying Kamakura (1221).

A large force was promptly dispatched from the military capital to deal with the situation; the imperial troops were speedily overthrown by the seasoned warriors of the Kanto region, and Kamakura's triumph was complete. All the nobles and courtiers that had taken part in this uprising were shown scant mercy, their estates being confiscated, and many met with violent deaths. Even the imperial family were accorded ruthless treatment; while the sacred person of the emperor Go-Toba himself was exiled to the rocky and barren island of Oki—where he suffered great hardships and died some three years later; a disloyal and sacrilegious action hitherto unheard of in Japan.

Another event of deep significance, and one that brought his rule into great prominence, occurred under Tokimune, sixth Hojo regent, in the defeat of the Mongolian invasion in 1281. This was the first occasion in her long history that Japan was attacked by a foreign foe. The huge armada arrived off the coast of Japan in May—the campaign lasting some two months, and the aggressors being finally scattered on August 14 of that momentous year.

The earlier Hojo regents ruled wisely and well. A council was organized by which strict justice was dispensed; the condition of the populace was ameliorated, their wrongs and oppressions being righted, while they enjoyed the benefits of an admirable government and kind treatment, as well as the blessings of peace and tranquillity after long devastation of war and bloodshed. However, after the death of the wise and pious Tokimune (1284) the Hojo prosperity began to wane.

The ascendancy of this family gradually dwindled until Takatoki (tenth regent, and last of the line) degenerated into a mere cipher and voluptuary, who devoted his time to the gratification of his own pleasures taking little heed of the affairs of state.

A quaint and entertaining description of this decadent condition of Takatoki's time is given in the *Taiheiki,* the so-called classical record of the time. On one occasion some fierce dogs started a fight in the ground adjoining the Hojo mansion. This incident afforded such gratification to the sporting instinct of the regent that he instituted dogfights as a regular pastime. Orders were issued for a vast number of powerful dogs to be collected: these huge beasts were housed in kennels richly decorated with gold and silver, fed upon dainty fare, and even carried abroad for exercise in *kago,* or palanquins! The number of these luxurious animals amounted to between four and five thousand: they were clad in garments of brocade and glittering tinsel, their presence causing the city of Kamakura to assume a new and unfamiliar aspect to the surprised inhabitants.

Any sort of amusement appealed to this indolent and dissipated man. Two companies of popular actors were summoned from Kyoto, and absorbed in their performances he was all indifferent to the flight of time, relegating the duties of his high position entirely to unworthy and corrupt ministers. These actors he quartered upon various noble families in Kamakura, compelling the latter to supply the mountebanks with gorgeous costumes and valuable equipment for their shows. Moreover, during the performances, the regent and the other spectators would mark their appreciation by divesting themselves of their robes of costly brocade and hurling them at their favorites! Naturally, this state of things could not last. A Japanese historian describes the Kamakura of those decadent days as a tree still green and beautiful to the eye, but crumbling and rotten at the core: the days of the Hojo dynasty were numbered.

At the command of the emperor Go-Daigo loyalist troops were raised to attack the rebels—as the military government was described: two of the leading spirits of this movement being the famous Kusunoki Masashige and Nitta Yoshisada. The campaign was waged with varying success until the fall and destruction of Kamakura was accomplished by Nitta Yoshisada. This great general hurled his troops upon the city in three divisions—the army commanded by himself advancing across the sands from Inamuragasaki; the death-knell of the military capital was sounded on July 5, 1333—a day traced in blood and ashes upon the pages of Kamakura's past.

Takatoki, although so wanting and worthless as a ruler, gave ample proof at the time of this catastrophe that the warrior spirit of his race was still alive. Together with almost a thousand of his officers and adherents he died the hero's death upon his sword that was the inevitable sequel of a ruined cause from the viewpoint of medieval chivalry: all perished in a scene of dauntless valor that stands out in high relief from the pages of history, even in those heroic days. When the people of Kamakura became aware of this tragedy that marked the overthrow of the Hojo line, so strong and unwavering was their fidelity to their fallen ruler that large numbers of them resolved to accompany the spirit of their lord in his journey to the land of shades. Over six thousand of them thus died the death of loyalty upon this dreadful day, whole families destroying themselves, and numerous priests participating in the general orgy of slaughter and extinction.

These events resulted in the emperor's restoration to power for a short time, but the military regime was not destined to suffer a long eclipse. Another of his generals—one who had been effective in fighting for the imperial cause, and who enjoyed the emperor's confidence in a marked degree—turned traitor, and determined to succeed the Hojo as head of the military rule at Kamakura: this was Ashikaga Takauji. His demands being naturally repudiated at Kyoto, this bold and treacherous usurper determined to assert his claim to the shogunate by force, and at the head of a vast army attacked the western capital. This campaign resulted in the flight of the emperor Go-Daigo, (who afterward died in exile), and the establishment of Takauji as shogun and founder of the Ashikaga dynasty, which lasted for fourteen generations, extending over a period of almost 240 years (1335–1573).

When Takauji proclaimed himself shogun he installed his residence upon the same site that had formerly been occupied by Yoritomo's mansion; but during the next year (1336), the new *bakufu* ruler left Kamakura in charge of a *kanryō*, or governor-general, and set up his own headquarters in Kyoto, where he established himself on a scale of great luxury and magnificence, in marked contrast to the austere simplicity and economy that had been the leading motives of the Hojo.

By this time Kamakura was beginning to rise from the holocaust of Nitta Yoshisada's invasion, and became a sort of secondary base where the laws and regulations were drawn up, and the administrative code was dispensed along the lines of Takauji's predecessors. But the Kamakura period was at an end. The erstwhile brilliant capital never really recovered from the chaos of Nitta's attack, and the conflagration started upon that day proved the funeral pyre of Kamakura's greatness, the renaissance under the Ashikaga regime being but a pale reflection of its departed glories, and barely exceeding the duration of a century.

During that period, a condition of great and increasing strife existed between the governors of Kamakura (*kanryō*) and their representatives (*shitsuji*): members of great Uesugi family holding the latter office, which became so powerful that it would be difficult to decide which wielded the greater authority, *kanryō* or *shitsuji*. This truculent state of affairs culminated in 1445, when the representative openly attacked the governor Nariuji. The latter fled to Koga in Shimousa (now Chiba–Ibaraki prefectures), Kamakura losing much prestige by this undignified condition of internal discord. The populace, hoping that the fugitive governor would return and be reinstated in office, preserved his estates in readiness and kept the land cultivated; but the departed *kanryō* died in exile, this fact constituting a potent factor in the final decline of Kamakura.

The city suffered extensive damage in the siege of 1454, and later on was again almost reduced to ashes by the great fire of 1526. Large numbers of its inhabitants transferred their residence to Odawara when the latter town rose into prominence as the seat of the powerful Hojo family, Kamakura receiving its final *coup de grâce* in the year 1603, when Edo was founded as the capital of the Tokugawa shogun.

The former brilliant city gradually declined into the little fishing village of the pre-Yoritomo period. However, the fortunes of this historic spot were not doomed to retrograde into permanent obscurity, and later on another renaissance was to develop, although based upon more prosaic lines.

The Restoration of 1868, with Tokyo established as the imperial capital; the rapid expansion of other adjacent towns into large and flourishing cities; increased facilities of communication; and various other reasons, all conduced to call attention to Kamakura's obvious and indestructible assets—its charming and picturesque scenery; the glorious sweep of blue ocean fringed by its crescent of sandy beach; its easiness of access; its teeming associations with ancient history—of which, like Rome, it has been said that "legends and romances cluster around every stone, and every cave is heavy with the bones of dead heroes"; its innumerable walks and excursions in every direction; and finally its pure bracing air and exceptionally fine climate.

However, the Restoration was not an unmixed blessing, for at that time the temples were dispossessed of their lands, and consequently fell upon very hard times; the high-water mark of their distress being reached about the year 1886 or 1887, when it is even said that some of the great structures were demolished and the timbers sold for firewood.

In 1890 the railroad, which before then had not come nearer than Ofuna—the junction upon the main line four miles distant—directly linked Kamakura with the capital, this fact being naturally conducive to a new era of prosperity. Since that time the *bessō* (seaside villas) of residents of Tokyo and Yokohama have increased and multiplied apace—Yuigahama gaining wide celebrity as a bathing resort and acquiring a high degree of popularity with the swarms of summer visitors, who transform the beach into a scene of liveliest animation. Three years after the advent of the railway the *shihan gakkō* (school for the training of primary school teachers) was removed from Yokohama to its present quarters at Kamakura on the eastern side of Hachiman. According to tradition the spacious playground of this academy is said to be the identical site of Takatoki's dogfights. Other scholastic institutions are the girls' school in the main avenue, with some 150 pupils; the large primary school almost opposite, two kindergartens, an orphanage for poor children, etc.

Although so many temples and shrines have been overtaken by various calamities and have disappeared since Kamakura's palmy days, yet there still remain the considerable number of forty Buddhist, and nineteen Shinto temples: eighteen of the former being associated with the Nichiren doctrines, and from their intimate connection with the life and teachings of the saint attract large numbers of the devotees of this most popular sect.

Two versions are extant regarding to origin of the name Kamakura. According to one theory the first emperor, Jinmu, visited this district during the course of his punitive expeditions in the eastern part of Japan. The enemy to the number of some thousands were slain by the imperial warriors—the corpses being piled up like mountains: hence this district acquired the name of *kabanekura,* or repository for dead bodies, which later became Kamakura. But a less sanguinary derivation, and the one that is generally accepted is the following. Fujiwara no Kamatari, the celebrated soldier and statesman of the seventh century, while on a pilgrimage to a distant shrine, passed one night at the little hamlet of Yui. Here he dreamed a sacred dream in which he was instructed by the powers above to bury his emblem, the *kama,* or large sickle that he carried, upon a hill in the district. This height is said to be the eminence behind Hachiman and which to the present day bears the name of Daijin-yama, or Hill of the Minister: thus the district became known as the repository of the *kama,* or Kamakura.

❋ KAMAKURA ❋

Here still dwell the ancient gods
    in the great silence of their decaying temples,
without worshippers, without revenues,
    surrounded by desolations of rice-fields;
where the chanting of frogs
    replaces the sea-like murmur of the city
        that was, and is not.

—LAFCADIO HEARN

Egara Tenjin

❀

T HIS SMALL SHRINE, situated near the main road to Kanazawa, is of extreme antiquity, being one of the few relics of the pre-Yoritomo period; a long and imposing avenue of ancient pines forms the approach, spanned by a large stone *torii*. The exact date of the foundation is unknown; records of it doubtless existed at the time of Yoritomo, when this shrine was of considerable importance and on a much more elaborate scale. In those days three temples were situated in a grove of *ume*, or plum trees, upon the high terrace of the present shrine; with a vassal building in the enclosure below the hill.

It is recorded that in front of the main gate there was moreover a place called the *sekitoriba*, or barrier, and there all worshippers and visitors to the temple were requested to make a contribution of money by order of the regent (Hojo Ujinao): the funds thus raised being employed for the temple repairs. The original document embodying this command is still preserved among the treasures of Egara Tenjin. The dedication is to Sugawara no Michizane, a statesman and distinguished scholar of the ninth century: descended from a line of erudite literati, Michizane was the most renowned for his profound literary achievements, and was universally revered as the most brilliant man of the age. He

1. Egara Tenjin.

was also a minister held in high esteem by the emperors Uda and Daigo: but at the height of his career, owing to the jealousy and intrigues of his enemies, he was unjustly banished in the year 901. Two years later he died in exile at the age of fifty-eight.

After the death of Michizane a series of misfortunes befell those who had compassed his downfall. The Imperial Palace was struck by lightning, and the chief agents in the conspiracy, one after another, all mysteriously died: these occurrences were interpreted in the popular mind as the spirit of Michizane wreaking vengeance upon his foes.

Forty-five years after the death of the exiled statesman, he was deified under the name of Tenjin, and the first shrine was raised to his memory in Kyoto: this resulted in the erection of memorial temples throughout the land. Since that time Tenjin has taken his place amongst the national divinities, and has been universally worshipped as the patron of learning and scholarship.

The present building is considerably affected by the flight of time, but in recent years certain repairs were carried out, including a new roof, on the occasion of a festival to commemorate the one-thousand-year anniversary of the death of Michizane: a large stone monument recording this fact stands on the left of the ascent. The shrine is embowered in a dense grove of lofty cedars and other ancient trees—on the right a superb old *ichō* (ginkgo tree) towers up into the sky, a veritable giant: through the solemn green twilight, upon the mossy sward

> The slanted sunlight weaves
> Rich-flickering through the dusk of plenteous leaves
> Its ever-tremulous arabesques of gold.

The *ume* trees of former days have all passed away. The memory of the departed scholar is invariably entwined with these poetic and fragrant blossoms, of which he was an ardent worshipper; for this reason the shrines to his memory are always planted with his favorite flowers, which have come to be universally recognized as the emblem of Tenjin. On the elaborate roof of the shrine, embellished with fish, lions, etc., one finds countless plum blossoms designed on the gray tiles, in addition to a long black panel with three of these flowers painted in white—the family crest of the deified statesman: this device also ornaments the entrance gate to the enclosure. Severe simplicity marks the interior of this little structure. Painted in dull red, with the two black doors marking the inner sanctuary hermetically closed; the sole decoration is a faded gold panel upon which the characters *Tenman-gu,* or Shrine of Tenjin, are inscribed in black.

In former times a long list of treasures were accredited to this shrine, but their numbers have been lamentably decimated by the various conflagrations that have proved fatal to so many priceless possessions of the Kamakura temples. However a few notable exceptions still remain. Within the sanctuary is preserved an ancient statue of Michizane garbed in his official uniform: this effigy moreover is possessed of remarkable features, for it is said to contain all the organs of the body shaped according to the physiological ideas of that period—inside the mouth a little bell is suspended in place of a tongue, and within the head is carved an eleven-faced Kannon, the Goddess of Mercy. The knees and lower portions of the statue have become scorched and blackened by its presence in various fires.

An interesting incident recorded in connection with this temple is that in February of 1213, a samurai of literary tendencies named Shibukawa, being convicted of an offense, was condemned to be executed. In his anguish the doomed man composed ten poems and presented them to the shrine of Egara Tenjin. These being brought to the notice of the shogun Sanetomo, who was himself a poet of great renown, he was so touched by the beauty and pathos of the poems that a free pardon was accorded to the delinquent.

The residue of the Egara Tenjin treasures are kept at the neighboring Kamakura Shrine, as there are no means of preserving them where they rightfully belong. These consist of several paintings of the tutelar deity, and various other antique objects. Amongst them is an ancient record which accounts for the existence of the shrine in the following legend:

In the first year of Choji (August 25, 1104), Kamakura was visited by a mighty tempest. Great winds shrieked; the earth was shaken by the thunder's crashing artillery, while incessant flashes, like hissing serpents, seemed to rend the heavens in twain. When the war of the elements was at its height, the black clouds opened, and a scroll, upon which was painted a portrait of Michizane, descended upon the spot where the present temple stands. This demonstration was regarded by the populace as signifying Michizane's desire for a shrine to be constructed in his honor upon this site. Consequently an appeal was made to the emperor

{ 46 }

Horikawa (reigned 1087–1107), and he consented to erect the temple, with the mysterious picture enshrined as the chief object of worship. Although obviously of great age, this ancient painting is well preserved, and is popularly supposed to be the work of the divinity himself: he is represented as standing upon white clouds arrayed in the court official costume—wide black robes lined with scarlet, a large and elaborate sword, and holding a *shaku,* or baton of office. It is recorded that during the course of the civil war then being waged, an attacking general (Imagawa Noritada) created great havoc in several temples in Kamakura, amongst which Egara Tenjin was included: the picture was carried away by him to Suruga (September 1455), but thirty-two years later it was restored to the shrine. Records also state that Yoritomo, when constructing his residence in Kamakura (in the district known as Okura) made this temple of Egara Tenjin his tutelary shrine to guard against the entrance of demons—and consequently ill luck—to the new building. Yoritomo also caused the curious statue, that is still preserved within the little temple, to be sent from Tsukushi, Kyushu, and installed for the veneration of the faithful. According to the *Azuma Kagami,* in September of 1202, a memorial service to Michizane was performed here in honor of the 300th anniversary of his death, by order of the shogun Yoriie, eldest son of Yoritomo. Amongst the various personages of exalted rank that did homage at this temple, it is stated that in 1590 Hideyoshi visited Egara Tenjin and caused it to be redecorated and beautified. During the Tokugawa period it was customary to renovate the shrine with the material left over when the temple of the Hachiman was repaired.

Sugimoto-dera

❀

A SHORT DISTANCE farther along the Kanazawa road leads to another temple of exceeding antiquity and unusually romantic approach. Founded in the year 734 by the priest Gyoki, this dedication is one of the most ancient of the pre-Yoritomo period in Kamakura, and was in existence for centuries whilst Kamakura was still but the most insignificant fishing hamlet.

Steep mossy steps—thickly bordered with azalea bushes, and here and there old gray stone lanterns—lead up to a picturesque lychgate, on either side of which stand the moldering but still fierce and threatening figures of the Nio, or the Two Deva Kings, whose mission is to put to flight all enemies from the sacred spot. Somewhat above this gate a *torii* marks the entrance to a sequestered little grassy plateau gay with flowers, wherein are divers ancient monuments and moss-encrusted tombs. The fern-grown wall of rock is cleft by the cave of Benten, whose floor is formed by a pool of water: according to tradition this cave was once the abode of a mighty serpent. At the back a niche is hewn in the rock which formerly enshrined a statue of the goddess, but owing to deterioration due to atmospheric influences the effigy has been removed to the temple above. Benten, the sea goddess, is always represented as a beautiful woman, and is supposed to have the power of assuming the form of a serpent: she is the patroness of music, the fine arts, and good fortune in general; her shrines are almost invariably in the neighborhood of water—the sea, a river, or a pond, in which a snake consecrated to her is supposed to dwell. Another flight of steps leads up to a plateau in the hillside, where in the dense shade of its solemn grove stands an old thatched building—generally solitary and deserted, but with its doors hospitably open to any stray worshipper that may be tempted by the beauty of the place to scale the steep and somewhat formidable approach. However, for those to whom precipitous steps form no attraction, a more appealing method of ascent will be discovered in a winding path lying to the left, and which gently conducts the pilgrim to the high terrace upon which the temple stands. A beautiful and peaceful spot, lying in the deep green shadows of tall forest trees: the screen of rock enclosing the level is pierced with tiers of caves containing venerable tombs. At the rear, framed in bushes and undergrowth, lies a small still pool of almost circular shape and great depth—indeed the aged guardian of the temple avers that it could not be fathomed, even with a rod the length of eighty people standing with outstretched arms!

The path to the left leads through the woods—past beautiful old lichened tombs, and affords a panorama of the neighborhood, including the distant purple mountains and, in clear weather, the snows of Mount Fuji towering into the blue sky. The steep track leading upward ascends to the top of the hill, where, in a glade musical with birds, is a venerable monument dedicated to Amaterasu, the Sun Goddess, who is believed to be the primeval ancestress of the imperial family of Japan.

Although the temple of Sugimoto is so ancient as to be approaching dilapidation, some most valuable relics of its early days still remain in its possession. The chief object of worship enshrined upon the altar—a large gilt statue of the Eleven-faced

Kannon—is a striking work from the chisel of Unkei, and is moreover of historic interest; it was presented to the temple by Yoritomo in the twelfth century. It is recorded that this statue was repaired in the Tempo era (1830–43), and unfortunately lost much of its original charm during the process. A large and beautiful figure of Jizo stands on the left. The saint's head is framed with a golden aureole and he is equipped with his customary symbols, the *shakujō*, or staff, and the *hōshu no tama*, or jewel of good luck. This effigy was carved by the priest Eshin and was also the gift of Yoritomo: in former times it was separately enshrined in the Jizo-do (Hall of Jizo) nearby, but was brought to the main temple to replace a statue of Kannon that has been removed to a shrine in Meguro, in Tokyo. The vigorous and striking representation of Bishamon (on the right) is highly esteemed by connoisseurs; it was carved by Takuma, and is considered a fine example of his art. A wheel-like halo studded with flames encircles this fierce divinity, who is trampling underfoot two demons of powerful appearance: here also the workmanship has greatly suffered by later repairs, which were executed in the Bumpo era (1318–22). Originally a Hindu deity, Bishamon was considered the protector of treasure. In Japan he is one of the seven gods of luck (*shichi fukujin*), and in feudal days was worshipped as the patron of good fortune in war. Bishamon is moreover one of the Four Deva Kings, or "gods of the four directions," and is supposed to guard the north against evil influences. At the back of the temple is arranged a group of deities—the thirty-three *keishin*, or incarnations of Kannon; these quaint little figures are ascribed to Unkei.

On the extreme right is the statue of Benten that was formerly in the cave below—an interesting figure well worth its rescue. The Fudo that stands nearby is a fine work of art, and is beautifully carved. But the *pièces de résistance* of this temple are enshrined in the *zushi*, the sanctum sanctorum immediately behind the main altar and screened from the vulgar gaze by locked doors. Here are deposited three exceedingly valuable statues of the Eleven-faced Kannon; two of these ancient works are enrolled upon the list of National Treasures, and are considered of high merit. The right-hand figure dates back some three hundred years before the Kamakura period: it is said to have been carved by the celebrated priest Jikaku, who died in the year 864, at the age of seventy-one. This pious and gifted functionary was on a pilgrimage to these parts, and by chance made the discovery of a mysterious piece of wood that was floating in the sea and emitted a sort of luminous halo, thereby proving its sacred character: with this trophy the Goddess of Mercy was fashioned. Legend asserts that when the temple was destroyed by fire in 1189. As rescue was not forthcoming, the statue proved its miraculous nature by leaving the altar on its own account; it was subsequently discovered safe and intact, placidly reposing beneath a large cryptomeria beyond the danger zone! Hence the name of the temple—*sugi* (cryptomeria), and *moto* (base, or beneath). It is further related that another conflagration occurred in the year 1257: on that occasion the residing priest Joki Shonin braved the flames and rescued the statue at the risk of his life, but miraculously escaped uninjured.

The figure in the center is also a National Treasure, and was carved by the priest Eshin in the year 985. Eshin was a famous sculptor of ancient times; he was the son of Tada Manju and an ancestor of the Minamoto family. This statue was executed according to imperial command and was presented to the temple by the emperor Kazan (died 1008). The third Kannon is the most antique of these valuable relics, but the workmanship is not so skilled, owing no doubt to the more primitive state of art in those faraway days; it was the work of Gyoki—the famous priest of the eighth century and founder of this temple.

The Japanese Madonna Kannon, Goddess of Mercy, is one of the most popular divinities, and is said to have refused the rest of Nirvana to save the souls of men. She is generally supposed to possess miraculous powers to deliver mankind from the dangers and perils of this mortal life: she hears the pleadings of the afflicted and assuages their sorrows, being especially considered the refuge of the distressed. Kannon is an abbreviation of her real title Kanzeon. *Kan* means to be possessed of spiritual insight, *ze* signifies the world or universe, and *on* is sound or voice; this deity hearkens to the world-sound and represents the principle of universal lovingkindness.

According to Chinese tradition Kannon was the young daughter of the governor of a town in Szechwan. When she was eighteen years of age the maiden repaired for worship to a temple where there were five hundred priests: the latter refused to let her return home, detaining her by force. Her father, infuriated by this act of treachery, caused all the priests to be slain and the temple was set on fire, his daughter ostensibly perishing in the general destruction. But the following night she appeared in a vision to her sorrowing parent, saying she had risen from the flames to paradise and was immortalized as a goddess. From that time she has been venerated by countless multitudes: in Japan she is represented as a beautiful idealization of womanhood, usually enthroned upon the lotus, the sacred emblem of Nirvana.

Another version of this legend, also of Chinese origin, relates that the parent of the goddess was enraged because his beautiful young daughter steadfastly refused all offers of marriage and was firm in her determination to enter religion as a nun. Various methods of compassing her death were attempted and averted by miraculous means: however, at last she was suffocated, and her pure soul descended to the underworld. But Enma, dread judge of souls, finding his hell was converted into paradise by her angelic presence, restored her to the upper world, where she lived for nine years practicing good works upon a mysterious island known as Fudarakujima—ostensibly in the vicinity of China—healing the sick and preserving mariners from the perils of tempest and shipwreck. Often this divinity is represented with eleven faces (Juichimen Kannon) symbolic of shedding sweetness and mercy in all directions; and also with a thousand arms (Senju Kannon), in reality but forty, to embrace the earth and to alleviate the sufferings of all mankind.

In eastern Japan there are thirty-three temples sacred to Kannon. Pilgrims believe it an act of great merit to visit these in order, and those who make the complete round of all the eighty-eight temples dedicated to the Goddess of Mercy have achieved such a supreme act of merit as to preserve them from Hell, and to open the gates of life everlasting! The Sugimoto Kannon is the first in importance on the round of Eastern Japan, the second being the Iwadono* Temple of Zushi; the An'yo-in (Kamakura) is the third; while the colossal statue at Hase comes fourth on the list. These pilgrims leave behind a printed slip, or label, as a proof of their visit; multitudes of these will be observed attached to the walls and pillars of the temple.

Another form of the divinity is the Bato, or Horse-Headed Kannon, when she is represented with a horse's head carved upon her headdress, and is supposed to exercise a protective influence over horses and cattle. Hence, offerings to Kannon are presented by farmers and peasants: adjoining the sanctuary of this temple a somewhat decayed white plaster horse stands in a wooden stable that was undoubtedly deposited for this reason.

The annual festival is observed on August 10th, upon which occasion the doors of the inner repository are opened and the

* This venerable temple is picturesquely situated, hidden away in the hills behind Zushi: it was also founded by the eminent Gyoki Bosatsu in 720, and belongs to the Sodo doctrines, the most powerful branch of the Zen sect. Ancient records state that the third shogun Sanetomo occasionally repaired to the Iwadono Kannon for worship. This woodland solitude is well worth a visit for its romantic environment: a mountain track at the rear—known for many centuries as the *junrei michi,* or pilgrims' road—leads to the Kanazawa highway, a few paces beyond the Sugimoto Kannon.

scene assumes a very gay aspect, crowds of devotees assembling to pay their respects to the beloved divinity, "who looketh down above the sound of prayer,"

> Storms and hatred give way at the sound of her name,
> At the sound of her name demons vanish:
> By her name one may stand firm in the sky like a sun.

Hōkoku-ji

❁

S OMEWHAT FARTHER along the Kanazawa road will be seen the approach to this small temple; a wooden bridge is crossed, spanning the rocky upper course of the Nameri River and shaded by the spreading branches of a fine old fir tree. A lychgate roofed with moldering thatch and piercing an open-work stone wall marks the temple precincts. Although all that was best and most valuable has passed away, and become "portions and parcels of the dreadful past," yet this lovely spot is well worth inspection for the charm of its romantic setting—the ancient trees; the rocks and caves; the riot of every shade of luxuriant green; the carpet of ferns and wild flowers; the densely wooded valleys—beyond and around the hills rising up to the rocky height of Kinubari-yama: above all for the indescribable atmosphere of peace and solitude, and mystic remoteness from the things of earth that seems to envelop like a dream so many of these old-world shrines and temples in Japan.

A small courtyard lies beyond the gate, shaded by lofty and dignified old trees; a flight of well-worn stone steps, thickly coated with moss, confronts the visitor with the sole remaining fabric that the inroads of successive centuries have left to the temple of Hokoku-ji.

Founded some six hundred years ago by Ashikaga Ietoki—grandfather of Takauji, first of the Ashikaga shoguns—the temple derived its name from Ietoki's nom de plume. In its bygone days of prosperity there were five edifices, with a bell tower, that have by degrees ingloriously dwindled to a solitary small and insignificant building. The last stroke of fate fell as recently as some thirty-five years ago, when the fine old *butsuden* (hall of images) was completely destroyed by one of the disastrous fires that these wooden structures are so unfortunately liable to, and with it perished all its priceless contents, including many highly prized statues and other important works of art. Of this calamity, so deplored by art lovers, not a trace remains. The site of the holocaust is as completely effaced by the finger of time as though it never existed, and the little valley of the vanished treasures has degenerated into placid ricefields. The centerpiece of the present altar is a very ancient figure of Buddha; another of the few remaining possessions is a curious statue of Kannon crowned with a jeweled head-ornament and said to be of extreme antiquity. On the right-hand side of the altar is preserved an interesting relic in the realistic and life-sized statue of the first priest who officiated at this temple—a disciple of the first priest of Engaku-ji, known as Tengan. This effigy is painted in natural colors and reposes in an ecclesiastical chair, the robes being lacquered a dull red hue.

Owing to the various calamities, extending over many hundred years, the treasures belonging to the temple have become sadly reduced. The existing remnants include an antique metal mirror which is said to date from the beginning of the Kamakura period (twelfth century); a finely carved Chinese *suzuri,* or writing box—made of black stone and ornamented with a design of quaint and nondescript animals according to the zoological ideas of that period; ancient seals of the temple; and various venerable objects that are supposed to have been the property of the sculptor Takuma. This famous artist is said to have resided in the vicinity of Hokoku-ji, hence this district was known as Takumagayatsu, or the Valley of Takuma.

Immediately facing the temple stands a graceful old pine which is said to date back from the early days of the temple. Its shape is superb, and as yet happily unimpaired by its great age: in this sheltered valley, immune from the storms that prove fatal to so many of these ancient landmarks, its boughs remain still fresh and green, manifesting no system of decay. According to the priest of Hokoku-ji, the preservation of this beautiful old tree constitutes a serious drain upon his income, the attentions of numerous gardeners being necessary to minister to its needs and to preserve it in a flourishing condition.

A little path thickly overgrown with ferns and wildflowers, and overshadowed by huge boulders of rock, leads the pilgrim to what must surely be one of the most sequestered and solitary abodes of peace in the world—an old cemetery. So ancient indeed are some of the venerable gray tombs, and so thickly covered with moss and silvery lichens that scarcely a trace of the original stone is visible; however, here and there a new monument with its inscription in fresh vermilion—and sprays of scarcely withered flowers, with little offerings to the soul of the departed—indicate that the spot is not wholly dedicated to the ghosts and spirits of remote ages, but now and again new inmates come to join the silent throng beneath the leafy rest and peaceful silence of this "dreaming garden of the dead."

High up in the overhanging cliffs, and shaded by the cloistering boughs of tall cedar and ginkgo trees, are two niches hewn out of the solid rock: here, beneath these rounded monuments, repose the ashes of the early priests of this temple. Although so safely sheltered from the fury of wind and rain, some of these venerable tombs are almost reduced to lacework by the flight of centuries, and seem as though the ebbing of the waves of time have imprinted corresponding little ribbed and stony wavelets upon their rugged surfaces. The solitary monument in the left-hand niche marks the resting place of the first priest of Hokoku-ji, Tengan. It can be approached by some worn steps almost concealed in the verdant undergrowth, and a more picturesque spot could hardly be found for the last long sleep than this mossy, fern-shadowed crevice in the rocky wall of the mountainside; one instinctively breathes a prayer that in the land of shades the soul of that ancient divine may find the tranquillity and beauty that surround his ashes in this mortal world of strife below. A grove of solemn cryptomeria forms the background to this sequestered graveyard. A short distance beyond, on the hillside above, is a cave containing two ancient tombs concerning which there is a tragic history.

The fourth Ashikaga regent, Mochiuji, was keenly ambitious to succeed to the shogunate, but fate willed it otherwise. When he was superseded, Mochiuji formed the plan of assembling an army in order to assert what he considered to be his rights by force of arms. However, the plot was betrayed before it could materialize. On realizing the collapse of his hopes and plans the unfortunate aspirant, together with numbers of his retainers, committed suicide in a nearby temple (Eian-ji) which has since disappeared, in the neighborhood of Zuisen-ji; on the same day his wife, with many of her ladies, was accidentally burnt to death. Now their eldest son, a boy of ten years of age named Yoshihisa, had been deposited for safety in the temple of Hokoku-ji. This child possessed the indomitable spirit of the samurai, and although of such tender years, he resolved to anticipate the fate that was surely impending from his enemies. So here, in this temple, he stabbed himself to death: his kinsman (Mochiuji's brother) who was in charge of the unfortunate boy followed suit, and died upon his sword. Their ashes lie beneath these old gray tombs, the smaller one which is of the Ashikaga shape being the memorial of the young Yoshihisa.

Kinubari-yama, the lofty height beyond, partly belonged to

Hokoku-ji in the old days. Its name—Silk-spread Mountain—is derived from the fact that its peak was plainly visible from Yoritomo's residence, and in the heats of summer the shogun is recorded to have caused white silk to be spread upon the summit, creating the effect of snow. From the neighborhood an accessible, although somewhat steep path winds upward to the great cavern above, which commands one of Kamakura's most beautiful panoramas. Near this cavern are three other large caves in the rock. Legend connects one of these with the days of Yoritomo; it is still well known in the neighborhood as *Karaito no tsuchi no rō*, or the earthen prison of Karaito.

It is a historical fact that the first shogun was on notoriously bad terms with his cousin Kiso Yoshinaka, whose territory lay in the north of Japan. Karaito was the daughter of one of his generals, who had entered the household of the shogun at Kamakura: she managed to hold secret communication with the enemy and cherished the idea of making away with Yoritomo. To this end she kept a small sword concealed in her dress and possibly her scheme of vengeance might have been accomplished, for she had been appointed to serve her master as one of his personal waiting-maids and opportunity would doubtless have occurred. But her design was discovered and she was imprisoned in this cave. Regarding her ultimate fate—whether Karaito managed to flee from her doom, or whether she shared the fate of Yoritomo's many victims—is left to the imagination and tradition is silent.

Jōmyō-ji

❀

A FEW PACES beyond the little bridge of Hokoku-ji brings the pilgrim to a monument of exceeding antiquity. This is a *gebatō*, which in past times was a sign to mounted worshippers that they are approaching holy ground and that at this point their steeds must be left behind. A long avenue, from which many of the gnarled old pines have passed away, leads to a short flight of steps and a thatched gate, from whence one emerges into the precincts of all that remains of the once great and famous monastery of Jomyo-ji.

Although now of somewhat less than ordinary exterior, and little suggestive of its ancient glories, in bygone days Jomyo-ji was one of the five most prominent temples of Kamakura, ranking in importance with the great foundations of Kencho-ji and Engaku-ji. In those palmy days there were seven main edifices with numerous satellites, an especially fine bell tower, and many other attributes, which alas, have gradually shrunk to the little measure of a single lowly building supported by a solitary offshoot.

Founded by Ashikaga Yoshikane in the year 1188, and established as one of the five monasteries in Kamakura of the Rinzai sect of Buddhism, in those remote times the temple was known as Gokuraku-ji, but in the year 1321, with imperial permission, the name was changed in honor of the founder, who was the ancestor of the first Ashikaga shogun, and whose posthumous name was Jomyo-ji.

The age of its prosperity only lasted for a period of somewhat over two centuries, then it was stricken by the relentless enemy that has reduced to a heap of ashes so many priceless structures all over Japan, and the knell of its decay was sounded.

Twice destroyed by fire and twice rebuilt, the temple never recovered from these calamities: according to records, toward the end of the fifteenth century Jomyo-ji had greatly declined, and even in those early days remained but a shadow of its former splendor. Although the views of the surrounding mountains and densely wooded landscape are picturesque, the actual enclosure of this temple may strike the visitor as being commonplace, and somewhat unattractive: however, in spite of the deterioration that the flight of centuries has wrought upon this ancient foundation, much still remains that may interest those to whom the relics of bygone ages make any appeal.

The present temple stands upon the site of the guest room of former times: the interior is plain, but cheerful and inviting, the only note of color being some sprays of painted flowers that decorate the panels.

The two chief treasures in the central division of the main altar are both of historical interest and extreme antiquity. The large statue of Buddha is supposed to have been a gift to Sanetomo, younger son of Yoritomo; beside it stands an ancient gilded figure of Amida. This latter image is said to have been carved in sandalwood by the Chinese sculptor Chinwakei, and was one of the sacred possessions of Masako, wife of Yoritomo, until she presented it to this temple.* It is recorded that in a dream the Inari of Okura (this part of Kamakura) appeared to Sanetomo in

---

*Now stored in the Kokuhokan (Kamakura National Treasure House) in the precincts of Tsurugaoka Hachiman Shrine.

the guise of a venerable man, advising the shogun to reestablish the temple of Gokuraku-ji (as Jomyo-ji was then called). The work was begun in 1212 and completed the next year, when Sanetomo and his mother marked the occasion by the presentation of the images.

The niche to the right is occupied by a large wooden statue of skilled workmanship, representing the celebrated priest who first officiated at this temple, Gyoyu. In front of this work are two smaller figures of priests. The division on the left contains, amongst other objects, a small statue of Kamatari, the sponsor of Kamakura and who, according to the claim of the Jomyo-ji authorities, is said to have buried his *kama* on the hill near this temple; however, the spot where the *kama* was deposited is generally supposed to have been the hill called Daijin-yama, behind the shrine of Hachiman.

A most interesting possession is a large colored map or chart of Jomyo-ji at the height of its prosperity: by its aid the imaginative visitor can gaze down the dim vistas of departed centuries and conjure up a vision of what the halcyon days of this great monastery must have been, when the now-deserted ricefields were gay with stately edifices, lofty trees, beautiful gardens, and busy throngs of priests and worshippers.

One of the chief treasures of Jomyo-ji is preserved in a small detached shrine to the right of the temple entrance. A large case is unlocked, revealing a curious and striking effigy of Kojin:* an avenging deity—fierce and bellicose of aspect and possessed of mighty strength, who is supposed to exercise the powers of punishing wickedness and crime. Equipped for that purpose with three faces to facilitate the detection of delinquents, this truculent god is moreover provided with three pairs of hands wherewith to control his weapons and effectively compass the

---

*This statue is now stored in the temple's treasury, the small shrines having been destroyed in a typhoon.

doom of the guilty: the two upper hands hold respectively a red and white disk representing the sun and moon and illustrating the wide sphere of his supernatural activities.

Regarding this figure, tradition relates the following: Yoshikane, founder of the temple, was the possessor of two pictures of the gods Kojin and Fudo, painted by the famous Kobo Daishi. In the first month of 1198, Yoshikane dreamed that the two deities became endowed with animation and descended from their frames. So to commemorate this dream he commissioned Unkei to fashion two effigies of Kojin and Fudo exactly as they appeared upon that occasion. The great sculptor set about his work in a reverent spirit, it being recorded that each time the wood was incised he accompanied the labor of his chisel with fervent prayers; at the end of the same year both statues were completed. The following year Yoritomo died. Masako marked the demise of her lord and master by becoming a nun: when her hair was cut off she caused part of this symbol of her retirement from the stage of life to be buried in the temple enclosure of Jomyo-ji—and above this relic a shrine was erected wherein were installed the statues of Kojin and Fudo.

Adjoining this valuable memento of the Yoritomo period is an overgrown mossy path leading up to a shrine of very small proportions. Although of such insignificant appearance this shrine of the fox-god Inari is of exceedingly remote foundation and was dedicated to the worthy to whom Kamakura owes its name—Kamatari. Indeed, a legend is extant to the effect that when the latter went forth on his nocturnal sortie in accordance with a dream, a mysterious white fox appeared, leading the way to the spot where the *kama* was to be deposited! In the vicinity of the little shrine is pointed out a rocky cave which is supposed to be the lair of the phantom fox. Moreover, tradition asserts that whenever this spectral animal makes an appearance it invariably heralds some species of good fortune for the temple.

Behind the main building is a miniature lake intersected by a rustic bridge. Just above, upon the hill a curious old pine will be observed—although not of large size, it is of weird shape and of a great age. Recently however, the burden of its years seems to be telling upon the strange clawlike branches, and unhappily its decay appears to be impending. Beyond this small landscape garden lies the cemetery, the centerpiece of which is the beautiful old gray monument which marks the resting place of the founder of Jomyo-ji, the shape of the tomb being typical of the Ashikaga period.

On descending from the graveyard, a footway to the right leads to a steep path. A multitude of stone steps ascend through the green twilight of foliage, and ultimately land the enterprising pilgrim upon a small enclosed level surrounded by ancient trees and tall bamboo so thickly as to preclude any distant view. The building that confronts one is called Kumanosha; it formerly belonged to Jomyo-ji. However, at present, the object of this small structure has become obscured by the mists of time—it is now detached, and is vaguely designated as the village shrine. When its festival days recur the whole neighborhood is *en fête*, and gaily decorated with lanterns and fluttering banners.

Beside the entrance to Jomyo-ji, the Nameri River ripples down to the sea in its rocky bed. Although so small, this stream is the chief river of Kamakura, and moreover is rendered historical by an incident concerning it which is known to every man, woman, and child of Japanese birth.

In ancient days there lived a magistrate of Kamakura named Aoto Fujitsuna, a man of lofty character and noted for his wisdom and strict integrity. He exercised his judicial talents under two of the Hojo regents, and one evening on returning from his duties at the Regency Office, he accidentally let fall some small pieces of copper money into the stream. Determined that government funds, however trifling, should not be allowed to disappear in this manner, Fujitsuna at once procured pine torches and enlisted the services of assistants, so that the coins were all successfully recovered. But as the cost of retrieving them naturally far exceeded the slight value of what was lost, the people criticized the worthy magistrate for his zeal in what seemed to be a wasteful and senseless proceeding. However, Fujitsuna, disgusted at their ignorance, indignantly pointed out that the coins if left in the riverbed would be permanently useless, while the money expended upon the torches and rewards to the assistants went into the pockets of the tradespeople, who would certainly be able to benefit therefrom.

The actual scene of this well-known incident appears to have been lost sight of: according to the temple authorities it took place in the immediate neighborhood of Jomyo-ji, but a notice is erected adjoining the temple of Hokai-ji claiming this part of the stream as the original spot.

Kōsoku-ji (Jūniso)

光
触
寺

❀

ABOUT TEN *chō* (a little over half a mile) beyond Jomyo-ji on the Kanazawa high road is the small village of Juniso. The chief feature of this insignificant cluster of farmers' cottages is the temple of Kosoku-ji, wherein is enshrined a famous statue of great antiquity, known as the Hoyake, or Cheek-branded Amida.

Founded in the thirteenth century, the building was gradually falling into decay, when in a severe storm some sixty years ago the old temple was completely wrecked by the violence of a typhoon. However, shortly afterward it was rebuilt, various of the original timbers being retrieved from the debris and used in the reconstruction. Above the entrance hangs a valued symbol of imperial patronage—the ancient tablet whereon the name Kosoku-ji was inscribed by the emperor Go-Daigo (1318–39). The interior is inviting and quite attractive, with carvings painted in gay colors. Before the sanctuary is suspended an elaborate gilt canopy with long glittering pendants.

At the rear, an unexpected object reposes upon a side altar in the shape of a gigantic head of the Buddha, black with age, and which is said to be a memento of the Kamakura period. According to the story, to commemorate the third anniversary of

Yoritomo's death, his widow Masako caused a huge statue of Buddha to be constructed and installed within a temple erected for that purpose. However, at a later date, the building caught fire and was entirely consumed. The body of the sacred figure shared the same fate, but the head was rescued from the flames and is venerated today as a relic of those remote times. Another side-altar is embellished with an excellent and convincing effigy of the first priest and founder of this temple—the famous Ippen Shonin (p. 118) who was also the spiritual founder of Yugyo-ji, the temple of the wandering priests at Fujisawa. Many stories and legends are related regarding this celebrated priest. It is recorded that on one occasion he made a pilgrimage to the Kumano Gongen (Shinto deity), and there practiced rigid austerities for the space of one hundred days. At the end of his penance the holy man implored the Almighty that a sign might be granted to prove his ministration had found favor in the sight of heaven. That night in a dream the sacred figure of Amida appeared in a luminous vapor near the bedside of the sleeping priest, offering him with extended hand a small paper. On awakening, Ippen Shonin found the paper of his dream lying beside his pillow, and inscribed with the words *Namu Amida Butsu*—the formula that has since been so fervently declaimed by countless numbers of pious enthusiasts. Thereupon in joy and triumph the priest bore his precious message on a proselytizing tour throughout the land, by its virtue gaining large numbers of converts to the faith.

The main altar is simplicity itself. A gilt figure of the Buddha keeps guard before the locked doors of the sanctuary wherein is enshrined the holy treasure of the temple—the Hoyake Amida, and to which no lesser functionary than the head priest has sole access. From the dim recesses of its sanctum the large spiked aureole glimmers with reflected luster from the tapers lit before it; the gleaming eyes of jade seem to flash in a weird and threatening manner upon the invaders of its peace and solitude.

The sacred figure is three feet in height. With one hand uplifted as though in benison, this venerable and impressive statue has stood upon the petals of its tarnished lotus for the long space of seven centuries. A fine work of art, it is said to be one of the masterpieces of Unkei, and to which a quaint and unusual legend is attached.

An early record to Kamakura relates the following tradition:

In the days of the emperor Juntoku (1211–42) a sculptor called Unkei was practicing his art in Kyoto. His skill in carving sacred images achieved such fame that the shogun Sanetomo summoned him to Kamakura, in order that the temples and shrines of the military capital might benefit by his genius.

It happened that amongst the ladies residing in Kamakura was one Machi no Tsubone, well known for her piety and spiritual proclivities. On the arrival of the great sculptor, this lady specially requested him to carve a figure of Amida Nyorai (a personification of the ultimate reality of the universe—*nyorai* signifies benevolence and love), to install as the chief object of worship in her private shrine; moreover she desired the artist to complete the work within the space of forty-eight days, to commemorate the forty-eight desires of Amida for the rescue and salvation of mankind. The figure of the divinity was duly executed within the appointed time, to the great satisfaction of the lady Machi; the new acquisition was duly deposited in her shrine with all appropriate offerings of flowers and incense.

Now amongst the inmates of this lady's household was a priest of low grade named Manzai: this man, although of pious tendencies, was apparently not without his weak points.

Some time after the carving of the image, the inmates of households frequented by this priest began to miss certain of their possessions; gradually an insidious tongue circulated the report that the disappearance of these articles was connected with the ministrations of Manzai. These scandalous rumors at last assumed such proportions that the neighbors' indignation reached a climax—the priest was arrested, and by order of his incensed patron was placed in confinement during her absence, urgent business having compelled her immediate departure for a place called Shibuya.

After his mistress had set out the priest was seized, and as a mark of the public horror at his supposed crime, he was branded with a heated iron upon the left cheek. Whilst Manzai was undergoing this torture he cried in a loud voice to the compassionate Amida to preserve his servant from the hand of the enemy. Lo! a miracle was wrought! All traces of the seared flesh immediately disappeared, leaving the cheek of the outraged priest smooth and immaculate as before. Astounded at his non-success, the assailant repeated his cruel action; each time pressing the hot iron deeper into his victim's face—but as before, after each impression the scar miraculously vanished as though by magic.

That night the lady Machi had a strange dream. A vision of her statue of Amida appeared, and sorrowfully indicated his left cheek, as though in amazement at having been accorded such persecution. On awakening, Machi no Tsubone experienced such alarm and consternation that she decided to immediately return to Kamakura. Her first action upon arrival was to purify herself with water and fresh apparel and to repair to her shrine.

There by the light of a candle she gazed upon the holy features of the Amida, and was horrified to discover the verification of her dream. Not only was the brand deeply impressed upon the sacred countenance, but a thin stream of blood was flowing from the wound! From the priest she realized what had taken place; the pitiful Amida had miraculously substituted himself for his falsely accused servant and faithful worshipper.

In deep repentance for her hasty action in crediting the priest's traducers, and not wishing evidence of this ruthless deed to go down to posterity, Machi consulted with another priestly adviser; a sculptor from the part of Kamakura called Kamegayatsu was summoned to repair the statue but his efforts proved of no avail. After all traces had been obliterated and fresh gilding applied, the mark of the brand invariably reappeared. When the sculptor had failed in twenty-one attempts he abandoned the undertaking and the fame of the statue was spread abroad through the succeeding centuries, even at the present day being known and venerated as the Hoyake, or Cheek-branded Amida.

The narrative states that Manzai—naturally preferring to eschew a neighborhood connected with such painful experiences—migrated to a temple at Oiso, where he spent the remainder of his life in the practice of piety and good works, dying in the odor of unimpeached sanctity at a ripe old age. As for the lady Machi no Tsubone, she embraced religion and became a nun, assuming the name of Hoami in commemoration of this incident (*hō* meaning cheek and *amida*, the Buddha). It is moreover recorded that on September 26th, 1251, at the age of seventy-three, she passed away in the attitude of prayer, kneeling before her beloved figure of the Hoyake Amida.

The celebrated poet Fujiwara Tamesuke evinced such deep interest in this strange occurrence that he wrote a detailed account of it, the manuscript being embellished with profuse and graphic illustrations in color by a famous contemporary painter of the thirteenth century named Tosa Mitsuoki. This valuable work is enrolled as a National Treasure and is carefully preserved at the temple as a history of the miraculous event.* It is in the form of two lengthy *makimono,* or scrolls, mounted on brocade with crystal rollers—each scroll being deposited in a separate lacquer case.

Near the main exit of the temple is a small wooden shrine wherein is preserved a venerable stone image of Jizo. This is the

*Now stored at the Kokuhokan.

Shioname, or Salt-tasting Jizo—an object of great antiquity and some renown, being specially described in a primitive record of Kamakura. A benign and compassionate expression is still distinguishable upon the crumbling features of the divinity. In earlier days he stood beside the high road to Kanazawa, but has been rescued from further vicissitudes and tricks of naughty men to placidly end his days under the protection of Kosoku-ji.

This somewhat enigmatical name was conferred upon the image from the fact that the purveyors of salt from Mutsu-ura, near Kanazawa, on their way to Kamakura made it an invariable custom to offer a sample of their ware to the compassionate deity as they passed, with a view to ensuring good luck in their business. Originally a luminous halo was said to surround the saint's head, but on one sad occasion a miscreant merchant was returning home, and incensed that the god had not presided over his transactions with more auspicious effect, vented his wrath upon the defenseless effigy, overthrowing it, and with sacrilegious hand cramming the Jizo's mouth with salt! After this indignity the aureole is, not unnaturally, said to have disappeared and was beheld no more by the rough traffickers of those regions.

Zuisen-ji

❀

THIS FAMOUS old temple stands back from the Kanazawa road some distance beyond Daito-no-miya; the narrow road leading to it intersects the pine avenue of Egara Tenjin. Formerly ranking second of the ten leading monasteries in Eastern Japan of the Rinzai sect of Buddhism, it was founded in 1327 by Ashikaga Motouji, and was distinguished by becoming identified with the Ashikaga shoguns.

The approach gradually ascends between high grassy banks until the thatched gate is reached which marks the temple enclosure: the grounds are beautiful with lawns and flowers, rocks and caves, and many interesting old trees. The fragrant foliage of an exceptionally large eucalyptus towers in front of the temple, the seed of which was brought from Australia in 1878.* The small cavern behind the lake** contained the statue of Benten and was known as the Angel's Cave. Beyond this, on the extreme left steps are hewn in the mossy rock. This route gradually ascends through charming environment to the top of

*Alas, this living relic has since perished.
**The site of the lake is now occupied by the original rock garden, restored in 1970.

{ 72 }

the mountain; from its winding nature the path is called the Juhachi-mawari, or Eighteen Curves. In olden times the distant view commanded from this small plateau was highly renowned amongst poets and nature lovers, its beauties having been immortalized in many songs and poems. Beyond the irregular ridges lies the deep blue ocean, distant purple mountains closing in the picture with lovely effect. In spring the masses of red and crimson azaleas lend a brilliant note of color to the scene; the groves are musical with the cry of the *uguisu* (nightingale), the little brown bird whose note is supposed to be a text of scripture—*hō-hokekyō*—while the trees and bushes of this thickly wooded region are gay with newly budding foliage, the delicate shell-pink and pale green hues presenting the felicitous appearance of giant clusters of blossoms. In bygone days Zuisen-ji enjoyed a high reputation for its maples; their "flaming brocade" is still effective and beautiful. But of late years their number has somewhat decreased. In 1328, shortly after the temple was founded, the first priest—the celebrated Muso Kokushi—caused a pavilion called Ichirantei to be erected upon the summit of the hill in order to afford rest and appreciation of the landscape. Poets have compared this little structure to a miniature Elysium from which one could gaze down upon the vision of the world below. When in the course of time this fabric fell into ruins, a new structure was erected some two hundred years ago by the enlightened scholar and philosopher Mitsukuni, lord of Mito, who was also a constant visitor and patron of Zuisen-ji. This building was modeled upon the Chinese pavilion Suiotei, built by the Chinese Emperor Kiso, of the Sung Dynasty (420–79). Around the interior panels of lacquered wood were suspended upon which a collection of poems—inspired by the beauty of the scenery and composed upon the spot—were inscribed: these panels are still preserved in the guest room of the temple. About a century after its construction, this second pavilion was destroyed in a severe storm but its site is still plainly to be seen. Within it was installed a "thousand-handed" statue of Kannon that is now enshrined upon the altar of the temple below.

The centerpiece and place of honor upon the main altar is occupied by a large and interesting effigy of the first priest of Zuisen-ji, the erudite and renowned Muso Kokushi. The tints are considerably faded and the flight of centuries has left its mark upon this ancient work; it is said to have been executed during the lifetime of the original, and has therefore been in existence some six hundred years. In the left-hand division is the chief object of worship, a valuable statue of Shaka; on either side are small but realistically painted images of Ashikaga Motouji and Ujimitsu, the third Ashikaga shogun. The right-hand division is occupied by the above-mentioned Kannon, in front of which is a fierce little statue with gleaming yellow eyes. This is the ever-popular Daruma (Sanskrit: *Dharma*), the Indian missionary priest who founded the Zen sect in China in the sixth century. Much depicted in popular art, and generally with a ruffianly countenance strangely belying his saintly character, Daruma was the great exponent of the doctrine of "Thought transmitted without utterance"; he is said to have remained in profound religious abstraction for nine years, after which his legs withered away from disuse, and disappeared!

In olden times a high tower was erected in the grounds to the right of the entrance gate. This was used as a repository for the most valuable statues, but when the tower was attacked by fire they were rescued and removed to the main temple. Behind the site of this structure is a large cavern in three divisions; the rocky chamber on the left is dimly lighted by a natural opening like circular windows, shaded with ferns and greenery. In the congenial gloom of this retreat, the ancient priest Muso Kokushi was in the habit of practicing *zazen*, the mystic art of detaching the mind from the body in religious meditation. The sequestered path to the right of this historic cave—between the cliffs and a grove of bamboo—leads to the graveyard, where interest centers in the

{ 74 }

fine old tomb of Motouji, founder of the temple. This archaic monument has a beautiful setting; it stands in a mossy cave surrounded by wet and glistening pebbles, upon which drops of water continually percolate from the rock above, conveying a strange symbolism of purity and peace. A little beyond is the solitary rounded tomb of a former priest of the temple, but amongst these venerable sepulchers no relic exists of Muso Kokushi. This great divine had been summoned to officiate at Tenryu-ji, the temple of the first Ashikaga shogun at Kyoto; there he died at the age of seventy, and there his ashes were interred.

Originally another temple, Eian-ji, stood in close proximity to Zuisen-ji, built and dedicated to the memory of Ujimitsu after his death in 1398. On February 10, 1439, the fourth Ashikaga regent Mochiuji, on the betrayal of his plans, committed suicide in this temple together with over thirty of his retainers. On that tragic day, the battle raged fiercely in Kamakura and unhappily a strong wind fanned on the flames that were the inevitable feature of these conflicts. It is recorded of this calamity that many temples and vast numbers of dwellings perished in the holocaust.

The wife of the ill-starred regent, with many of her attendant ladies, had taken shelter in the three-storied tower of Zuisen-ji, but it was impossible to avert their doom: the tower caught fire and all the unhappy fugitives were burnt to death. The two little princes alone had managed to escape, but as a sequel to this disaster the Ashikaga family entirely disappeared for nine years. At the end of that time the family was forgiven and Mochiuji's son Nariuji returned to take up his quarters in Kamakura. However in 1445—while Nariuji was officiating as *kanryō*—he was attacked by his too-powerful representative, and from whose violence he fled to Koga in the north of Japan. This feud caused the termination of the office of governor of Kamakura, a fact that materially conduced to the decline of the city.

Just within the entrance gate of Zuisen-ji is a new Jizo-do. This small structure is a recent erection, the opening ceremony having taken place on June 26, 1916. It was built to enshrine a fine old statue of Jizo—a standing figure sculpted in dark wood; this image dates back from the Kamakura period and is considered a representative example of the art of that age. Upon either side are ranged six small figures of pugilistic demeanor, armed with various weapons: these are the twelve Shinsho, or guardian ministers of Yakushi Nyorai, the god of wisdom and healing. These valuable images have only recently been acquired by the temple. In past times there were twelve vassal shrines attached to the temple of Hachiman, but at the Restoration these buildings gradually fell into decay and disappeared. At that time the statues were acquired by a resident of Kamakura named Jimbei Yoshimura; he presented them to Zuisen-ji and the Jizo-do was erected under his auspices.

An interesting fact in connection with this temple is that for a time its tranquil seclusion afforded a shelter to the celebrated patriot and martyr Yoshida Shoin, whose uncle was then officiating as head priest of Zuisen-ji (a celebrated scholar named Chikuin). Some writings of the former are still preserved as treasures of the temple—mementos of his loyalty to the imperial cause and of his tragic fate.

This young samurai was an ardent loyalist. When the American envoy Townsend Harris came to Shimoda for the second time in 1859 to conclude the commercial treaty between Japan and America, Yoshida Shoin was deeply incensed that the treaty was concluded by the shogun's minister, Ii Naosuke, the emperor's authority being practically ignored. With a little band of enthusiasts (the translation of whose motto means "Revere the sovereign, expel the barbarians") they determined to attempt to overthrow the shogunate. With that end in view, Yoshida resolved in spite of the national edict that meted out death to any Japanese subject who should leave the empire, to go abroad secretly in order to make a careful study of foreign customs and methods.

His preparations were made at Zuisen-ji. One dark night he

attempted to conceal himself on board one of the American ships of the Harris expedition, but was discovered, and the Americans gave notice to the Tokugawa government at Edo. Orders were promptly issued for his arrest; he was seized and beheaded at the early age of twenty-eight, many of his associates suffering the same fate.

Nevertheless, this little group of talented and ardent patriots have been described by historians as the real motive force that led up to the Restoration of 1868.

Kamakura Shrine

❀

THIS IS the only temple in Kamakura of modern foundation. It was constructed as recently as the year 1869 by order of the emperor Meiji, and is of pure Shinto architecture. Prince Morinaga, to whom the shrine is dedicated, was formerly the head priest of a temple on Hiei-zan, near Kyoto, and was also known as Daito-no-miya from the name of his place of residence. A stone bridge spanning a small stream gives access to two courtyards, shaded with a grove of pines, maples, and many cherry trees.

On the right-hand side of the upper court is a building enclosed within a high dark palisade. This sanctum was specially erected as a rest-house for the emperor Meiji when he visited this shrine in 1873. It consists of a wide matted verandah with two rooms—the apartment on the right contains the raised dais upon which His Majesty reposed. The tokonoma is decorated with an interesting work of art in the shape of a life-sized and vigorous equestrian statue of Prince Morinaga, in which the spirit of medieval times is well reflected. The ill-fated prince is clad in picturesque armor, equipped with a case of arrows, and grasping a long bow. This carving was the work of a modern sculptor, Kisai Yamada, and was executed in 1893.

Kamakura Shrine is of historic and tragic interest, for here the unfortunate Prince Morinaga, third son of the emperor Go-Daigo, was imprisoned for seven months in a dark cavern behind the temple and there cruelly assassinated in 1335 at the age of twenty-seven. This gallant prince had been the mainstay of the revolution which had for its object the overthrow of the military government and the restoration of the imperial ascendancy, which had been divested of all power by the military rule at Kamakura. However, the crafty and ambitious Takauji (who became the first Ashikaga shogun), realizing that the prince was a serious obstacle to his design of establishing himself at Kamakura as the military governor and practical ruler of the empire, conspired to poison the emperor's mind against his own son, and falsely concocted a plot to the effect that the innocent Prince Morinaga was scheming to depose his imperial parent and to usurp the throne in his stead. Unhappily, the emperor Go-Daigo was over-susceptible to the influence of his advisers, and, lending a ready ear to these sinister reports, in November 1334 he caused a warrant to be issued for his son's arrest.

In answer to the accusation, Prince Morinaga inscribed a pathetic appeal to the parent whose cause he had so loyally served, and passionately asserted his innocence. He concludes with the following words:

"In spite of all this I have unwittingly offended. I would appeal to heaven, but the sun and moon have no favor for an unfilial son. I would bow my head and cry to the earth for help, but the mountains and rivers do not harbor a disloyal subject. The tie between father and son is severed and I am cast away. I have no longer anything to hope for in this world. If I may be pardoned, stripped of my rank, and permitted to enter religion, there will be no cause for regret. In my deep sorrow I cannot say more."

Go-Daigo's heart might have been melted had he received this affecting petition, but the messenger feared the wrath of Takauji, thus it was never delivered, and the doom of the ill-starred prince was written in the book of fate. He was exiled to Kamakura, where he was put under the charge of Tadayoshi—brother of the enemy who had accomplished his ruin—who confined his victim in this dark and gloomy cavern. Seven months later, just before the invasion of Kamakura by Hojo Tokiyuki (son of the last Hojo regent), as Tadayoshi was leaving Kamakura he determined to put an end to his royal prisoner. Accordingly he instructed one of his followers named Fuchibe to return, in order to execute this deed as speedily as possible.

History thus describes the tragic scene that ensued. With an escort of seven horsemen the assassin arrived at the "earthen prison." Although in the outer world the morning sunshine was clear and invigorating, the air of the dank cave was dark as night; by the light of a flickering taper the captive was reciting the scriptures. Fuchibe announced his presence, informing his victim that a palanquin was in readiness to bear him from that place. Straightaway the prince grasped the ominous significance of this message for which, doubtless, he had long been waiting. Springing forward he cried, "Thou art the messenger of Death," and essayed to wrest away the assassin's sword, but Fuchibe was too dexterous; parrying the attack he felled the prince to the earth, inflicting a sharp wound upon his knee with the weapon. However the imperial spirit was not yet quelled. When the murderer leapt upon his victim's chest to consummate his evil purpose, the frenzied prince seized the dagger in his teeth, breaking off part of the steel—but furiously grasping another sword the emissary twice stabbed Prince Morinaga in the heart; then raising the dying prisoner by his long black hair he slashed off his head. As Fuchibe was bearing away this trophy as a sign that the grim and bloody deed had been accomplished, the expression of the dead face, with its mournful eyes widely opened, was so appalling that the courage of the murderer failed him, and he cast away his dreadful burden a few paces beyond the cavern. A pathway leads to this place; the actual spot where the head was thrown is railed in, and a notice is erected whereon the circumstances are recorded. Later on, the remains of Prince Morinaga were buried on top of a hill a short distance eastward of the shrine amidst surroundings of great natural beauty, the tomb lying in the shadow of a mighty pine tree. The hill is now enclosed with a palisade by order of the imperial household, and entrance is forbidden.

As the temple is of such modern foundation, naturally its treasures are few. But they comprise a few memorials of the prince in the shape of various manuscripts, including one in his own handwriting; also, a realistic painting of the severed head, pale and cadaverous of aspect, in which harrowing representation the artist has rendered full justice to the suffering of the imperial victim.

Kakuon-ji

❀

O N THE LEFT of the large *torii* marking the gateway of Daito-no-miya runs a grassy path intersecting a valley between densely wooded hills. At the outset is a large stone monument recording the fact that this path leads to one of the eighty-eight resting places of the famous abbot and saint Kobo Daishi: it culminates, in about half a mile, in a slight eminence planted with a grove of plum and cherry trees.

Here is situated a venerable temple of unimposing exterior, Kakuon-ji. In former times this tranquil valley presented an aspect of considerable animation, the approach being lined with ten subsidiary temples. Moreover, the Kakuon-ji of those remote days consisted of numerous edifices studding the level terrace and the adjoining hillsides; much is recorded in ancient writings concerning the elegance of its original aspect. As the result of a sacred dream, Hojo Yoshitoki (afterward second regent) constructed a shrine in the part of Kamakura called Okura (1218), installing therein a statue of Yakushi Nyorai fashioned by Unkei. Owing to the fame of this figure the district became known as Yakushi-dogayatsu, or Valley of the Yakushi-do. This shrine was damaged by fire in 1250, repaired in 1263, but later again fell into decay. The temple of Kakuon-ji is supposed to occupy the identical site. Founded by the eighth Hojo regent Sadatoki in 1296 and placed under the direction of a famous priest named Chikai, the chief objects of worship were the set of large figures consisting of Yakushi attended by his satellites—all said to be the work of Takuma.

An interesting feature of the existing temple is its great age. In December 1352, the *butsuden,* or hall of images, was repaired by Takauji (first Ashikaga shogun), many of the fine old timbers of the declining vassal building being used in the process of reconstruction. So thoroughly was this work carried out that it has lasted until the present day—between five and six hundred years—and is consequently one of Kamakura's most ancient buildings. The space of the main altar is entirely occupied by the three huge images—the centerpiece being the famous Yakushi Nyorai, or Healing Buddha, enthroned upon a gigantic lotus, the petals of which are beautifully shaped. To this deity—the Aesculapius of Buddhism—is also attributed the power of giving sight to the blind. On either side he is supported by the solar and lunar divinities Nikko and Gekko Bosatsu, who represent sunlight and moonlight and are generally associated with Yakushi. In former days these statues were richly tinted in colors. Alas, this embellishment has shared the general fate of annihilation and extinction and but the merest traces remain. Below the main altar is a great effigy of the Buddha sculptured in wood; the boss on the forehead, from which the radiance that illumines the universe is supposed to emanate, is of crystal. This figure is said to date back from the Ashikaga days—sculptor unknown. The walls are flanked on either side by twelve mighty warriors of pugnacious and threatening aspect; some appear to be singularly ferocious, brandishing swords and various weapons with long hair bristling erect, others are of more reposeful demeanor. These are the Juni Shinsho, the twelve guardian ministers of Yakushi Nyorai, who serve as messengers to execute his purposes and desires. This divinity is supposed to have made twelve vows to succor human beings who are afflicted with illness or suffering from various perils and distresses.

It will be remembered that Yoshitoki—founder of the Yakushi-do—held the office of bearer of the sword of state to Sanetomo, the third shogun, on the occasion of the latter's visit of thanksgiving to Hachiman, when the assassination took place. The ghostly dog that Yoshitoki beheld, warning him to turn back, was supposed to be one of these messengers to the god Yakushi. Tradition states that on that occasion one of the twelve known as Inu no Kami (the dog divinity) was missing from his accustomed place!

The ceiling of the temple is decorated with a large blue dragon surrounded by white clouds—this design was executed in the Tokugawa period by an artist named Tenshin. But the *pièce de résistance* of Kakuon-ji is the famous Kuro Jizo, or Black Jizo, who occupies the place of honor in a small shrine within the temple precincts. This statue is also said to date from the Kamakura period. It is a National Treasure and is considered an admirable work of art, the worshippers of this dusky but popular deity being numbered by thousands. Sculptured in dark wood and adorned with a golden breast-ornament of archaic design, the Jizo has a gracious and benign countenance; a most effective background is afforded by the elaborate golden mandala—known as the *funa-gokō*, or boat halo, from its resemblance to the shape of a boat. This is beautifully carved with a design of flames and is further embellished with pale blue disks upon which Sanskrit characters are inscribed in gold, surrounded by the infernal fire.

A record of many centuries ago avers that this celebrated statue was endowed with miraculous powers. Although with the object of beautifying the figure it was repeatedly painted in lighter colors—on each occasion during the night—the Jizo, repudiating such meretricious embellishments, mysteriously returned to his original somber hue. According to another tradition this Jizo once made a special descent into the infernal regions, in order to witness the punishment and tortures of the condemned souls. The kindly nature of the benevolent deity was so affected by the agony of these miserable wretches that he undertook for a time to take the place of their relentless custodian, greatly reducing the intense heat of the purgatorial fires and thus lessening the torment of the writhing sufferers. For this reason the Black, or Hitaki (fire kindling) Jizo as he is also called, has many devotees amongst firemen.

In former times July 13 was supposed to be the day when the lid was taken off the fires of hell and the ghosts of the departed were allowed to return to the upper world; this is still celebrated as the Festival of the Dead.

It is recorded that on that day there were special rejoicings at this Jizo-do, thousands repairing to the shrine for worship, and many sacred dances taking place upon that festal occasion.

On either side of the dominant central figure (which is somewhat over eight feet in height) are myriad images arranged in twelve rows; at first sight their identification is not apparent, but a nearer inspection proves them to be figures of Jizo. Some appear of great antiquity, some are wearing little bibs, while others have labels attached upon which a date is inscribed. Occasional gaps are also visible where certain of the small effigies seem to have been removed. The reason for the vacancies in the long lines of the little gods is as follows: To be childless, and therefore to have no successor to carry on the name and family traditions, is considered almost in the light of a calamity in this land, where the family is of paramount importance. Consequently, when a wife has been married some years and the joys of motherhood appear to have passed her by, as a last resort she may apply to the temple for the loan of one of the "Thousand Jizo." This she reverently carries home and deposits in the *butsudan,* or household shrine, with daily prayers that her hopes may be granted. Should the gods lend a favorable ear to her supplications, after the successful birth of the child the borrowed Jizo is returned to the temple with due rejoicings. But in the reverse case—when all petitions before the little children's god have proved of no avail—he is kept a reasonable time and then sadly brought back to rejoin the miniature army of saints in the dim twilight of the Jizo-do.

Jizo (who has been identified with the Sanskrit *ksite garbha*) is one of the most popular and widely venerated deities in Japan, and has been described as the most Japanese of all the Japanese divinities. He is certainly the most lovable figure in the popular faith, being the protector of children in particular, and of expectant mothers, as well as of travelers and pilgrims. For this latter reason little groups of Roku (Six) Jizo may be constantly seen on the high roads. As he is universally revered as the guardian of dead children, frequently sorrowing mothers bring the little garments of their lost ones to deck the statues hoping that in return the kindly god will specially protect the poor little wandering ghost in the shadowy and demon-haunted *Sai no Kawara,* or dry bed of the river of souls in purgatory. Occasionally however, a little hat or bib has been gratefully offered by a rejoicing parent whose child has been cured of dangerous sickness by intervention of the benevolent deity. The heaps of little stones that are always in evidence around the statues of Jizo signify that if a stone is offered with faith, it helps the tiny wanderers in the dusky regions to perform their long penances, and shortens the time of their suffering in the underworld.

In the little valley a few paces to the rear of the main temple is one of Kamakura's ten celebrated wells—Munetate-ido. Its claim to celebrity lies in the fact that because of the exceptional purity of the spring, Kobo Daishi is said to have dug the well and used its waters to offer to the gods. A path behind the main building, intersecting a grove of cherry trees, gradually ascends to another small vassal temple situated on the hillside, also of great age and weather-beaten exterior. This is known as Dairoku-ji. Here, in the center of the altar, a deity of menacing appearance is enshrined in a huge case of black and gold lacquer.* A near inspection will reveal his extreme antiquity, for the figure is constructed of metal that seems to be crumbling away with the flight of centuries. With fiercely gleaming eyes and brandishing a sword, this divinity is not so alarming as he seems. He is Fudo, the god of wisdom according to some exponents, the god of fire according to others. The fire is for the purification of the mind; the sword is to make war on the devil—the purpose of the rope in his left hand being to bind them up when vanquished.

The sword is supposed to be typical of intellect, or enlightenment; the rope signifies mastery of the evil passions and desires of unregenerate mankind, and subjecting them to the sway of reason. The Lord Buddha truly said, "Fudo dwells within the mind of every man."

This effigy is said to be the work of Gangyo—a famous sculptor of the time of Hojo Sadatoki (1284–1300)—and was known as the Kokoromi, or Experimental, Fudo because the artist subsequently constructed a second statue of the same divinity, an exact model of the present figure but on a larger scale. This is still worshipped in a shrine on the mountain of Oyama (adjacent to the Hakone range).

A strange square stand will be observed below the image, with an iron depression containing ashes: this is the *gomadan,* or receptacle to contain holy fire for invocation, and is said to have been used by Kobo Daishi. On special occasions fire is kindled, it being supposed that the smoke is typical of prayers ascending to heaven and that the flames scare away demons, otherwise known as the unruly passions of erring mortals.

On the hill just above the Fudo temple is another small shrine, the exterior of which is also much weathered and decayed.** But

*This structure has since collapsed from age. The statue of Fudo can now be seen at the right of the entrance to Kakuon-ji.
**This building has, unfortunately, been lost with the passage of time.

the interior was renewed (in 1905), thanks to the munificence of the faithful. This little structure is the home of thirteen gods. It is full of rocks and perched here and there are small figures, bearing a strong family resemblance, but are displayed with their various names attached on labels to prevent confusion among worshippers.

The rocky path winds up, with ever-varying views, to a plateau at the top of this height which is railed in and provided with seats, inviting the wanderer to repose awhile in enjoyment of the prospect. A long vista of wooded hills and valleys, in every shade of luxuriant verdure, rolls away to meet the distant blue expanse of ocean melting into the paler turquoise of the sky above. The white sails gleaming in the sunshine seem no larger than butter-flies dancing across the quivering wavelets; while in spring and summer the little brown birds (*uguisu*) serenade in chorus from the surrounding glades and tempt the pilgrim to unduly linger in this sylvan corner of the earth, lying so far aloof from the "world's wide din."

At the rear of the plateau is another shrine dedicated to Kobo Daishi and containing a larger stone image in his likeness. The fact that during this holy man's wanderings he rested in this spot is a cause of great pride and felicitation to the temple, several other images and various mementos being preserved of that remote occasion. This celebrated priest (774–835) and great religious instructor of medieval times was the founder of the Shingon sect of Buddhism, the mystic formula of which he was commissioned to propagate by the erudite Chinese abbot Huiko during his sojourn in China. This occult creed made a strong appeal to the public taste and soon achieved an extraordinary popularity, numbering millions of adherents; its center was established on the summit of Koyasan amidst scenery famed for its natural beauty, becoming the largest and most powerful monastery in Japan. Such was the sanctity of this most popular saint that many of his followers are said to believe he is not really dead, that his body is incorruptible and preserved in a state of repose within the tomb awaiting his next reincarnation. This sepulcher is the Mecca of his numerous devotees, and every year thousands of worshippers repair to do homage to the great departed.

Kobo Daishi is also renowned as the inventor of the Japanese *hiragana* syllabary. A marvelous calligrapher himself, as well as a skilled sculptor, there are many stories extant of his supernatural achievements. A typical legend of this wizard of the brush relates that when he was in China the emperor desired him to inscribe the name over one of the palace doors that had become effaced by time. Kobo Daishi at once took five brushes, one in each hand, one between the toes of either foot, and the fifth in his mouth. With simultaneous strokes he traced with exquisite delicacy the desired inscription, then from a distance he spattered drops of India ink upon the wall, where they alighted in the form of beautiful characters!

Upon a large slab of gray stone beside the shrine the following is recorded: On Kobo Daishi's return from China in the year 816 he traveled all over Japan in search of a suitable site whereon to found this monastery. During his stay in Kyoto the emperor bestowed upon him as a gift a piece of valuable wood. The priest fashioned therefrom a statue of himself and offered it to the emperor as a souvenir of his sojourn in the capital. It was a somewhat unusual image—the arms and legs being jointed with chains to render them moveable, so the figure could be made to rest either in a sitting or standing posture; hence it was known as the Kusari (chain) Taishi (great instructor). The present statue is a copy in stone of the original work.

Behind this shrine a wooden gateway marks the exit from the plateau. The narrow path on the left leads up over mossy crags to the summit of the mountain, an unexpected feature being the large number of irregular and picturesque caves that honey-comb the rock crest. They are said to number over one hundred.

From the fact that bones and relics of human remains have been discovered, it is inferred that in former times they were used as a mausoleum—a more ideal spot for that purpose could hardly be imagined. Eighty-eight of these caves contain statues known as the "Eighty-eight Kobo Daishi," while within many others are ancient monuments.* The track that winds toward the west leads gradually up to the Washi no Mine, or Eagle's Peak. Upon the summit, enthroned upon a high stone base is a large and well-carved statue of the saint—it has evidently been protected from the elements by a roof, but storms have swept away the outer covering, and only the iron supports are left. The steps leading up to the small rocky level upon which the figure stands are steep and somewhat difficult, but the vast panorama commanded from this height is enchanting, and should on no account be missed. On either side of the peninsula lies the sea—the bays of Tokyo and Sagami respectively, studded with white-sailed craft—while the undulations of the landscape billow away into the far horizon with indescribable effect. If the path is continued in a south-westerly direction it leads to the summit of Hansobo—the goblin mountain behind Kencho-ji—its rounded peak being visible for some distance as a guide. A descent can either be effected from the track on the western side, from which the main road can be regained in the vicinity of Meigetsu-in; or by the route between the chains, which steeply descends to the platform in the hillside upon which is perched the little shrine of Hansobo.

This is one of Kamakura's most beautiful walks. The scenic effects are greatly enhanced in spring, when the mountains are gay with wild flowers and the new shoots of the luxuriant foliage; also in the fall, when the joyous tints of the autumn leaves and the rich crimson and scarlet maples paint the landscape with vivid coloring.

*This picturesque route was badly damaged in the great Tokyo Earthquake of 1923, and is now closed.

The Tomb of Yoritomo

❀

A SHORT DISTANCE to the east of Hachiman is a
wooded eminence called Okurayama. Here, in a lonely
grove high upon the hillside, lies the historic site where
the great Yoritomo, founder of Kamakura, was buried. Embowered
by tall forest trees, whose interlacing boughs cast a tracery of
heavy shadows upon the mossy sward beneath, it is a beautiful
and tranquil spot well befitting the long sleep of a hero.

The tomb is impressive in its extreme simplicity. Enclosed
within a massive stone fence is a stone pagoda-shaped monument
of some five feet in height, heavily coated with the rich velvet of
dark green moss; a stone lantern stands on either side, and
before it an incense burner for offerings to the soul of the
departed. These simple emblems are all that mark the sepulcher
of one of the greatest warriors and statesmen Japan has ever
known, and one of the greatest names of the most heroic period
of Japanese history. Upon the level ground below—now a net-
work of ricefields and gardens—was situated Yoritomo's official
residence; it is recorded that during his lifetime the family shrine
was erected upon this terrace on the hillside where his monument still exists. In the course of time the shrine disappeared and
the tomb was gradually falling into decay, but in 1779 Prince

Shimazu came to the rescue—restoring and embellishing this important link to those early days when Kamakura was at the zenith of her glory. Prior to that time the tomb was only three feet high, but at the prince's instigation it was raised to its present height; the fence was added, with the stone lanterns, and also the font for the holy water of purification.

It is recorded in ancient writings that after the death of Yoritomo in 1199, it was customary for the Hojo regent, and many other distinguished personages, to repair to this tomb to pay homage to the illustrious departed. To the right of the plateau upon which the monument is situated, a small and precipitous track ascends the hill. This leads into a comparatively broad and easy path gently winding upward to the tombs of two other important functionaries belonging to the same epoch. However, should this track be considered too steep and forbidding, a short distance to the right (from below) lie two imposing flights of steps spanned by large stone *torii*, which form the orthodox approach to these historic monuments.

The cave on the left contains the ashes of Yoritomo's celebrated counselor Oe Hiromoto. This distinguished scholar is said to have been the most important factor in the conception and organization of the Kamakura system. Indeed, according to some historians, without his assistance and wise counsel Yoritomo would hardly have risen to fame. When the shogunate was first established, Oe Hiromoto held the position of supreme adviser to the shogun, but the power was gradually assumed by Yoritomo's father-in-law—Hojo Tokimasa. This great statesman and legislator died in the same year as Yoritomo's widow Masako, 1225, at the age of seventy-eight; he is said to be an ancestor of the house of Prince Mori. To the left of the enclosure stands a stone monument upon which his history and virtues are recorded. The cave on the right marks the grave of the illegitimate son of Yoritomo, Shimazu Tadahisa, said to be an ancestor of the house of Prince Shimazu.

Below the approach leading up to the tomb of Yoritomo is a large railed-in space suggesting a cemetery containing numerous stone lanterns and monuments. This is a memorial to the soldiers from this district of Kamakura who fell in the Russo–Japanese War (1904–5), and reads: "In memory of loyal souls."

2. Statue of Yoritomo, founder of Kamakura shogunate. Courtesy of the National Museum, Tokyo.

Tsurugaoka Hachiman Shrine

鶴岡八幡宮

❀

THIS LARGE and important shrine—so closely connected with the family of Yoritomo, and the theater of many dramatic scenes of ancient history—occupies a commanding site upon the eminence known as Tsurugaoka, or Hill of Storks. From earliest times Hachiman, the Japanese Mars, has been the deity specially worshipped by warriors and the military classes, the original dedication of the shrine receding through the centuries to fabulous antiquity.

The first temple of Hachiman was established at Usa in Kyushu (Province of Buzen); the deity worshipped therein seems to have been a direct descendant of Amaterasu, the primeval goddess of the sun. According to the legend, at the ceremony of dedication eight white banners were seen to descend from heaven, fluttering down upon the shrine. From this miraculous demonstration the temple was known as Yahata no Yashiro (Shrine of the Eight Flags), and which according to Chinese pronunciation becomes Hachiman. Later on, in about the sixth century, the emperor Ojin, son of the valiant empress Jingo, came to be identified with the deity of this temple. The empress Jingo—a lady "intelligent, shrewd, and with a countenance of blooming loveliness"—is said to have reigned for the lengthy period of sixty-eight years (201–

69) and was famed as the leader of the celebrated military expedition to Korea.

In the year 859, the emperor Seiwa transferred from Usa and established at Iwashimizu, in the Province of Yamashiro (now Southern Kyoto), the original of the present shrine. The family of Minamoto being descended from the emperor Seiwa, and the deity Hachiman Ojin and the empress Jingo being associated with such warlike distinction, Hachiman came to be identified as the patron divinity of the Minamoto. When the temple was erected in Kamakura, it later assumed the aspect of the tutelary shrine of the military capital. This was effected in the year 1063 by Minamoto Yoriyoshi, ancestor of Yoritomo. On the occasion of an expedition to the north of Japan he had the shrine of Hachiman established in Kamakura in order that special prayers might be offered for his victories and the success of the campaign. Yoriyoshi's eldest son Yoshiie (1041–1108) was possessed of such brilliant military qualities that he was regarded in the light of being a reincarnation of Hachiman. It is a well-known fact that before the birth of Yoshiie, his father specially prayed before the Hachiman shrine for an offspring who should be a worthy son of Mars. The war god apparently lent a favorable ear to his petition, for the child that was born was of such magnificent valor and so renowned for his skill as an archer that the family of Minamoto owed much of its supremacy and distinction to Hachiman Taro—or the firstborn son of Hachiman, as he was known to posterity, and which name was ceremoniously conferred upon him by his father. This heroic ancestor played an important part in laying the foundations of the Minamoto power that culminated four generations later in the whole of Japan lying beneath the sway of his great-great-grandson Yoritomo.

This first temple of Hachiman to be erected in Kamakura was of less imposing proportions and upon a considerably smaller scale than it assumed later; its site was also different, being much nearer to the sea. This site is still in existence, the historic spot being marked by a small shrine that also bears the name of Hachiman. However, when Yoritomo took up his abode in what was afterward to be his capital and the most important city of the empire, in 1180 he removed the shrine to its present site, which was originally known as Matsugaoka (Hill of Pines), but was rechristened Tsurugaoka after the former locality. At first this remodeled edifice was situated in the courtyard below the hill. However, in March 1191, a disastrous conflagration occurred in Kamakura and the buildings of Hachiman were entirely destroyed. After this fire, Yoritomo caused the shrine of his patron god to be rebuilt in its present commanding situation. This was so speedily accomplished that the main temple and all the vassal buildings were completed in the same year, and on November 21, 1191, the restored shrine was dedicated with an opening celebration of great splendor and general rejoicing. In spite of its lofty and isolated situation the temple was again attacked by fire in 1821, and again destroyed. On this occasion it was rebuilt and reestablished under the auspices of the eleventh Tokugawa shogun Ienari, the present structure dating from 1828.

Formerly the Hachiman shrine was classed under the compromise between Buddhism and Shinto known as *ryōbu shintō* (two religions), a system originated by Kobo Daishi, who claimed that the Shinto gods were incarnations of Buddhist divinities, and thus amalgamated the two creeds, the austerities of Shinto becoming merged in the ornate decoration and gorgeous ritual of the imported faith. Thus the former aspect of Hachiman was on an entirely different scale; ancient records describe in detail the vast numbers of elaborate structures that surrounded the main shrine. These included the Hall for the Recital of the Scriptures; the great Bell Tower; the Goma-do, or Incense Temple—enshrining the statues of five saints carved by Unkei, and from whence thin spirals of the sacred smoke ascended ceaselessly by day and by night; the Chinese Pagoda; Benzaiten, or Temple of Benten, erected on an island of the lotus pond; the temple dedicated to the martyred Sanetomo; and the Rokkakudo, or six-sided pavilion. West of the great *ichō* tree, behind the Incense Temple, stood the Rinzo (Hall), where the holy books of the scriptures were kept: this building was some thirty feet square, and the sacred writings are said to have been brought from Korea at the request of Sanetomo.

Another temple was dedicated to Takeshiuchi no Sukune, faithful retainer of the empress Jingo, and who carried in his arms when a babe the emperor Ojin. But the downfall of the shogunate and the restoration of imperial power in 1868 brought about the reaction in favor of restoring the national faith to its original simplicity. Shinto again became the state religion, and Buddhism was disowned and disendowed. All the glitter and ornamentation disappearing from the shrines, they returned to the unembellished austerity that forms such a strong contrast to the Buddhist temples and the great shrine of Hachiman assumed the aspect of mysterious solemnity and beauty unadorned that it presents to its stream of visitors and admirers in the present day.

Of all the numerous vassal temples and subsidiary structures, two important ones alone remain. Below the broad steps upon the eastern side—with its beautiful carvings and paintings sadly impaired by time and the ravages of the climate—stands the Waka-miya, the temple dedicated to the emperor Ojin's son, who became the emperor Nintoku (313–99). A short distance to the right is the Shirahata-no-miya (Shrine of the White Flag), dedicated to Yoritomo. This building—painted black and decorated with the gold crest of the Minamoto family—is of a unique and highly artistic style of architecture, the four main pillars being made of iron, and the doors of the sanctuary are gilded with a curious black design. This shrine was originally on the same level with the Hachiman shrine and was rebuilt there after the fire of 1828—which destroyed both edifices; however, it was established upon the present site September 20, 1887. Within the sanctuary is a statue of Yoritomo, concerning which the following anecdote

3. First *torii* leading to Tsurugaoka Hachiman Shrine.

is universally known: In the year 1521, after the battle of Odawara, the great Hideyoshi visited Kamakura and came to pay his respects to this shrine. Tapping the effigy of Yoritomo familiarly upon the shoulder, Hideyoshi is said to have declared that himself and Yoritomo were the sole rulers of Japan who had arisen from the ranks of obscurity to wield the scepter of power over the whole country. But whereas Yoritomo had great ancestors, he was enabled to attain his object with less difficulty. Hence Hideyoshi proclaimed himself to be the greater of the twain.

The approach to Hachiman is over a mile in length, leading through the long and stately avenue of splendid old pines arched with three great stone *torii*—the Shinto gateways—directly from the beach of Yuigahama. The first *torii* was erected before the temple under the personal supervision of Yoritomo, December 16, 1180. Originally they were all made of wood, which occasioned a repeated dispensation of destruction and repairs until the year 1668, when under the Tokugawa auspices they were reconstructed in their present form. Especially imposing is the Great Torii—the massive structure that spans the avenue with majestic effect; the stone from which it was fashioned was brought from Inunoshima, Province of Bizen (now Okayama). In ancient days it is said that a mighty *torii* stood in the sea at Yuigahama (as at Miyajima) flanked by a *haiden* (hall of worship). The *Azuma Kagami* states that on October 30, 1215, a new *torii* was erected at Yuigahama to replace the former one which had been destroyed in a storm two months before. But on this wild coast the second seagate was soon doomed to share the fate of its predecessor. It is further recorded that in the disastrous earthquake and tempest of April 3, 1241, both the gate and its adjacent building were completely wrecked, the debris being swallowed by the great waves in the fury of the storm.

From a short distance beyond the station a raised approach divides the road into two, leading to the entrance of the shrine. It is now an avenue of cherry trees that in April presents the ethereal effect of a long tunnel of bloom. This special way is of great antiquity. It was originally constructed by Yoritomo and is known as Dan-Kazura. History states that this approach was an offering to propitiate the gods before the birth of his eldest son Yoriie, in order that his wife Masako might be accorded an easy and safe delivery of the expected heir.

Even at the present day, many old willow trees may be observed in the neighborhood of Waka-miya. In former times they grew in such profusion that this district was known as Yanagiwara, or Willow Field, and Kamakura is said to have been poetically described as *yanagi no miyako,* (willow-capital) in contradistinction to Kyoto, the *hana no miyako* (flower-capital). The semicircular stone bridge leading into the lower court is called the

Akabashi (Red Bridge), as formerly it was constructed of red-painted wood. In olden days it was customary for the shogun, on repairing to the temple for worship, to leave his equipage near this bridge and to proceed on foot. In past ages this beautiful curved way—lying in the shadow of gnarled old pines whose lichened boughs seem to be guarding it from the desecration of ordinary footsteps—was considered sacred and, like the Red Bridge at Nikko, it was intended for the entry of the highest in the land, the flat bridge beside it being for the benefit of mere commonplace human beings to cross into the sacred precincts.

The historic ponds they span are transformed into a vision of beauty in the summer—a glory of the pink and white lotus flowers that seem to possess such an inscrutable affinity with the mysteries of religion, death, and the joys of Nirvana. The blossoms' purity of form and tint are scarcely less wonderful than the solemn gray-green cups of the mighty leaves, with their exquisite shell-like tracery and within whose curves lie iridescent beads of water that sparkle like jewels in the sunlight—to the Buddhist mind symbolizing the evanescence and fleeting nature of the life of man.

These ponds owe their existence to Yoritomo's consort Masako, and were made at the time of the great attack upon the Taira, a retainer called Oba Kageyoshi undertaking and superintending the work. Four islands were constructed in the western pond while the eastern sheet of water contained but three. The Japanese word *san* means three and also birth: while the character *shi* signifies death as well as the number four. The pond of birth was planted with pure white lotus flowers, but the lake of death contained red blooms only, the Minamoto flag being white, while the banner of the enemy was of scarlet hue. Hence the ponds were considered symbolic of the conquest and extermination of the Taira and the birth of the power and glory of the Minamoto. However, another tradition attaches a milder and more merciful significance, asserting that Masako caused the western pond to be planted with red lotus flowers as a tribute to the memory of the heroism and valor of the defeated foe. The *Taiheiki* states that on the occasion of Nitta Yoshisada's victorious entry into Kamakura (July 5, 1333) he caused the bloodstained sword to be washed in this pond after the gruesome ceremony of examining the heads of the enemies, a formality to which in those days the highest importance was attached. The pair of huge stone lanterns just beyond the curved bridge were presented to the shrine in the Tokugawa period by the sugar merchants of Edo and Osaka respectively.

The open building known as the Maidono, or Dance Hall, is situated in front of the broad flight of steps leading up to the main shrine. This famous spot is associated with the dance of Shizuka Gozen, the well-known incident in the history of those times that is so perennially dramatized and related in song and story. Shizuka, originally a beautiful dancer of Kyoto, was the mistress of Yoshitsune, the famous youngest brother of Yoritomo, and was one of the four undying heroines of the twelfth century. When Yoshitsune became a proscribed exile and his enemies were on the alert to take his life, he refused to allow Shizuka to accompany him on his precarious flight as it would mean her almost certain death. Hence he attempted to send her back to her home in Kyoto under the escort of a trusted servant. In the wilds of Yoshino the latter robbed his defenseless protégé of all her possessions and escaped, leaving her penniless to battle with storms of snow and wind in that desolate mountain region. However, some kind priests rescued the unfortunate girl and with their assistance she managed to reach Kyoto. There she soon fell into the hands of the foe and was brought to Kamakura, where every means was resorted to in order to induce her to disclose the whereabouts of her lord and master, but with fruitless results. As she had achieved considerable fame as a dancer, Yoritomo commanded that she should be forced to give before him a public exhibition of her skill. At first strenuously opposed to being used as a toy to amuse her bitter enemy, she was finally compelled to submit, but her indomitable spirit made use of the occasion to defy the despotic shogun. There in the presence of all that brilliant assembly, instead of the expected performance, Shizuka, to her waving fan, chanted a love song extolling the virtues and heroism of her lover and, lamenting the cruel fate that had torn them asunder, anticipated the joys of reunion!

It is said that Yoritomo retired in wrath, while all the witnesses of this scene fully expected that the daring girl had signed her own death warrant. However, the beauty and the sorrow of the graceful captive had touched the heart of the lady Masako, who intervened to save her life. Shizuka was discovered to be *enceinte,* and was detained in prison until the expected one was born. This unluckily proved to be a son, which was slaughtered by the relentless command of Yoritomo—but an order of release was signed for the mother and she was permitted to disappear into obscurity.

A broad flight of over sixty stone steps ascends to the shrine. Beside this ascent stands a noble *ichō* tree, which is said to be over a thousand years old, and which played a part in the tragedy that was enacted upon these steps in the year 1219. At that time Yoritomo's second son Sanetomo was the reigning shogun, while an officiating priest of high rank at the temple of Hachiman was Kugyo, nephew of Sanetomo (son of Yoriie, his elder brother). Now some time before Yoriie had fallen a victim to the malignity of his enemies, the same enemies had trained the young Kugyo to regard his uncle Sanetomo as the assassin, and incited him to cherish the scheme of avenging the murder of his parent. The real agent was supposed to have been Hojo Yoshitoki, who was aiming at the entire extinction of the Minamoto and their partisans as a necessary prelude to usurping the supreme power for himself.

At the beginning of the year 1219, Sanetomo received the honor of a high appointment conferred upon him by the emperor, so according to custom he repaired to a service of thanksgiving at the shrine of his patron deity. It is recorded that the unfortunate young shogun (he was but twenty-eight) had some presentiment of his impending doom, for just before the ill-omened expedition, while his hair was being dressed by an attendant named Kinuji, he playfully offered a hair to the man saying it would serve as a memento when his master was no more. Moreover, on setting out, Sanetomo (who achieved such celebrity as a poet that many of his verses are still universally known and are considered of high distinction) composed a little stanza that might well be interpreted as a farewell, and which has been translated:

> Though I am forth and gone,
> And tenantless my home;
> Forget not thou the spring
> O plum tree by the eaves.

The service was arranged to take place in the early evening of January 27. The day had been wild and stormy, and it is recorded that a mantle of snow lay upon the ground to the depth of two feet. Contrary to the advice of his counselors, Sanetomo refused to take the precaution of wearing armor under his robes of state and also declined to postpone the ceremony until daylight. Escorted by a large retinue of high officers of state and a thousand horsemen, the procession started on its way. The shogun, leaving his escort in the lower court, proceeded to the shrine above attended by a single member of his suite—Naka-aki, the bearer of the long sword of state. The sword-bearer should have been Yoshitoki (son of Tokimasa and afterward second Hojo regent), but near the entrance to the shrine a mysterious white dog was in evidence. Yoshitoki, at this apparition is said to have been seized with sudden illness and returned, requesting Naka-aki to carry the sword in his stead.

The ceremony was a protracted one, lasting on into the night. On his return, as Sanetomo and his sword-bearer were descending the broad steps, Kugyo—who disguised in female garb had been lurking in concealment behind the *ichō*—suddenly rushed upon his prey. "I am Kugyo, my father's murder is avenged!" cried the assassin, and seizing the head of his victim from the blood-stained snow, disappeared in the darkness and made his escape. However, he was pursued and ultimately slain by the emissaries of the regent and thus perished the last survivor of the direct line of Yoritomo, the rule that the great originator hoped to establish upon secure foundations for all eternity passing away in three generations, after the brief period of barely forty years.

The shrine upon the plateau above consists of the Tower Gate, wherein keep guard the quaint warriors in medieval costume armed with bows and arrows, Udaijin and Sadaijin, figures that in Shinto replace the more formidable Nio of Buddhism; the main building; and a large roofed colonnade running around three sides of the edifice, which is utilized as a museum to contain the treasures and abundant historical relics belonging to the temple. A place of honor is accorded to the gift of the late emperor Meiji, consisting of a gold-mounted sword and some beautiful lacquer boxes. The following mementos of bygone ages are listed as National Treasures:

Two gold-mounted swords presented to Yoritomo by the emperor Go-Shirakawa over seven hundred years ago. A set of five silk robes presented by the emperor Kameyama in the year 1281: the outer garment is of pale fawn color, and embroidered with a design of phoenixes in various tints. This gift was accompanied with a request that special prayers should be offered for the conquest and expulsion of the impending Mongolian attack.

A carved wooden mask to be used in sacred dances, representing a *bosatsu,* or saint, presented by Yoritomo. Bows and two flat cases of arrows presented by Minamoto Yoriyoshi, Yoritomo's ancestor, 860 years ago. A *suzuri,* or writing box, presented to Yoritomo by the emperor Go-Shirakawa.

Amongst a variety of exhibits the following are of interest:

A quaint war drum ornamented with a design of golden dragons and which is said to have belonged to Prince Morinaga (1308–35). A wooden camp candlestick, a metal bell, and an iron helmet of Kusunoki Masashige. A beautiful canopied boat made of dark wood and ornamented with mother-of-pearl, presented to Hideyoshi by the emperor of China, Ming dynasty. In the same case is a large leather warrior's hat brought by Kato Kiyomasa from Korea—also, curious tall gilt ornaments surmounting flags, and used upon the same expedition.

Two large painted statues, both attributed to Unkei; the goddess Benten, who is playing the *biwa,* attired in silken robes; and a venerable Shinto deity known as Sumiyoshi, a bearded worthy whose robes are decorated in Chinese style. Tall green porcelain vases, gifts of Hideyoshi; various relics of Yoshitsune: his armor and two primitive effigies of himself and his henchman Benkei; and a set of antique dance masks.

In the western corridor are many survivals of the Kamakura period. Here also are kept the *mikoshi*—highly decorated palanquins that are carried about the neighborhood in procession on the occasions of the festivals of Hachiman. These occur around mid-April and September, when the spacious courtyard and approaches to the shrine are thronged with visitors, and the scene becomes one of great animation.

Before the entrance gate above are two beautiful metal receptacles for water, each being ornamented with the quaint design of a stork and carved inscriptions. These thank-offerings were presented to the temple of Hachiman by citizens of Kamakura in commemoration of the success of the Japanese forces in the Russo–Japanese War (1904–5).

On the western side of the terrace is a small eminence called Maruyama, or Round Mountain. Upon the summit, shaded by a grove of lofty trees, is a shrine that stood formerly in the courtyard below. According to an ancient record it contained a statue of Kannon, also a species of Bacchus—the curious wooden effigy of an inebriated figure known as Sake no Miya, an emblem that made a sympathetic appeal to devotees of:

> The cup that clears
> Today of past regrets and future fears.

The latter somewhat incongruous offering was presented to the shrine by a carpenter named Totomi, who appears to have been an ardent disciple of the alchemist that transmutes "Life's leaden metal into gold." However, when in the course of time (Kanbun era 1661–73) the shrine was removed and erected upon the top of the hill where it now stands, the carpenter's gift was repudiated as unorthodox and detrimental to the sacred atmosphere—so the Goddess of Mercy alone ascended to her present home.

At the rear of the Waka-miya temple an easy path leads up to the terrace of the main shrine, gradually winding up to the summit of Shirahataoka (Hill of the White Banner), which commands beautiful views of land and sea through the great boles and drooping branches of the mighty pine trees. Nearby is the famous spot known as Daijin-yama (Minister's Hill) which is immortalized as the supposed site of the interment of the *kama* in accordance with Kamatari's sacred dream.

Kenchō-ji

❀

MANY CENTURIES ago this temple was the head and chief of Kamakura's five great monasteries and, according to records of its earlier aspect, the halcyon days of Kencho-ji must have been magnificent indeed. Ancient writings and the charts that are still preserved amongst the temple treasures reveal that, in addition to the more important structures, this vast enclosure contained the large number of almost fifty vassal buildings scattered here and there amongst the hills and valleys of its romantic site.

Like Engaku-ji, there are three gates shadowed by groves of ancient trees before the temple is approached. The third tower-gate—a huge structure with the same superb austerity in its vast curves and gables of thatch—bears unmistakable traces of kinship with the same Chinese models.

Kencho-ji was founded in 1251 by the fifth Hojo regent Tokiyori, who took the tonsure himself in 1256. The temple owes its name to the fact of its establishment during the Kencho era; the process of construction occupied two years, being finally completed in 1253. Prior to this, Tokiyori had specially invited from China a celebrated Chinese priest to become the first lord abbot of the projected monastery. He arrived in Japan in the year

1245, presiding over the administration of Kencho-ji with distinction and success until his death occurred in 1278. This famous divine was known as Doryu (Chinese: *Tai-chao*) but is often alluded to by his posthumous name of Daigaku Zenshi, which was bestowed upon him by the emperor Go-Uda in special recognition of his abilities.

Flocks of tame doves wheel and circle in the soft air around their home beneath the huge roof of the tower gate; below its spreading eaves is suspended a large panel bearing the inscription *kenchō kōkoku zen-ji,* traced in vermilion and signifying the full name of the temple. From ancient times it has been customary as July 15 recurs (the festival of the dead) to hold beneath this gate a *segaki,* or requiem mass for the souls of the departed, when alms are distributed to the poor. In addition to this service a supplementary mass was celebrated known as the Kajiwara Segaki; this originates from a legend which is supposed to have occurred in the days of Doryu. Upon one occasion the requiem rites had just terminated when a pale and spectral warrior on horseback rode up. On discovering that his arrival was too late, he appeared so perturbed and downcast the benevolent priest was moved by compassion, and held a second mass for the benefit of his belated visitor. The warrior was duly grateful for this consideration and proclaimed his mystic origin—he was the ghost of Kajiwara Kagetoki, a favorite retainer of Yoritomo, well known in popular history for his crafty and unscrupulous character, and especially as the betrayer of his master's famous brother Yoshitsune. The present tower gate was rebuilt by Mochiuji (fourth Ashikaga shogun) some five hundred years ago, when the original was destroyed by fire.

To the right of this structure, in a low belfry with a thatched roof, hangs the Kencho-ji bell, the most ancient in Kamakura, registered as a National Treasure. Constructed in 1255 at the command of Tokiyori, upon two of its beautiful green bronze panels is engraved a poetical inscription written by Doryu; its height is between six and seven feet, with a circumference of some fifteen feet, the tone being exceptionally mellow and penetrating.

The main temple is embowered in a grove of wonderful old trees of a striking and hoary antiquity, *byakushin,* or Chinese junipers. These veterans as small saplings are said to have been brought from China about the time the temple was founded, and have therefore stood sentinel in the courtyard for between six and seven centuries. Beneath the spreading shade of the largest juniper stands a tall stone monument enclosed by chains; this was erected to commemorate the heroes from this part of Kamakura who perished in the Russo–Japanese War (1904–5). The characters of the inscription *chūkonhi*—memorial of loyal souls—were traced by General Count Nozu, a brilliant officer who gained high laurels upon the same field of battle.

A charming legend is recorded of these same Chinese trees in their early days. At the time of the first lord abbot's demise, the funeral pyre was kindled in a spot not far distant from the temple court. A dense smoke arose, enwreathing the outstretched branches: when the sacred remains had been reduced to ashes, *shari* of five different hues were revealed. Moreover, when the smoke died away from the trees it was found to have crystallized upon the dark foliage into *shari,* also of five colors, which remained suspended until they were eagerly gathered and treasured as relics of the departed by the crowds of his followers and admirers.

A *shari* is a beautiful pearl-like object which is occasionally discovered amongst the ashes of a dead person after cremation and is considered an emblem of holiness. From this incident these junipers were known as the *shari-ju,* or trees of the *shari.*

Before the entrance of the main temple is a graceful fountain of green bronze fashioned in the shape of a huge lotus leaf and which is always brimming over with clear water supplied by a natural spring. The *butsuden* (hall of images) is said to have been removed to its present position from Kunosan. This mountain near Shizuoka, so famed for its beautiful view, was selected by Ieyasu as the site for his own tomb, from whence his mortal remains were removed to the mausoleum at Nikko.

In former times this temple was brilliant with rich decorations of which but the faintest traces remain. The natural tones of the old timbers, the fading spectral grays and yellows of wall surfaces, the eccentricities of the joints, the carvings of waves and dragons and demons, once splendid with lacquer and gold, now time-whitened to the tint of smoke and looking as if about to curl away and vanish, are all very striking. The panels are beautifully carved with a design of floating angels holding musical instruments, but the coloring has long faded. The ceiling is better preserved; it is beamed and coffered, each caisson being gilded and decorated with phoenixes, peacocks, and other birds; this work is said to date from the Ashikaga period.

The chief object of worship is a gigantic statue of Jizo enthroned upon a mighty lotus; it is carved in wood, lacquered, and originally gilded, but the latter has almost entirely disappeared leaving the dark lacquer, which invests the great figure with a somber and forbidding appearance. The saint is represented with his customary emblems the *shakujō*, or staff, and the *hōshu no tama*, or jewel of good luck, upon his outstretched palm; his aureole of green and gold is also ornamented with these latter emblems. It will be observed that to the upper end of the *shakujō* metal rings are attached. The object of these rings was to make a little sound to frighten away any insect or small animal that might be in the path of the pilgrim, in accordance with the first precept of the Buddhist that he may not slay or take life in any form.

This huge effigy was originally constructed to enclose a small miraculous figure of Jizo. In ancient writings it is recorded that the site of this temple was the old execution ground for criminals, and was known as Jigokugayatsu, or the Valley of Hell. During the time of Tokiyori, a man named Saita committed a severe offense and was sentenced to be executed upon this spot. As the executioner attempted to cut off the head of the condemned man, twice the stroke failed—the sword miraculously breaking in twain at the second attempt whereupon the mystified functionary demanded if his victim could offer any explanation. The criminal proceeded to state that he had always cultivated a great and special veneration for the holy Jizo, preserving a tiny image of the deity enclosed within his topknot of hair. This was found to be the fact; moreover examination of the little figure revealed a newly inflicted wound upon its back! Saita's guilt was pardoned, this supernatural intervention being interpreted as a proof of his innocence. When the temple of Kencho-ji was established, this same miniature effigy of Jizo was said to be enshrined within the head of the large idol, which had been constructed for that purpose by the family of Saita as a token of gratitude. Its height is about one and a half inches; this little relic is no longer enclosed within its former sanctuary, but is preserved with the other valuable possessions of the temple being annually exhibited at the "airing of the treasures," which takes place in the latter part of August.

Yet another legend is recorded of this great statue: In ancient days in the vicinity of Kencho-ji there lived a woman, wife of a man called Soga, who made her living by keeping silkworms and reeling their silk for the market. This pious woman also cherished a special devotion to Jizo, constantly repairing to the temple of Kencho-ji for worship. One bitter winter's day it occurred to her that as the shaven head of the deity had a bleak and frigid appearance, it would be a charitable action to make a covering to protect it from the cold. Consequently she wove some silk and constructed a cap which she reverently placed upon the head of the divinity, with many prayers and apologies that poverty prevented her weaving a silken robe to protect his whole form from the freezing weather.

Some time afterward the woman was suddenly stricken with

illness and died; but, although all animation was suspended and no sign of life could be detected, the body remained warm. Consequently, no steps were taken for her interment. After lying in this comatose state for three days she suddenly revived and gave an account of her experiences in the underworld. On appearing before the judgment seat of Enma, king of those dusky regions and judge of the dead, he upbraided her for spending all her time in destroying the lives of silkworms, whereas the Lord Buddha has expressly prohibited the destruction of any form of life. For this crime and contempt of holy writ she was condemned to be burnt in molten metal until purified of her sins. But whilst crying aloud in anguish amidst the flames, suddenly her torment was alleviated; the benevolent Jizo appeared beside her, drew her from that hissing place of torture and obtained her pardon from the dread judge by reason of her kind action and relation to the Jizo through her act of sympathy.

In a small chamber on the right of the temple are preserved two historic relics of stirring times. These are said to be the identical mighty war drum and large bell of green copper that were used at Yoritomo's famous hunting camps at the base of Mount Fuji, renowned in history as the Fuji no Makigari. Inside the huge drum are three spearheads of metal (originally silver) to increase the penetrating qualities of its sonorous thunder. Beyond these trophies a most valuable possession of the temple and a National Treasure is enshrined in the celebrated statue of Tokiyori, fifth Hojo regent. This image is considered a fine example of the Kamakura period. The regent is represented in his thirty-third year and is arrayed in ceremonial robes holding the *shaku*, or baton of office. Within the same recess is an interesting antique statue of Prince Shotoku, who in the reign of Empress Suiko (503–628) caused Buddhism to be adopted as the religion of the court—this quaint image is painted and lacquered in well-preserved colors.

The adjoining recess enshrines a large ancient statue of the

Goddess of Mercy, with a thousand hands holding certain Buddhist emblems—the lotus flower, the wheel of the law, the sun and moon, a skull, a pagoda, and an axe—the latter typifying severance from the world. The celebrated Kannon that is venerated in the shrine of Ishiyama on Lake Biwa is said to be an exact reproduction of this image, having been fashioned by the same sculptor from wood of the same tree.

The recess at the back is occupied by another effigy representing the looped hair and mild countenance of Prince Shotoku, also some boldly carved large figures of the disciples of Buddha ascribed to Unkei. In the adjoining compartment are deposited all the *ihai,* or memorial tablets of the departed priests of this temple, carved in a curious design with gilding and colors. The great Jizo, unlike many important images, possesses no mandala, his background being formed by glimmering multitudes of small gilded images arranged in tiers, the Thousand Jizo; these figures are said to have been carved by the priest Eshin. Above him hangs a gilt canopy ornamented with dragons and in former times gay with long fringed pendants of bright hues, which have shared the general fate of extinction.

To the rear of the *butsuden* stands another spacious building with a noble thatched roof; this is the hall where services are held, lectures and instruction being also given to students of theology. On entering the temple precincts, a gate on the extreme left leads to a building founded in 1885 as a theological college for the training of priests. Beyond the lecture hall a gate leads to the guest chambers—a large thatched building enclosed within a walled courtyard and known in olden times as the Ryuoden, or Hall of Dragons, from its scheme of decoration; this is the scene of the annual display of the temple treasures.

At the rear, framed in by large trees, lies a peaceful and picturesque garden that attained great celebrity in ancient days. It was the first landscape garden laid out in the Zen style and served as model to later designers. At the northeast corner of the lake there stood a celebrated pine tree of beautiful shape, the Yogo no matsu, or Shadow Pine. According to the legend, upon one occasion the inmates of the temple were assembled in a chamber overlooking the garden, when to the amazement of all, suddenly one of the branches of the tree—that had hitherto been quite straight—dropped in a strange manner toward the observers. The Lord Abbot Doryu immediately exclaimed that he beheld a stranger in rich attire resting upon the bough. This mysterious apparition conversed with the Lord Abbot, to whom alone he was visible. When questioned regarding his abode he made answer, "Tsurugaoka." All the witnesses of this strange scene concluded that as a mark of special favor the god Hachiman had revealed himself to the priest Doryu—Tsurugaoka, or the Hill of Cranes, being the eminence upon which the temple of Hachiman is situated. After that occult visitation the tree was known as Reisho, or the Cold Pine. This famous old tree flourished until some sixty years ago, when unhappily it perished of old age—pictures of it occur in earlier records of the temple.

A flight of stone steps leads off from the left of the guest hall, beside an old monument and a very ancient celebrated well, shaded by ferns and greenery. This is the Kinryu-sui, or the Well of the Golden Dragon, the pure water from its spring supplies the lotus leaf fountain before the main temple.

Above, upon the small plateau is a quaint shrine containing an interesting specimen of old Chinese art in the shape of a venerable and curious image of the Senju (thousand-handed) Kannon. The goddess is seated, not upon the customary flower of the lotus, but upon its leaf. This romantic spot overlooks and affords a fine view of the landscape garden below. The broad flight of steps gently sloping upward to the left leads to the beautiful old thatched and vine-wreathed gate of Tengen-in, the residence of the head of Kencho-ji.

The main road toward the north winds up past the teahouses, to the shrine Hansobo. The straight path gradually rises through a grove of cryptomeria to the small temple of Shoto-in. Beneath the shade, and almost concealed by the drooping spiked plumes of a fine old white-cedar tree (*kujaku hiba*), an ascent of stone steps on the left leads up to a little gemlike graveyard lying beneath the rock cliff. A beautiful and calm-faced figure of Jizo— shrouded like a garment in the delicate green and crimson leaves of a miniature vine—seems to be keeping watch over that place of peace, where the old gray tombs, so strangely beautified with moss and lichen, symbolize the resting place of an ancient noble family of whom the name has disappeared and all traces have lapsed into obscurity.

Beyond, within the temple enclosure, another flight of mossy steps ascends to another small shady plateau. Here one is confronted with a cave containing a solitary tomb. The setting is most romantic, the sheer screen of rock being almost covered with broad ferns and verdant growth, and wholly overshadowed by tall trees in which the wind ceaselessly murmurs. This picturesque spot marks the passing of an imperial scion—son of the emperor Go-Saga (who ascended the throne in 1243). This prince officiated as lord abbot of Kencho-ji in its early days, being known as Bukkoku Zenshi. Of this priest of royal lineage tradition records that he studied with a gifted Chinese priest, who imparted the secret of a medical remedy for women's ailments which was highly prized in those times. The efficacy of this compound holds good even in the present day: it is still prepared in the temple and finds a ready sale. This historic sepulcher is specially preserved under the supervision of the imperial household—the central figure in the temple opposite being a colored effigy of this prince garbed in his priest's robes.

At the end of the teahouses on the road to Hansobo, a broad path branches to the right. This leads to another old offshoot temple which must have been of great charm in bygone days, judging from what remains of a small landscape garden and its beautifully trained pines. But the unique feature of this temple,

Kaishun-an, is that it stands on high ground overlooking a lake. This romantic sheet of water—Daigaku-ike, or Lake of Enlightenment—is enclosed by wooded hills and fed by a mountain-spring. In ancient times it was known as Kame no ike, or Tortoise Lake, owing to the fact that its waters were said to be inhabited by a giant reptile whose shell was over five feet in length. According to an ancient record, a samurai named Harada came to Kamakura seeking his father's bones amongst the warriors slain in a battle near Yuigahama. These mementos of his parent he reduced to fine powder and from this unusual material fashioned a statue of Jizo. This figure was known as the Harada Jizo and is said to be buried on the summit of a hill adjoining this lake.

Returning to the main path, through a wooden *torii* and a grove of cherry trees—that in early April fills the valley with fragrance and clouds of diaphanous blossoms—a series of stone ascents amidst a picturesque environment conduct the pilgrim to the terrace on the hill (Shojoken) whereupon perches aloft the shrine Hansobo, Should the number of steps be considered too formidable, to the right, half-concealed beneath the trees, an unobtrusive path will be observed that winds gradually upward to the platform just below the shrine. Hansobo is a highly popular little temple of gay and attractive interior; it is dedicated to a *tengu*, a mythical deity described as a goblin for lack of a more descriptive epithet. These mysterious beings are supposed to inhabit the deep shade of lonely mountains and forests, and are considered to exercise a protective influence. They are also regarded as the patrons of martial arts and occur in many of the legends of ancient times. A clear day is essential for an expedition to this shrine, when the view from the terrace is enchanting—a wide prospect of hills and valleys, the distant mountain ranges, above which float the snows of Mount Fuji, and beyond, the deep blue stretch of ocean. Far out in the bay, beyond the tawny demilune of Kamakura's beach, the lilac-shaded island of Oshima lies upon the horizon like a huge amethyst. From its crater a shaft of pure white smoke is ceaselessly poured into the azure dome above, hovering over the island like a snowy cloud. This is one of the most active volcanoes in the world; like the fiery-hearted little Stromboli, it slumbers not, nor sleeps.

The steep face of the hill below the temple has been converted into a species of landscape garden profusely adorned with ornamental rocks, stone lanterns, bronze statues, carved tablets variously inscribed, and divers monuments interspersed with bushes and flowers. Another unusual feature of Hansobo is the vast number of small paper flags inscribed with prayers, which are in evidence all along the approach below, for the propitiation of the deity. A lighthouse stands at one end of the terrace to guide nocturnal visitants to the shrine. In ancient times an ornamental pavilion stood upon this rocky ledge to serve as a resthouse and also to afford facilities for admiring the landscape; this quaint structure was known as a *kanran-kaku,* or place for viewing the waves. At the extreme right of the terrace is a shrine for Jizo. From here the steep path, past the belfry and over the gnarled and twisted roots of ancient trees, ascends between the chains to the summit of the peak Oku no In, commanding a panorama said to be over a thousand square miles in extent.

The air here is sweet with piney odors and surcharged with charm and a wondrous tranquillity. One path from the crest leads to Kakuon-ji, another to Ofuna, and a third to the hamlet of Imaizumi, famed for its ancient temple dedicated to Fudo, and also for its picturesque lake. From the terrace where the shrine is situated it is not necessary to redescend the steep flights of steps—the romantic path on the western side, with a fine view of Mount Fuji, gradually slopes down to the teahouses below.

On the hill of Shojoken behind the Hansobo shrine a cave pierces the rocky wall, wherein is a stone statue of Doryu. Around this cave—with its inspiring vista of the glories of mountain, sea, and sky—historic memories are entwined, for this was the retreat in which the first priest Doryu was wont to retire from the world for the practice of religious abstraction, zazen. It is recorded that upon a certain occasion the lord abbot was seated in the cave in the prescribed attitude of zazen, and deeply absorbed in meditation. Suddenly a famous contemporary priest Ippen Shonin (died 1289) appeared in the cave before the master and recited the following ironical poem:

> *Odori hane*
> *Mau shite danimo*
> *Kanawanu o*
> *Inemuri shite wa*
> *Ikaga arubeki*

meaning: "In this world even the most strenuous exertions bring small results, so what fruit can one hope to obtain by mere idle dozing!" With ready wit Doryu parried the attack:

> *Odori hane*
> *Niwa ni ho hirou*
> *Kosuzume wa*
> *Washi no sumika o*
> *Ikaga shirubeki*

which may be interpreted as: "The tiny sparrow picking up grains upon the earth can never soar to the abode of the eagle!"

Ippen Shonin was so impressed by this retort that he was converted to the "idle dozing," becoming a distinguished pupil of Doryu. Another retreat to the right was dedicated to his meditations and became known as the Cave of Ippen Shonin.

Returning to the court of the main temple, in the vicinity of the great bell is a thatched gate and a grove of cedars. A path slants upward through the trees; this leads to a very interesting part of the temple, dedicated to the devotees of religious abstraction. Three venerable buildings form a courtyard, the hall on the left being for lectures and instruction. Directly opposite is the *zendō*, or chamber of meditation. As in Engaku-ji, a statue of Monju—personification of wisdom—faces the door. The floor is tiled, with raised and matted platforms for the priests and students, who in the attainment of their spiritual education sit there hour after hour, detached from the things of earth, and soaring beyond the present into "the path which leads unto Nirvana, where the silence lies."

At the end of the court, overshadowed by the dark foliage of two fine old Chinese junipers, stands a large pillared hall of sacred aspect. Paved with stone, the whole floor is lightly flecked with moss of a pale emerald hue, and appears undefiled by the foot of man; to the sanctum entrance is strictly forbidden. Four tall stands for candles, lacquered in dull vermilion, lend a striking note of color to the somber interior. At the further end where one would expect an altar, are closed doors, before which stands a metal incense burner of archaic design—a lamp above that is never extinguished, diffusing a soft golden light upon the scene. This forms the antechamber to an inner sanctuary, upon whose altar is enshrined a statue of the first priest of Kencho-ji.

Although so many centuries have elapsed since the construction of this temple its origin seems merged in the medieval haze, and almost fabulous to the present era, nevertheless this sacred spot forms a direct link to the remote epoch. Every morning of the year the scriptures are intoned and prayers offered before the shrine dedicated in perpetual devotion to its spiritual founder. Immediately behind, narrow flights of stone steps (136 in number) ascend the hill, and lead up to the small green amphitheater which lies just below the summit of the ridge. Here, embowered in a thick canopy of foliage high above the world and vested with an atmosphere of indescribable tranquillity and solitude, repose the ashes of the long-departed priest. The only sounds that break the silence are the music of the doves that flutter and circle around the gate tower's massive roof, and occasionally a rich melodious boom from the great bell below quivers through the stillness of the valleys. Indeed, the remoteness of this upland glade seems to symbolize the ineffable peace of the "mansions that were not made with hands." The tomb is beautiful in its extreme simplicity. An old gray-lichened monument of the conventional ecclesiastical form rests upon a carved stone lotus—emblem of purity, and the life beyond the grave. Especially impressive is the effect toward late noon, when shadows deepen and yet the dying rays "thrill wood-glooms to gold," while the sunset glory paints the surrounding hills with all the rose and crimson glamour of unreality.

Kencho-ji, as its former importance would suggest, is the possessor of a vast accumulation of treasures. Like those of Engaku-ji, every year in August they are displayed in the guest rooms of the temple, and are of great attraction to those interested in rare and curious relics of bygone ages.

In the first room are a set of ten ancient and realistic paintings representing the judgment of sinners before Enma, king of the underworld. Represented in the clear and minute style of the old Italian school of painters, the torture of the unfortunate miscreants is graphically presented, and is being carried out with enthusiasm by demons of alarming and ferocious appearance. The front hall is fragrant with incense: there sits the grim figure of a large green bronze lion with wreaths of pale blue smoke issuing from his formidable jaws. This is an ancient Korean work of art, said to have been brought back by Kato Kiyo-masa, Hideyoshi's famous general, after the Korean invasion in 1592.

The central room contains abundant relics of the first lord abbot Doryu amongst which many proofs of the talents of this gifted priest are in evidence. These include a book of seven volumes written and illustrated by himself, and bound in curious Chinese brocade. Each page bears a beautifully executed representation of one of his contemporary priests, and forms a monument of painstaking labor, reminiscent of the missals and illuminated books that were executed by Western monks and priests of early times. The more personal relics of Doryu include his ecclesiastical robes; his rosaries; his flute; his *hossu* (a long brush of pure white hair symbolic of the spiritual power of the priesthood); his incense boxes of pierced wood; a book of prayers inscribed by himself; and many of his writings, rules, and instructions to the temple inmates. A more intimate memento of his daily life is the plain bronze bowl resting upon a lacquered stand that was used for the priest's private ablutions.

In this section are two highly prized objects connected with the great saint and proselytizer of the thirteenth century, Nichiren, founder of the Hokke sect of Buddhism, who is said to have made a sojourn at Kencho-ji during his student days—a lacquered case containing eight rolls of the scriptures (*Hokekyō*) said to have been inscribed by Nichiren's own hand—also a green bronze incense-burner of tripod shape presented by the saint to this temple.

Above the altar hangs a large colored portrait of Doryu, date and origin unknown. Immediately below is a gold and lacquer case containing the tiny figure of Jizo that according to the legend so miraculously preserved its owner from death; the mark of the sword-cut is said to be still in evidence upon its back! On the left is an object of interest that has also become historic from the legend connected with it. Resting upon the lotus of an elaborate and beautifully carved stand is a small metal mirror in the shape of a flower vase. This is said to have been an item of the lord abbot's personal property, brought by him from China. After the death of Doryu, it is recorded that some person had a dream in which it was revealed that the mirror contained a portrait of the deceased lord abbot. As no vestige of such a thing had existed during the priest's lifetime, the regent Tokimune (who had been greatly attached to the departed) was naturally skeptical regarding the matter. However, examination proved the mirror to have clouded over, and faint marks had appeared upon the surface, formerly so clear and reflective. An expert was summoned to polish the metal, when a picture of the goddess Kannon was clearly revealed. The doubts of the regent were dispelled by this apparition, for the holy priest was supposed to have been a reincarnation of the Goddess of Mercy, and this remarkable incident attracted much attention in those times.

The representation of the goddess—with a crown upon her head and holding a fan—is plainly visible to this day; and however the picture may have originated, its soft and misty effect certainly suggests that it was dreamed into the mirror rather than the work of human hands. Three ancient descriptions of this mysterious occurrence, with pictures of the ghostly mirror, are hanging on the wall to the left. In the corridor a huge painting represents the *nehan,* or death of the Lord Buddha. This work dates from the year 1697. The Blessed One reclines upon a dais in the center, surrounded by his disconsolate disciples, who are grouped in various attitudes of anguish and despair; forming the outer ring are the quaint forms of animals and insects, who have assembled to mingle their lamentations at the passing of the master. Above, in the heavens, a procession of angels are appearing to escort his soul to paradise.

Opposite this work of art hang two valuable relics in the shape of the ancient charts of Kencho-ji as it existed in the flower of its long-faded glory, and graphically representing the vast number of edifices comprised by this great monastery. However, in spite of the gradual dilapidation and neglect of centuries, Kencho-ji is not doomed to become extinct, for the authorities are collecting funds and project the erection of various large edifices. The illustrated plans are exhibited below the large two-storied gate; if the scheme is realized, these buildings will in all probability go down to future generations as a landmark of the present era when many of the existing memorials of the past will have shared the fate of such a melancholy number of Kamakura's temples, and have vanished into dust and oblivion.

Arai no Enmadō
(Ennō-ji)

新
居
閻
魔
堂

❀

ALMOST OPPOSITE the entrance gate of Kencho-ji mossy steps ascend to a small and ancient building known as Enno-ji, or Arai no Enmado; the temple dedicated to Enma (Sanskrit: *Yama),* the dread regent of the Buddhist hells—king of the dead—prince of the underworld.

This alarming deity is supposed to preside over the courts of justice in the dusky region to which souls repair after the death of the body in the upper world. According to their deeds judgment is pronounced; through varied punishments and terms of purgatory the purified soul is led back to the right path, and finally to paradise. "If the departed has been a hardened sinner he is set still further backward in his way to Nirvana, and must pass through the two most wretched states of hell and of the hungry spirits before he reappears upon earth in an animal shape. King Yama decides not only as to the mode of this transition but also as to its duration. He who has toiled as a slave, teaches Buddha, may reappear as a prince; he who has ruled as king may perhaps, on his reappearance, wander in rags. Everyone makes his own prison; his actions prepare him for joy or pain."

The temple was erected in 1250, and was first presided over by the priest Chikaku. In early times it was situated near the seashore, southeast of the great *torii* in the pine avenue approach to Tsurugaoka Hachiman and was then known as Hozo-in. However, in the days of the Tokugawa shoguns, the structure was moved to its present site upon the hillside—sequestered from the havoc of storms and tidal waves—and rechristened as Enno-ji.

Enshrined within the sanctuary is the celebrated statue of Enma, judge of souls, said to have been carved by the famous Unkei and regarding which there is a well-known legend. When the great sculptor died some seven hundred years ago and duly made his appearance before the judgment seat, the lord of darkness demanded why in life no effigy had been carved of his own majesty. Unkei being unable to reply, the soul judge thundered forth, "Whereas in life thou hast made no image of me, return to the earth; now thou hast beheld my face canst thou fashion a true likeness of him before whom all must appear!" To the bewilderment of his friends the defunct sculptor found himself suddenly resurrected into the world of living men. There, in obedience to the deity's command, he executed the present work as the memento of his purgatorial sojourn and which is said to be the first presentment of the dreaded Enma ever wrought by human hands.

This statue—esteemed as a masterpiece and enrolled as a National Treasure—occupies the place of honor and is surrounded by his satellites, the Ju-O, or Ten Kings. "Everything is worn, dim, vaguely gray; there is a pungent scent of moldiness; the paint has long ago peeled off the pillars. Throned to the right and left against the high walls tower nine grim figures—five on one side, four on the other—wearing strange crowns with trumpet-shapen ornaments, figures hoary with centuries." These are the ten kings of the Buddhist hells, Enma himself being the tenth. It is said that the condemned souls working out their sentences in purgatory are further judged every seven days and their misdeeds reviewed by these lesser arbiters for the term of three years.

These denizens of Hades are also attributed to the chisel of Unkei and were considered fine works of art. But alas, what we see today must be mere phantoms of the Ten Kings as they left the master's workshop bearing the virile impress of his genius. It is recorded that in the days when the temple stood in close proximity to the shore, all these valuable statues suffered great damage in the disastrous tidal wave that ruined the building toward the end of the fourteenth century.

In the year 1673, the large image of Enma was found to have deteriorated to a marked extent, and was entrusted to the hands of a contemporary artist for repairs. During the process of renovation, this functionary discovered an ancient document inserted in a cavity within the statue, and which proved to be (in a literal sense) internal evidence of its origin. This paper states that the figure was carved by Unkei in 1250, but 270 years later its reconstruction had been undertaken by a celebrated maker of idols named Joen. Hence it is only too probable that with these successive disasters and repairs but a small proportion of the original work can be in evidence, yet it still remains a thrilling and effective presentment of savage wrath.

Among the images on display at this temple is an interesting statue of the fearsome Shozuka no Baba, also attributed to Unkei. This old hag, together with the *oni*, or demons, is supposed to be the persecutor of the ghosts of children. She forces the little ones to pile up heaps of stones in the Buddhist Styx—the Sai no Kawara, or dry bed of the river of souls—and torment the frightened little spirits until the compassionate Jizo comes to their rescue.

This great fierce statue of the judge of souls has been thus described by Lafcadio Hearn:

> The guardian lifts the veil with a long rod. And suddenly out of the blackness of some mysterious profundity masked by that somber curtain, there glowers upon me an apparition

at the sight of which I involuntarily start back— a monstrosity exceeding all anticipation—a face.

A face tremendous, menacing, frightful, dull red as with the redness of heated iron cooling into gray. The first shock of the vision is no doubt partly due to the somewhat theatrical manner in which the work is suddenly revealed out of the darkness by the lifting of the curtain. But as the surprise passes I begin to recognize the immense energy of the conception—to look for the secret of the grim artist. The wonder of the creation is not in the tiger frown, nor in the violence of the terrific mouth, nor in the fury and ghastly color of the head as a whole: it is in the eyes—eyes of nightmare.

When this awe-inspiring monster is approached and compared with the placid benevolence of Jizo, the beholder will appreciate the felicity of the caustic Japanese proverb:

> *Kariru toki no Jizo gao*
> *Kaesu toki no Enma gao*
>
> Borrowing time—the face of Jizo
> Repaying time—the face of Enma

Tōkei-ji

❀

PROCEEDING IN a northerly direction toward Ofuna, a short distance brings the pilgrim to the iron gates of Tokei-ji, a small temple of unusual associations, whose original founder is said to have been the kinswoman of Yoritomo— a lady known as Mino no Tsubone.

Reestablished in 1285 by the wife of Tokimune, sixth Hojo regent, Tokei-ji was a nunnery popularly known as the divorce temple, a peculiar feature of this foundation being that it afforded sanctuary to any woman who might be desirous of escaping the thrall of connubial woes. This prerogative was conferred by imperial sanction with the object of providing the unfortunate wife with a means of rescue in cases where the conditions were so infelicitous that, possessing no other alternative, she might be driven to desperation.

The fugitive was allowed to take refuge for three years on condition she helped to serve in the temple, and none could molest her. When that period had elapsed she was legally entitled to a divorce from the undesirable spouse. However, when the sympathetic Princess Yodo, daughter of the emperor Go-Daigo (1318–39) became the fifth abbess, she considered three years an undue length of time, and curtailed the period of service to two years. The nunnery enjoyed this privilege until the latter days of the Tokugawa regime. The wife of Tokimune herself was the first abbess and was followed by a long line of successors, certain of their number being of very exalted rank. The last abbess of Tokei-ji was named Junso. She died on May 7, 1902, and with her demise the nunnery became a thing of the past.

Tokei-ji was moreover distinguished by becoming the residence of the eminent and widely traveled lord abbot of Engaku-ji, Shaku Soen. To commemorate his recovery from an attack of severe illness the present beautiful and artistic belfry was constructed in 1916.

Without the entrance to the temple stands an ancient copper statue of the Buddha; the bell moreover found a temporary shelter beneath the eaves of the thatched roof pending the construction of the new belfry. These relics of the Kamakura period were acquired in a somewhat unusual manner, having been unearthed by farmers while laboring in some fields belonging to Tokei-ji in the part of Kamakura called Nikaido. From the inscription carved upon the bell it apparently had been in former times the property of a temple known as Fudaraku-ji—a foundation that was established upon an imposing scale by Yoritomo near the seacoast at Zaimokuza.

Although the temple of Tokei-ji is on a small scale, it is scrupulously well kept and inviting in appearance. The chief treasure, an ancient statue of Kannon attributed to Unkei, is enshrined in a large black case veiled with curtains of purple silk. Framed with an aureole of gold and blue, the Goddess of Mercy is crowned with a curious and elaborate head-ornament; a long archaic necklace reaches almost to her feet, near inspection revealing a beautiful design of flower tracery upon her garments. The lotus upon which the figure stands is resting upon a golden lion of somewhat mythological shape. This valuable statue is included in the list of National Treasures.

A large representation of the Buddha forms the centerpiece of the altar, whose golden mandala bears a design of flames and copper-colored disks, while below, the quaint figures of Fugen and Monju Bosatsu are poised upon their curiously carved elephant and lion respectively. The term *bosatsu* is applied to any saint who has attained a degree of enlightenment only one stage below Buddhahood itself. Twenty-five *bosatsu* are especially worshipped, each one being supposed to embody a virtue of the almighty and infinite Buddha. Fugen is considered to represent the supreme goodness which characterizes the ultimate reality of the universe; Monju is the personification of wisdom.

The right-hand section of the altar is of great interest. Here we find the statue of the founder and first abbess of the nunnery. With shaven head this saintly lady reposes in a chair of ecclesiastical design, her nun's habit being lacquered in red and gold. To the left is a larger figure of the daughter of the emperor Go-Daigo. Her well-preserved robes are elaborately gilded and lacquered in colors, but the face is somewhat impaired by the inroads of time. This imperial priestess died August 6, 1396, and was interred in the cemetery of the nuns on the hill behind the temple.

The central case contains Daruma in his customary attitude of abstraction, while the effigy on the left represents the daughter of Hideyori, only son of the great Hideyoshi. After the dramatic episode of the storming and fire of Osaka Castle when Hideyori lost his life in the flames, his daughter Tenshu (who had entered the novitiate at the early age of eight) escaped, safely reaching the peaceful haven of Tokei-ji where she spent the remainder of her life and was consecrated as the twentieth abbess of the convent.

Behind the temple, through leafy and shaded alleys a path ascends to the beautiful graveyard. Here beneath the green shadows reposes the mortal dust of those medieval abbesses, who in the dim centuries so long ago renounced the vanities and glamour of the world, seeking rest and peace where alone true peace is to be found: "Here are no storms, no noise, but silence and eternal sleep."

Should the spirits of those pious and long-departed functionaries be permitted to revisit the scene of their spiritual labors upon this earth below, surely they must rejoice at the poetry and tranquil beauty of their last resting place. These ancient monuments are feathered with silvery and dull golden lichens and deep mosses from which spring myriad fronds of little ferns, relieving the somber aspect of this silent spot with the paler green of their delicate lace traceries.

The tomb of the imperial lady, as befitting her royal descent, is apart from the others being enshrined within a mossy cavern hewn from the rock and secluded within the precincts of an inner and outer enclosure spanned by a large *torii*. The largest monument, resting upon a stone lotus blossom and enclosed within a lichen-crusted fence, is the burial place of Tenshu; while the tomb of the consort of Tokimune is of pagoda shape, and stands within a smaller cave near the more imposing sepulcher of the princess.

Engaku-ji

❖

A FEW PACES beyond Tokei-ji, on the high road to Ofuna, lie the precincts of the foremost of all Kamakura's Buddhist temples. The first roofed gate spans the road, shaded by a Chinese juniper so hoary and so pierced by rents and gaps that one marvels how such a time-corroded veteran still contrives to live and flourish. The path bearing to the right between the lotus ponds leads up to the entrance of the temple enclosure; now, alas, sadly desecrated by the march of progress in the shape of the double lines of the railroad that is no respecter of sanctity, and with its unlovely "ways of iron and webs of steel" so ruthlessly cuts through the grove of ancient cryptomeria, even encroaching upon the sacred lotus ponds themselves.

The site is an ideal one: a gently rising valley enclosed by the rock walls of the green hills, heavily shaded by majestic old trees and the feathery whispering of tall bamboo groves. The pilgrim could scarcely fail to be impressed by the monastic peace and solitude that seem to pervade the very atmosphere of this beautiful spot and symbolize emancipation from the dust and fetters of the world at the threshold of Nirvana.

This temple has always been a stronghold and sanctuary of Zen Buddhism—the contemplative sect whose doctrine teaches that every man may gradually purify his own soul and achieve the knowledge of Buddha through religious meditation and the gospel of silence. *Zazen* is much practiced by the Zen sect, that mysterious art by which the soul can be detached from its earthly prison to soar away beyond the problems of life and death, attaining through rigid discipline of mind and body enlightenment and assimilation with Buddha—the almighty and ineffable. "Life itself is a curtain hiding reality, as the vast veil of day conceals from our sight the countless orbs of space. But the purified mind, even while prisoned within the body, may enter for moments of ecstasy into union with the supreme."

Originally founded in India by the missionary priest Dharma in the year 513, Zen first reached Japan a century later; but those early days were not ripe for its reception and the new sect made no headway. However, at a later period in 1192, the Chinese priest Eisai (who is considered the founder of Zen in Japan) was successful in establishing these doctrines, which made a special appeal to the dauntless old warriors of ancient times—since the introspective philosophy of the Zen dogmas especially inculcated indifference to death and the manifold dangers and perils that beset life—hence it became a potent feature in the development of *bushidō,* or chivalry.

Engaku-ji was founded in 1282 by the great Hojo regent Tokimune, an ardent believer in Zen Buddhism, and whose rule was such an eventful and momentous chapter in medieval history. The name of this regent is renowned for his autocratic methods of dealing with the envoys of Kublai Khan, who had the temerity to menace the integrity of Japan and whose unfortunate emissaries were beheaded at Shichirigahama in 1280 according to the direction of Tokimune. The next year the Mongolian invasion that threatened Japan's existence was turned into an overwhelming disaster for the attacking armada.

It is recorded that when Tokimune formed the project of erecting an important temple and monastery (1278), in company with the celebrated Chinese priest Doryu he investigated the neighborhood of Kamakura in quest of a suitable site. When the present situation was decided on and workmen were engaged to dig the foundations, the religious zeal of Tokimune led him to assist at the excavations in person. During the process of his labors he unearthed a stone box which was found to contain the *Engaku-kyō*—a section of the Buddhist scriptures—hence the name of the temple.

In the following year (1279), Tokimune dispatched a small group of architects to China in order to make a study of the Chinese temples and to become familiar with the styles of architecture. On their return in 1282, the buildings of Engaku-ji were constructed. The grounds are on an extensive scale, comprising some 500 acres of hill and valley; at that time the number of temples and various edifices amounted to over forty, of which barely half that number survive to the present day.

On the death of Doryu in 1298, Tokimune invited another important priest from China, who was justly famed for his piety and learning, to assume the spiritual direction as first lord abbot of Engaku-ji. This functionary was known in China as Chu-Yuan, which according to Japanese pronunciation became Sogen; he is also referred to as Bukko Zenji, the title conferred upon him by the emperor after his death. Quaint legends are recorded concerning the arrival of this erudite divine. According to one tradition, when his procession was approaching Kamakura, a flight of snow white herons flew in front of the cavalcade and guided it to its destination, when they alighted in the lotus ponds that still exist below the second entrance gate of the temple. In the popular opinion this manifestation was an incarnation of Hachiman—the patron deity of Kamakura, who deigned to appear in the form of these birds as a sign of approbation and to welcome the newcomer to his appointed place. Another legend relates that at the time of the opening ceremony, while Sogen was delivering his learned discourse, a number of pure white deer mysteriously appeared and followed the priest's instruction with rapt attention. These unexpected guests were interpreted as sacred messengers of the gods and were considered a good omen; hence the part where the temple is situated is known as Zuirokuzan (Hill of the Sacred Deer).

From the second entrance a path leads up beneath the deep shadows of the lofty cedars to the great tower-gate. It is only possible to appreciate the full effect of this ancient structure from a distance, when the austere simplicity of the mighty curves and gables of its thatched roof conveys an extraordinary sense of majesty and power. The path leads on beneath a grove of trees hoary with the passing centuries to the *butsuden,* or hall of images—whose style of architecture bears a family resemblance to the Chinese tower-gate. The present *butsuden* dates from some three hundred years back, the original structure having been entirely destroyed by fire in 1558, after which calamity the temple was not rebuilt until 1625.

Paved with tiles that have assumed a mossy greenish hue—a coloring well suited to the dim light of the interior—the chief object of worship enshrined upon the high altar is a large and ancient statue of the Buddha, which was fashioned in 1381 by a Chinese artist named Kyoden. In the conflagration, however, the body of the image was consumed, the head alone being rescued intact. It is said to have been repaired with the funds left by a pious lady belonging to the court of Ieyasu, named Yogenin. Enthroned upon a gigantic lotus, the great figure is now almost entirely black—age and atmospheric influences having left scarcely a trace of the former gilding. The head moreover bears the impress of another disaster and was somewhat inclined toward the right side by the great earthquake of 1855.

Behind the high altar on the left is a recess containing four statues of various abbots of Engaku-ji; the figure on the extreme right is a representation of Sogen, the first head of the temple. Various images occupy the recesses on the right side of the exit.

These include a fine set of the Juniten, or Twelve Guardian Deities, who protect the different quarters of the horizon from malignant influences.

Above the entrance to the temple hangs a tablet inscribed by the emperor Go-Kogon; the characters reading "Treasure palace of the great light," a somewhat enigmatic text interpreted as signifying prayer. The inscription suspended from the tower-gate was traced by the emperor Hanazono (1308–48)—upon the tablet is recorded the full name of the temple. To the left of the *butsuden* is a railed-in space enclosing a granite monument poised upon the back of a huge carved tortoise. This was erected by popular subscription to commemorate the heroes from this vicinity who perished upon the field of battle in the Russian War (1904–5). The characters upon the memorial were inscribed by the lord abbot of Engaku-ji, and signify "For the protection of their country."

A path beside this enclosure leads to the rocky cliffs in the hillside, concealed by thick trees. Here are numerous caves; chambers hollowed out in tiers and containing myriad images of the Goddess of Mercy in various shapes and forms—the "Hundred Kannon of Engaku-ji." The upper tiers are accessible by means of a narrow enclosed stairway hewn in the solid rock. In the cave above the steps is a tablet of granite whereon is carved the inscription:

> Adoration to the great merciful Kanzeon who
> looketh down above the sound of prayer.

The upper caves command a fine view of the tower-gate's magnificent sweep of roof, embowered in the solemn foliage of the surrounding cryptomeria.

The main path gently ascends past a beautiful lake called Myoko-ike (Lake of Sacred Fragrance)—oblong in shape and bordered with ancient rocks—to the small temple of Butsunichi-an, dedicated to the memory of Tokimune, who died in 1284 and is said to have been buried in this spot. Above stands the *ihai,* or memorial tablet of the departed regent. Behind this sacred object a case encloses the fine painted and lacquered statue representing Tokimune at the age of thirty-four—the time of his entering the priesthood. Owing to the fact of its being protected from the havoc of the atmosphere, this valuable work is remarkably well preserved and is held in high esteem by art lovers. An oil painting of Tokimune garbed in his ceremonial robes has been executed by a modern artist (Yuji Takeo). A large photograph of this picture is suspended above the altar; on the left the illustrious founder is depicted in his more youthful days.

A short distance beyond this temple, somewhat screened by the trunk of a towering cedar, is a small round cave of curious chimneylike shape. This is connected with the legend of the mysterious white deer, who are supposed to have gained access to the temple precincts by this means; a venerable stone monument beside the cave bears the inscription *Hakuroku-do,* or place of the white deer.

The path from the upper side of the lake leads directly to the gem of Engaku-ji. This is the Shariden, the most ancient building in Kamakura, which has fortunately escaped all the catastrophes that demolished the neighboring structures and is the sole construction that has been preserved intact from the Kamakura period. As a perfect model of the Sung style of Chinese architecture, this small temple has been placed under special government protection. The Shariden was originally erected to enshrine a sacred relic, the Buddha's tooth, which was deposited within the sanctuary and enclosed in a pagoda-shaped casket made of crystal. The legend of the tooth dates back to hoary antiquity, even to the days when the Lord Buddha was yet upon earth. (Authorities agree that Buddha was born in the year 623 B.C., his death occurring in 543, at the age of 80.) According to tradition the great teacher promised to bestow upon the lord of heaven a relic; in the Nirvana Sutra it is recorded "Now will I give thee a relic—I will give thee a tooth from my right upper jaw"—which was obtained after the death of the Buddha to the accompaniment of miraculous demonstrations and is deemed of extraordinary efficacy in granting prayers. This relic came into the possession of a famous Chinese priest known as Senritsushi; it was held in highest reverence by the emperor of that remote epoch (who at first entertained doubts, but was convinced by supernatural occurrences of its validity), as well as by his successors. The treasure was enshrined in the temple called Nonin-ji in the capital of China, and attained a wide celebrity. Now in the days when Sanetomo, son of Yoritomo, was shogun, it is stated in an ancient record that he was visited by a strange dream wherein he imagined himself transported into a splendid temple in the kingdom of China. There he beheld an aged priest delivering a discourse to a vast assemblage of both priests and laymen, who were following his teaching with devout attention. The shogun inquired of a bystander the identity of the master who was thus instructing the multitude, and what was the name of the great temple.

The stranger made answer, "This is the temple of Nonin-ji, the founder of which is the holy priest Senritsushi you now behold."

"But how can he be here, since he is long dead?" asked Sanetomo.

"Who shall unveil and measure rightly the mysteries of life and death—he is dead and yet he lives. Today his soul lives in Sanetomo, ruler of Japan."

"Who then is the priest attending on the master?" inquired the shogun.

"He has also been reborn; the priest Ryoshin of the part of Kamakura called Yukinoshita is his present reincarnation."

When Sanetomo awoke he was deeply impressed by the vividness of his dream, and resolved to summon Ryoshin at once to his presence. Now it happened that this priest had also dreamed the same dream, and on his way to apprise Sanetomo he encountered the shogun's messenger upon the road. These occurrences moreover were confirmed by another priest—Senko, the lord abbot of Jufuku-ji.

Various accounts of the vision of Sanetomo are extant, but the present may perhaps be considered the most interesting version. The effect of all these coincidences was to create in the shogun a strong desire to repair to the sacred spot in China which had been the scene of his former incarnation. To that end he ordered a large ship to be constructed at Yuigahama (Kamakura beach), but this project was strongly discountenanced by his advisers, it being considered too hazardous a voyage for such an important personage to attempt in those day of primitive navigation. Nevertheless, Sanetomo remained firm in his determination and the vessel was constructed under the direction of the famous Chinwakei; however, on completion its launch was found to be impossible, so as the result of this mysterious fact the disappointed shogun was compelled to forgo his project. In his stead an embassy was dispatched to the temple of Nonin-ji bearing rich gifts for the priests, also valuable wood and metals wherewith to repair the temple. The priests were overjoyed at these attentions, but in the place of return offerings the messengers requested the loan of the sacred relic, the Buddha's tooth, in order that the shogun might be enabled to worship it in his own country.

Naturally it was a matter of great difficulty to induce the Chinese priests to part with their most cherished possession; but finally, on condition it should be returned after Sanetomo had done homage to the relic, the Japanese emissaries gained possession of the tooth and returned to their native shores in triumph. However, all was not yet smooth sailing, for these things having come to the knowledge of the emperor Juntoku, the sovereign was desirous of retaining such an important and miraculous object in his own proximity. According to his instructions the returning party was intercepted and the relic was deposited in the imperial palace at Kyoto. When the messengers returned empty-handed and related what had occurred, Sanetomo was so highly incensed that he contemplated journeying to Kyoto in person to try and retrieve the coveted treasure.

However, his counselors prevailed on the shogun not to resort to this extremity, one of his retainers of over eighty years of age, Adachi Morinaga, undertaking the mission in his stead. The efforts of this venerable emissary were crowned with success; Morinaga pleaded his cause with such effect that the emperor consented to hand over the holy relic. Sanetomo, attended by a brilliant retinue, met the returning party at Odawara and the Buddha's tooth was triumphantly installed in the family temple of Choshoju-in (which had been built by Yoritomo), amidst supernatural manifestations and general rejoicing. A special temple was constructed for its reception, the tooth being worshipped there until the time of Hojo Sadatoki (1284), when the oracles decreed that the position of Engaku-ji was the most auspicious spot wherein to enshrine the relic. Accordingly, the Shariden was constructed (by the versatile Chinese priest Chinwakei) and therein the holy tooth was ceremoniously deposited in the year 1301. Apparently the preservative influence has extended to its shrine, for curiously enough the Shariden alone has borne a charmed existence amongst the vicissitudes that have beset not only all the other buildings of this enclosure, but all the multitude of the Kamakura temples.

Numerous are the legends regarding its miraculous intervention and the blessings obtained when the aid of heaven was invoked at this shrine during natural calamities of all descriptions: tempests, plague, famine, floods, conflagrations, earthquakes, and wars—not only internal strife, but even invasion from foreign nations, for it is said that at the time of the Mongolian attack the aid of the Almighty was invoked and favorable omens obtained through the occult powers of the relic. It is further recorded that in 1391, Ashikaga Yoshimochi (fourth shogun) removed the *shari* from its shrine in Kamakura to Kyoto. About the year 1467, during the civil war, it fell into the hands of the enemy, but soon afterward mysterious gleams and glitters were observed to emanate from its crystal casket and lo, the tooth was discovered to have miraculously returned! In one of the Buddhist sutras it is written:

> In this world of suffering my relics shall change to an emerald jewel for the sake of the poor and unfortunate, and I shall scatter the seven treasures upon all mankind. I will grant their prayers.

The high altar in the center of the Shariden is also under government protection and is constructed of valuable Chinese wood, the doors of the inner sanctuary being of ornate design. On either side are ancient effigies of Jizo and Kannon that are said to have been brought from China together with the relic.

An interesting fact in connection with the Shariden is that this small structure is an exact reproduction in miniature of the original main temple of Engaku-ji, which was destroyed by the fire of 1558. Behind the Shariden and connected with it by a passage at the rear is the shrine dedicated to Sogen, original head of Engaku-ji and wherein the central object is a large and impressive statue of the departed. A miniature pond lies behind this structure known as Shuku-ryu-chi, or Abode of the Dragon. The mossy ascent to the left leads to a small level in the rocky hillside whereon is the tomb of the first lord abbot and spiritual founder of this great monastery.

Below, on the left of the Shariden, is a large square cave containing a monument of imposing proportions. Here rest the ashes of the priest Kosen Osho, who died in the year 1890. On the demise of that eminent scholar his most brilliant pupil, the lord abbot Shaku Soen, was appointed to preside over the fortunes of Engaku-ji in his stead.

4. Interior of Shariden at Engaku-ji. Photo by Takeshi Fujimori.

On the right of the cloistered courtyard of the Shariden is the entrance to the *zendō*, or hall where the mystic art of *zazen* is practiced by the priests and their pupils. The interior is of an austere simplicity—the large chamber being divided by a central pathway with a raised and matted platform on either side. Upon these mats the priests keep their long vigils. Wrapped in a pall of oblivion they find deliverance from the corroding influence of the world, and attain to the state of Buddhahood through the purifying virtues of meditation and silence within this abode of peace. The single figure of a saint is enclosed within a high shrine with latticed doors—a small but beautiful statue of Monju Bosatsu, typifying the highest wisdom.

The buildings beyond include the chambers where the scriptures are expounded—lecture hall, refectories, etc. A short distance to the main temple is a walled enclosure entered by a fine old roofed gate. This is enriched with elaborate carvings, the upper panels being decorated with bold designs of dragons and waves, birds, etc. The courtyard is shaded by venerable trees and forms the prelude to the guest rooms—a hall of imposing proportions consisting of a central space of polished wood surrounded by eighty-three tatami mats. The row of buildings leading off from the guest hall to the south are the offices of the temple. Beyond there, and almost opposite the *butsuden* stands the Yokushitsu, an old building with a thatched and gabled roof that in ancient times fulfilled the function of bathing establishment to the monastery; adjoining it is a deep square well that constituted the water supply.

Behind this relic of a bygone era grass-grown and somewhat dilapidated steps ascend steeply from a wooden *torii;* these lead up to an important possession of the temple—the great bell. High upon the hillside it hangs from the massive timbers of an open belfry, sheltered by a curved roof of Chinese shape; it moreover enjoys the distinction of being the largest in Kamakura, its dimensions measuring some eight feet in height by six feet in diameter. In days of yore this bell was esteemed a sacred object, a spirit being supposed to dwell within its massive green curves. This can be better credited when the great swinging beam is set in motion and a peal of rich musical thunder rolls into the valleys—the vibrations throb and quiver for an incredible length of time before the atmosphere gradually sighs back into the former stillness of that upland solitude.

The famous bell was cast in 1301, its panels bearing a poetic inscription in Chinese. With the receding centuries the huge mass of copper has assumed a lovely hue of green, in perfect accord with its surroundings and highly satisfying to the aesthetic instincts. Its origin is based in legend. It is recorded that Tokimune's son Sadatoki (eighth Hojo regent, 1284) who had entered the priesthood was desirous of acquiring a large bell for the monastery. With a ceremonial retinue he repaired to Enoshima, and there before the shrine of Benten he ardently besought the goddess that this design might be accomplished. His petition was favorably received; the divinity intimated that the lake lying beyond the temple should be explored. Investigations revealed a large quantity of metal deposited at the bottom of the lake; with this the great bell of Engaku-ji was constructed.

Other legends and fables also cluster around this bell. It is recorded that in ancient days a priest of huge stature mysteriously appeared on a pilgrimage throughout the land, with a loud voice exhorting the populace to repair to the great bell of Engaku-ji; whatsoever they prayed for with a pure uplifting of the heart should be granted them. This happened, and many following his advice obtained their desires. As this gigantic priest was such a conspicuous figure, jingling his little bells along the thoroughfares, it seemed strange that none knew aught concerning his origin or from whence he came—even his name was unknown. He vanished just as miraculously as he appeared. The mighty apparition was none other than the holy spirit of the bell—his mission ended he disappeared into the bell, becoming part of it! It is also written that in the year 1480, the bell of Engaku-ji was miraculously endowed with the power of volition, tolling of its own accord when no human being was near. All who accepted this fact in a reverent spirit met with good fortune and prosperity, but ill luck attended the scoffers and evil befell them.

In those days in a village called Tamagawa, there dwelt a man named Ono. This man was attacked by mortal sickness to which he succumbed, and thus cut off in the flower of his years he descended into the shadows of the underworld. However Enma, lord of death, instead of pronouncing judgment upon his soul remonstrated with the newcomer, and since the appearance in the land of shades was premature, the judge of souls commanded him to return from whence he came to finish his allotted span of life in the upper world. But Ono replied that it was impossible; he knew not where the road might lie in the twilight of the shadows. Then Enma instructed him, saying that if he went toward the south, the waves of sound that flowed from the great bell of Engaku-ji would penetrate even to the darkness of those gloomy regions and would guide him safely back. Ono obeyed these counsels, duly regaining his home in the world of living men. From that day he and his kindred cherished a great devotion to the bell of Engaku-ji, whose echoes had so well and truly guided the lost soul.

Nearby stands a small shrine dedicated to the goddess Benten, with whom the bell naturally claims affinity. To celebrate its successful construction a great festival was inaugurated at the Benten Shrine of Enoshima, on which occasion a long and motley procession wended its way from Enoshima to Engaku-ji. These proceedings have taken place ever since those remote times at the interval of sixty-one years. Within the little building a series of quaint and curious paintings are exhibited which are supposed to be of great antiquity, and which represent this festival of the goddess Benten and its remarkable procession.

The treasures possessed by Engaku-ji are manifold and price-

5. Enma at Enno-ji. Photo by Kobin Yukawa.

6. "Samurai on horseback." Scroll, Kamakura period. Courtesy of the Tokyo National Museum.

我身の栄花を極

7. *Mokugyo* block at Jufuku-ji.

8. Shariden gate at Engaku-ji. Courtesy of Kamakura City Hall.

9. Statue of Kannon at Hase-dera. Courtesy of Hase-dera.

10. Temple bell at Engaku-ji. Photo by Motoaki Sakamoto.

11. Temple gate of Kencho-ji. Courtesy of Kamakura City Hall.

12. Statue of Nichiren at Ryuko-ji, Katase. Photo by Fumio Sekiguchi.

13. Approach to Jochi-ji. Courtesy of Bon Color.

14. View from the grounds of Komyo-ji temple near Yuigahama, cliffs of Inamuragasaki in the distance. Courtesy of Bon Color.

15. Bamboo grove at Hokoku-ji. Photo by Motoaki Sakamoto.

16. Early spring in Tokei-ji. Photo by Taro Nakamura.

17. Tsurugaoka Hachiman Shrine with its famous ginkgo tree.

18. Sunset at Sagami Bay with Enoshima and Mt. Fuji in the distance.
Photo by Taro Nakamura.

19. Statue of Buddha surrounded by autumn flowers, *higanbana* (cluster amaryllis). Photo by Fumio Sekiguchi.

less. Every year in mid-August these are all unearthed from their cases and wrappings to see the light of day for the space of about one week, being exhibited in the chambers and corridors of the large guest hall to all beholders who may present themselves in a reverent spirit. This is known as the annual *mushiboshi,* or airing to free from insects—and as practically all the temples in Japan follow this procedure, a visit at that juncture rewards the pilgrim with a view of many valuable and historical objects, often of great beauty, which are as a rule invisible on less auspicious occasions.

Amongst such an embarrassment of riches it is hard to individualize. The paintings of the sixteen disciples of Buddha make a special appeal to the lover of ancient art, with their Botticelli treatment and mellowed coloring. They date from between five and six centuries ago, being the work of a celebrated Japanese priest named Chodensu.

A vivid portrait of Sogen, first head of the monastery of Engaku-ji, constitutes a charming memento of the early days of the temple. The ancient divine is represented in his old age with two doves, one at his feet, while its twin nestles in the sleeve of his robe. According to the legend, when the priest was still in China before the summons of the shogun was delivered, a little dove came and pulled at his sleeve. After his arrival in Kamakura, when the newcomer was escorted to Hachiman and there beheld the doves sacred to the god of war—with whom the military capital was so closely identified—the priest recalled the incident, and interpreted the bird that had plucked at his robe to be the spirit of the god, and as a special messenger calling him to his new field to labor. After that occasion, the newly installed lord abbot expressed the desire that when his portrait should be painted he might be represented with doves. As its brilliant coloring would suggest, this picture is comparatively modern, having been executed some 150 years ago.

Many quaint Chinese objects are still preserved that were the personal property of Sogen. These include his priest's robes of curious material and design, the circular writing box used by him, and four large rosaries—one of glittering crystal that gives no hint of its antiquity, and will probably sparkle on in its wrapping of crumbling silk through all eternity. Another valued historical relic is the document traced in bold and sweeping characters by the emperor Go-Saga conferring the posthumous title of Bukko-Zenji upon the departed. Certain mementos connected with the arrival of the Buddha's tooth are also in evidence. These include a curious bag of green and gold brocade, with silken cords and tassels of faded purple, that enveloped the outer metal case of the crystal pagoda; also, the antique Chinese embroidery of strange design and stranger workmanship that was draped over the holy relic.

The temple possesses innumerable documents and writings inscribed by notable personages of the Kamakura period, and which seem to form a mysterious link across the centuries that have elapsed since that remote epoch—these include two letters (mounted on *kakemono*) from the shogun Tokimune, founder of Engaku-ji, and dated July 18 and December 23, 1278, respectively.

Suspended from the roof of the corridor is a quaint memorial of the days when life was more leisurely and considerably more picturesque than in the present era of rapid transit—the palanquin of black and red lacquer used by the former lord abbots when they emerged from the sacred seclusion of the temple precincts. Another item of special interest amongst the numerous National Treasures possessed by this temple is an ancient chart of Engaku-ji that was made soon after its completion and graphically presents the numerous buildings of the great monastery as they existed in all the pristine glory of those early days.

Meigetsu-in

❀

THIS SMALL temple lies a short distance to the southeast
of Engaku-ji and is worth inspection for its romantic
setting as well as for its association with Kamakura's early
history. Situated in a valley, the grounds are surrounded by rock
scenery fringed with bamboo groves and wooded heights with
natural amphitheaters—which in early summer are heavy with
the fragrance of the great white lilies that bloom in profusion,
starring the hills and dales with fairylike effect. The precincts are
entered by a pine-shaded gate with thatched gables; a long grassy
approach gradually rises to the rocky level where stands a forlorn
and meager building, the sole remnant of former times that is left
to mark this historic spot.

The environment of Meigetsu-in (Temple of the Clear Moon)
is intimately associated with the famous Tokiyori—fifth Hojo
regent—as his dwelling place when he retired from the world,
and the scene of his death. Upon this site he constructed a
temple called Saimyo-ji with a small abode for himself in close
proximity. Although all this has long passed away, on the Ofuna
high road nearby there still stands an ancient stone landmark
bearing the temple's name cut upon its rugged gray surface.
Tokiyori had a most interesting personality, indeed his life reads

{ 163 }

like a chapter of romance. An astute philosopher and possessed of great benevolence, many stories are related and also dramatized regarding his extreme frugality and contempt of luxury: in the disguise of a mendicant priest he would wander about the country to get in touch with the common people and ascertain at first hand their grievances. These pilgrimages abounded in incident and resulted in the rectification of many wrongs.

The spiritual side of this just and virtuous man was highly developed; from his youthful days he had been a devoted adherent of the Zen sect of Buddhism. Consequently, when his health declined he entered the priesthood in 1256, and retired to the congenial seclusion of the hermitage that he had prepared, with the intention of devoting the remainder of his life to practicing the rites of his religion amidst the rural surroundings of this tranquil retreat.

But Tokiyori's fervor for things spiritual did not obliterate his interest in things mundane. Nominally a relative was appointed, Nagatoki (his own son Tokimune being of too tender years), to rule in his stead; yet he kept his hand upon the helm of state—especially when any unusual or complicated matters arose—and practically ruled in camera until the day of his death, which occurred in 1263. It is recorded that Tokiyori's demise took place when arrayed in his priest's vestment and while practicing *zazen*. Realizing his end was at hand he knelt upon a rope mat and, assuming the attitude of mediation and communion with the unseen world, the great ruler thus serenely "abode his destined hour and passed into the life beyond."

So popular and so beloved by the common people was this shrewd and kindhearted regent that, according to ancient records, after his death such numbers of people imitated his example—from respect to his memory shaving their heads and becoming recluses—it became necessary to deal with the matter by law and instructions were issued to the governors of different provinces prohibiting this practice. After the decease of Tokiyori the temple of Saimyo-ji seems to have fallen rapidly into decay; later it was rebuilt on a modest scale by Tokimune, rechristened by the name of Zenko-ji, and placed under the direction of Doryu, first lord abbot of Kencho-ji, who had officiated at the ceremony when Tokiyori was ordained priest.

However, in 1379 a large and imposing temple was erected upon this site by Ujimitsu, second Ashikaga regent, which was of such importance that it ranked first of the ten great temples in the Kanto region (the eight provinces east of Hakone). The name of Zenko-ji was retained; from the ancient colored chart that it still preserves, these various edifices must have possessed considerable artistic beauty. They were surrounded by a charming landscape garden, a lake of fanciful shape spanned by a curved bridge facing the main buildings. Meigetsu-in was erected by Uesugi Norikata, who died in 1394. The Uesugi were a powerful and important family of ministers and statesmen during the Ashikaga regime, proving the prop and mainstay of the first four *kanryō,* or governors-general. On the death of the fourth regent Mochiuji in 1439, the Uesugi influence had become so potent that the authority was wielded by themselves until the fall of the Ashikaga shogunate.

In those days Meigetsu-in was a vassal attached to Zenko-ji and always mentioned in connection with the more important building. A record of some 240 years ago describes it as the guest chambers of Zenko-ji—it is claimed that some of the original timbers still remain in the present small building. But although declined to such barren and scanty proportions, it is noted as the possessor of an important National Treasure. This work of art is a statue of Shigefusa, court noble and first ancestor of the Uesugi family. He accompanied the emperor Go-Daigo's youthful son Prince Munetaka to Kamakura when, at the request of Tokiyori, the prince was appointed shogun in 1251. Carved in colored wood and garbed in the lofty and wide exaggerated pantaloons of official uniform, the effigy affords a vivid illustration of the picturesque costumes of those remote times and is considered a most valuable relic of the Kamakura period. This statue was sent to London in 1910, and exhibited in the Japan-British Exhibition as a representative example of the realistic style and bold chiseling of the sculpture belonging to that period of art. At the present time, however, the large empty lacquered case, as a sign and token, alone remains upon the altar; the statue having been lent to the National Museum at Ueno, where it doubtless commands a wider public than in the vague seclusion of Meigetsu-in.

Sundry other treasures remain in the possession of this small temple. On the left of the altar is an interesting and unusual bust of Tokiyori, which is said to have been constructed by the famous Chinese priest Sogen (first director of Engaku-ji), of a clay material in which Tokiyori's own ashes were mingled. Regarding the principal statue of Kannon, an early record states that it contains numbers of diminutive images of saints. On the right side of the building is a fine representation of the fifth Tokugawa shogun, Tsunayoshi, carved in dark wood and presenting the appearance of bronze. Five sets of lacquer bowls are still preserved that are widely known and esteemed amongst connoisseurs as the Meigetsu-wan. They are of a beautiful red and purple color, inlaid with the fitful fires of mother-of-pearl; with these are kept two other valued relics—a pierced scarlet incense box; and an antique Chinese *suzuri,* the dark stone being exquisitely carved with a design of grapevine clusters and monkeys.

Upon the altar is a quaint memento of the famous Yoshitsune, in the shape of a small carved metal reliquary containing a *shari* that is said to have been a prized possession of this ever-popular hero. The ancient chart of the temple is enrolled as a National Treasure and bears the seal of Ujimitsu (died 1398).

Beside the temple is the tenth and last of Kamakura's ten celebrated wells, the Kame no Ido, or Tortoise Well. To the rear, on the left-hand side, the surrounding screen of rock is pierced by a wide cavern, around whose walls are carved in relief a row of large dark figures; in the center stands a stone monument. This is said to be the tomb of the founder Uesugi Norikata, from whose posthumous title of Meigetsu the temple derives its name.

According to certain authorities the mortal relics of this worthy were dispatched to Gokuraku-ji for interment so possibly the cave tomb may be merely a memorial; but if not the whole, it is most probable that a portion of his ashes were deposited here according to an old-established and somewhat confusing custom in Japan, whereby an important personage may possess more than one gravestone reared over his remains. A path leads to the tomb of Tokiyori, which stands near the entrance gate and has recently lost its rustic aspect of former years, being now fenced in within a comparatively ambitious enclosure. Upon a hillock of rocks and grasses, shadowed by trees, stands a small lichened monument of the Hojo shape. Beneath this insignificant tomb sleeps the dust of the great and sagacious ruler who loved this peaceful spot so well that he renounced the tumults of the world in order to dedicate the last seven years of his life to the attainment of spiritual enlightenment in the dreamy repose and calm tranquillity of this sequestered valley.

Jōchi-ji

❀

ON THE Ofuna high road opposite the approach to Meigetsu-in is the gate of a very ancient temple, Jochi-ji. Although now in an advanced condition of oblivion and decay, in the days of old Jochi-ji was a foundation of high importance, ranking fourth on the list of Kamakura's five great monasteries. However, its origin remains shrouded in the mists of uncertainty and no exact records seem to have survived to the present day.

A long and gently rising avenue of cryptomeria leads to the courtyard, which is entered by a curious old gate and bell tower in one, the large bell being suspended in the upper story with quaint and medieval effect. The interior of the temple is of extreme simplicity, the sole adornment of the altar being three large figures of Amida, while below is a dark statue of the first Chinese priest to preside over the monastery.

A path running north of the bell gate leads to the deserted Jizo-do. This dilapidated structure contains a National Treasure in the shape of the celebrated Jizo ascribed to Unkei and which is supposed to be one of the best examples in Kamakura of this popular saint. The figure is time-stained and moldy, conveying the impression of centuries of neglect.

The Fudō Temple
Lake of Imaizumi

今
泉
不
動

❀

THE SMALL hamlet of Imaizumi consists of some dozen or more farmers' cottages and lies somewhat over two miles distant from Engaku-ji, across the hills in a north-easterly direction. Before the thatched gate of Meigetsu-in a path crosses the stream toward the tomb of Tokiyori. A few steps beyond the tomb a small raised graveyard will be seen upon the hill, immediately below which a track ascends, bearing to the left; if this footpath is followed it gradually rises to a pass commanding a wide panorama on every side and rewarding the climber with an enchanting prospect of the manifold glories of earth and sky and sea. From the summit on the northern side the scattered thatched roofs of Imaizumi are visible in the valley below. The path descends—gently at first, then more precipitously—to the little hamlet, which is intersected by a high road. After traversing this road (from Ofuna) for about a mile toward the east, the pilgrim reaches the enclosure of the famous Fudo; but half that distance brings one to the lake—a beautiful and picturesque sheet of water lying in a high valley and reflecting in its still green depths the thickly wooded peaks that rise steeply from its shores; the remoteness and inaccessible nature of this tranquil and poetic spot contributing in no small measure to its charm.

The characteristic also belongs in a marked degree to the venerable mountain temple that has stood for so many centuries enshrined in its Old-World setting of hills and rocks and noble forest trees, far from the haunts of man. Within the enclosure one is attracted by the loud rushing sound of water. Steps descend to a lower plateau; the waterfall leaps out of its rocky bed above that is credited with the unexpected attribute of restoring the insane to their senses! Nearby is a lodging erected for the accommodation of lunatics during the process of recovering their reason. The remedy is drastic, and consists of standing beneath the fall three times daily with the whole force of the water descending upon their defenseless heads.

A steep abundance of steps lead up to the ancient and hoary temple, standing remote within its sacred grove. Midway towers a huge pine encircled with a *shimenawa,* or rope with straw tassels, denoting an object of veneration. A short distance from the ground the mighty trunk divides into twain. This is the lovers' tree—a symbol of undying affection and marital fidelity—and is dedicated to En-Musubi no Kami, the god who hearkens to the woes of lovers. The great tree is supposed to be tenanted by the sympathetic deity and prayers offered here are considered efficacious in exorcising the frets and obstacles that beset the course of true affection.* The temple is dedicated to Fudo, the popular god of wisdom. A statue of the divinity sits aloft upon an adjoining hill; below are the thirty-six representations of his attendants, carved in stone and arranged in tiers. The path on the left winds up to the *shōrō,* or belfry.

The annual festival is held in March, when the priests give exhibitions of *hiwatari,* or firewalking, before the assembled crowds of worshippers and pilgrims, slowly wending their way barefooted across a bed of glowing charcoal. The site of this

*Both the lodging for the mentally infirm and the lovers' tree are no longer to be seen.

demonstration is near the cascade; before the rite takes place, the priestly actors in this fiery drama divest themselves of their robes and purify their bodies from the dust of earth by standing beneath the falling water.

The steep road ascending the hill opposite the temple, spanned by *torii,* is a popular route leading to the peak of Hansobo, and also to the cave-pierced heights above Kakuon-ji.

Jufuku-ji

❁

THIS TEMPLE is situated in a part of Kamakura called Ogigayatsu (Fan Valley), standing back from the main road some distance beyond the Imperial Villa.* The site of Jufuku-ji is of historic interest, as this locality was originally the home of Yoritomo's father, Yoshitomo. When Yoritomo entered Kamakura in 1180, he intended to establish his seat of government in the same place; but finding the grounds not sufficiently extensive for this purpose, the estate of his grandparent at Okura was ultimately selected for the official residence. In the same year, the first temple was erected by one of Yoritomo's important retainers, Okazaki Yoshizane. Ancient records state that in the following year (1181), Yoritomo held requiem services here in memory of his mother.

In the year 1200, according to the desire of Yoritomo's consort Masako, a large and important temple was erected upon this site, ranking third in the list of Kamakura's great monasteries. This edifice was highly esteemed by Sanetomo, who frequently attended for worship and to celebrate memorial requiem services

*Although this building no longer remains, the road is still named Onari-cho, meaning "Royal Visit."

20. Wooden statue of Myoan Eisai (1141–1215), the priest who brought Zen to Japan. Courtesy of the Kamakura Museum.

for his ancestors. Many and valuable were the treasures presented to Jufuku-ji, but the day of its prosperity was comparatively brief—for in 1395 the monastery was entirely destroyed by fire, and from this disaster little was retrieved.

The temple was consecrated by its first priest, Eisai (1141–

1215), famed as the introducer of the Zen sect into Japan, where he founded a seminary for the study of its doctrines. A beautiful avenue of old pines leads to the temple court, which lies in the shadow of very ancient trees, including four hoary specimens of Chinese juniper. The sole building that remains to Jufuku-ji is the *butsuden* (hall of images). The centerpiece and chief image of the altar is of unusually interesting origin—a large statue of the Buddha crowned with a tall headdress and apparently fashioned of ancient bronze. But appearances are deceptive. According to tradition the pious Masako caused this image to be constructed from countless slips of paper, whereon she inscribed with her own hands texts and portions of the Buddhist scriptures. The work of shaping the figure was entrusted to the Chinese priest and sculptor Chinwakei, whose skill was highly esteemed by Sanetomo and who had been specially invited from China to repair the huge Daibutsu at Nara—the head of the image having fallen off and suffered much damage in the destruction of the temple by fire.

The present statue was constructed on a frame of basketwork and is known as the Kago (basket) Shaka. When the work was completed, Masako is said to have traced and enclosed within the image six pictures of Kannon, the Goddess of Mercy. Two have disappeared, but the remaining four of these valued mementos of the wife of Yoritomo are still in possession of the temple. Below are statues of Monju and Fugen Bosatsu; on the right of the central image is a large and ancient Jizo encircled with a green halo that was chiseled from one piece of wood seven feet in length and is considered a valuable work. On the immediate left of the Buddha stands a dark and ghostly figure ascribed to Takuma and representing Kasho, an emaciated disciple of the Master.

On either side of the sanctuary tower stand the gigantic Nio, or the two Deva Kings Indra and Brahma, the ferocious sentinels who generally keep guard at the gates of Buddhist temples and by

21. Wooden statue of Jizo Bosatsu, 13th century. Courtesy of the Kamakura Museum.

22. Giant wooden statue of one of the pair of Nio guardian deities at Jufuku-ji. Photo by Motoaki Sakamoto.

their alarming appearance put to flight all demons and malignant invaders of the shrine. Originally these colossal figures were possessed by a vassal temple of Hachiman. But shortly after the Restoration, when the number of Hachiman's temples became considerably reduced, these two giants were acquired and removed to preside over the fortunes of Jufuku-ji. A side altar contains some interesting relics, including a statue of the first priest of the temple, Eisai; a small but realistic figure of Sanetomo; and the *ihai,* or memorial tablet of Masako.

The cemetery is a tranquil and beautiful spot, surrounded by thick woods and enclosed with huge boulders of rock, whose gray sides are honeycombed with mossy caves containing tombs, two of which are of great historical interest. A black gate encloses one of these rocky caverns. Here, in the dusky twilight, beneath an ancient monument are said to be deposited the ashes of Sanetomo, the youthful ruler who made such a tragic exit from this world upon the steps of Hachiman. According to tradition, this tomb was erected in Jufuku-ji by the lord abbot, to whom the ill-fated shogun is said to have been much attached. The cave is known as the Egaki Yagura, or Picture Cave, as originally the walls were carved and painted in colors with a design of peonies and decorative branches.*

A few steps from the resting place of her son is a beautiful green cave wherein it is said the mortal dust of the lady Masako is enshrined. She died in 1225, having outlived her illustrious spouse by twenty-six years; and this small lichened tomb, painted by the hand of time in loveliest hues, memorializes the intrepid spirit whose name stands out from the pages of Japanese history as perhaps the greatest female character—whose strong individuality and commanding intellect have exalted her into one of the imperishable memories of a heroine of the world.

On the opposite side of these shadowy courts of sleep, mossy

---

*The tomb of the author, Iso Mutsu, stands in this cemetery. —Ed.

and well-worn steps ascend to a small shrine dedicated to Konpira—a highly popular deity who is supposed to be the protector of mariners and seafaring fold. If the track is followed behind the shrine it winds on through the woods—past the beautiful statue of Jizo* beloved of the nuns of Eisho-ji below and skirts the historic Genji-yama with charming and ever-varying distant views. Eventually the path diverges in several directions to be followed according to the taste and fancy of the wanderer.

Behind the temple of Jufuku-ji is a hill called Ishikiri-yama, (stone-cutting mountain), upon which is a large stone known as Bofuseki, or Husband-Gazing Rock. There is a legend to the effect that when the brave warrior Hatakeyama Shigeyasu was slain fighting in a battle at Yuigahama (Kamakura Beach), his young wife ascended this hill from which the scene of her lord's death was visible, and the power of her grief was so intense and of so petrifying a nature, that like Niobe she was turned into stone, and there has remained ever since, a pillar of woe.

*This statue now resides at the Kokuhokan.

Eishō-ji

❀

THE ENCLOSURE adjoining the temple of Jufuku-ji on the northern side contains some picturesque copper roofs. These deserted buildings formed part of the nunnery of Eisho-ji, which from its original pictures and representations must have been indeed a thing of beauty in its palmy days. But alas, this ancient foundation has fallen upon evil times, its present condition being ruin and decay, tenanted by one single nun.

Eisho was a beautiful court lady and prime favorite of Ieyasu; she was cherished as the mother of Ieyasu's son Yorifusa, founder of the house of Mito. Her ancestor was the celebrated Ota Dokan who built the original castle in Edo upon the site of the present Imperial Palace in Tokyo, and whose residence was in Kamakura, situated upon the same spot that was occupied later by the nunnery. On the death of Ieyasu, the disconsolate Lady Eisho cut her hair and entered religion, this convent being founded in her honor in the era of Kan-ei (1624–44), and here she was buried. The first to preside over the administration of Eisho-ji was a daughter of the Lord Mito. A peaceful little graveyard a few paces north of the nunnery contains the large and imposing tombs of the departed lady abbesses. Sheltered from the world by a heavy screen of foliage and the green plumes of bamboo, this lovely and sequestered retreat is entered by a broad flight of steps ascending from the singularly inappropriate vicinity of the railroad.

It is recorded that these gentle nuns took great pleasure in the natural beauty of the wooded heights behind the convent, which were included in the grounds in the foundation. A memento of those departed days still remains in the shadowed remoteness of a thick grove of pines near the foot of Genji-yama. To mark their appreciation of this tranquil spot, a large and beautiful statue of Jizo—with peace and benevolence beaming from his stony countenance—was erected in this natural temple; and here, unseen and unknown, he holds his solitary court with apparently the little wild creatures and the birds of the air for his sole worshippers and devotees.

The hill of Genji-yama—whose summit, crowned with the solitary majestic pine that is such a familiar landmark of Kamakura—was also the property of Eisho-ji in those days, and was known as Hatatate-yama, or Hill of the Standard. This was due to the tradition that Minamoto no Yoshiie—ancestor of Yoritomo—planted his flag upon the crest of Genji-yama with special prayers to the gods for the downfall of his enemies, as he crossed this hill at the head of his warriors to encounter the attacking rebels.

The Tomb of
Tamesuke

❀

I N FRONT OF the nunnery of Eisho-ji a road branches in an
eastward direction. A few paces beyond, a path (on the left)
leads up to a weather-beaten temple lodged in the rocky
amphitheater above. Beneath a cherry tree at the entrance
stands a large stone bearing the inscription "The historic site of
Reizei Tamesuke." Tamesuke was a famous poet of the thirteenth
century belonging to the great Fujiwara family and was the
worthy descendant of a long line of poets and distinguished men
of letters. His grandfather was the celebrated and epoch-making
Teika, whose work ranks among the classics of Japanese literature.

His father Tame-ie also achieved such success that an estate
was conferred upon him by imperial favor. At his death a quarrel
ensued between the two brothers regarding the possession of this
estate, and as the efforts of Tamesuke to retrieve his property
proved of no avail, his mother—a lady of independent and
intrepid character and herself an author of distinction—undertook the long journey to Kamakura to refer the case to the court
of law, in the hope of obtaining justice for her son. This lady was
named Abutsuni; the diary that she kept on this journey, containing a poetic account of her experiences copiously interspersed

with verses, is written in admirable style and has become a classic widely read in the present day. This journal is called the *Izayoi Nikki,* or *Diary of the Moon of the Sixteenth Night,* the author having set out on the evening of that day.

An interesting passage relates to Mount Fuji: she is surprised to see no column of smoke rising from the crater as on her last visit to those parts (neighborhood of Okitsu). During her residence in Kamakura, she stayed near the great temple of Gokuraku-ji. She describes it thus in the *Izayoi Nikki:*

> My dwelling in the Azuma (a poetic term for this part of Japan) is in the Tsukikagegayatsu (Valley of the Shadowed Moon), which lies compassed by hills near a bay in the vicinity of a mountain temple. All is peaceful and sublime. The roar of the waves and the sighing of the wind is unceasing.

Abutsuni died in this sympathetic environment before the lawsuit was concluded, and her tomb is said to be in the nunnery of Eisho-ji. However, eventually the decision of the law court was pronounced in favor of her son. Meanwhile Tamesuke had followed his parent to the capital. He selected the present site for his abode and apparently found it congenial, for he spent all the remainder of his life in this part of Kamakura, which in compliment to this illustrious scion of the Fujiwara became known as Fujigayatsu, or Wisteria Valley.

The romantic scenery of the little nook—enclosed with rocks of fantastic shape, hill, and green distances—would make an appeal to any mind susceptible to beauty and it is not surprising that the poet found it inspiring to his muse. Here he composed the well-known "Hundred Poems of Fujigayatsu," and here he breathed his last in the year 1328, at the age of sixty-six. On the right is a small shrine dedicated to Fudo. In early times, the tract below, now covered with rice-fields, was an ornamental lake; but this has long vanished together with the gardens and the various vassal buildings belonging to the temple above.

Jokomyo-ji, or Temple of Sacred Pure Luster, was erected in 1252 by Hojo Nagatoki—who four years later became regent on the retirement of Tokiyori. The only building left is the Hall of Amida—a time-stained mildewed structure from which all pure luster appears to have long departed. However, the large statue of Amida is still enthroned upon its neglected altar—this figure was known as the Jewel-Crowned Amida* from its gem-studded headdress; on either side are effigies of the Goddess of Mercy which were considered works of great merit.

But the forlorn condition of the temple is atoned for by its delightful setting. Perched upon a little rocky plateau in the hillside and sheltered by fine old forest trees, the surrounding rocks are perforated with quaint caves of varied shapes and contain curious old tombs and monuments— apparently survivals of the very remote past. Indeed several are so incredibly ancient of aspect as to have become the mere ghosts and phantoms of tombstones. In some cases the surfaces have assumed the semblance of maps in high relief, seeming upon the point of crumbling into a puff of fine dust—yet to the touch these venerable relics remain hard and unresisting as when hewn from their native beds of rocks.

To the rear of the temple a steep ascent gives access to another terrace above. Here one is confronted with a huge rock pierced by a spacious cavern, the ingress being reminiscent of a cathedral door—the cave of the Amibiki Jizo. A divinity almost black with age, as his name implies (Amibiki means "drawn by nets"), he was retrieved from the depths of the sea by fishermen with nets, and is supposed to preserve a mysterious connection with the deep. He sits aloft upon his throne placidly smiling at the blue ocean in

*This statue is now kept in the treasure hall on the terrace behind the temple.

the distance; the depression at the back of the cave, behind the great stone halo of the deity, is said to contain salt water that rises and falls with the tides. A wooden ladle will be observed upon the statue's base; it is considered an efficacious prelude to orisons at the shrine of this divinity of sea origin to make him an offering, and to spray his body with the salt water.

The children of the neighborhood come and vigorously rub themselves with the piles of stones heaped up before their protector—this being supposed to grant immunity from disease. The Jizo's kindly countenance is crowned with a baby's hat, and around his stony neck are tied several moldy bibs—doubtless offerings from anguished mothers who hoped to gain some favor for their tiny wanderers in the dark ways of the underworld. According to some accounts the statue was placed here by the agency of Tamesuke. This may possibly have been the case, as an inscription carved upon the back of the figure states that it was consecrated by the priest Shosen in November 1312.

In the interior of this cavern is a sort of inner chamber hewn in the cliff, traversed by a stone ledge upon which is a tomb. It is said that in ancient days this grim enclosure was used as a prison and criminals were incarcerated within its rocky walk. Yet another path leads from this plateau; another flight of mossy and well-worn steps ascends to a third level. The centerpiece of this beautiful spot—enclosed within a stone fence with a standing lantern, a font for the water of purification, and an incense burner, for any stray admirer to do homage to the soul of the dead poet—is the old gray monument that marks the burial place of the departed. A charming and wholly appropriate spot for the last sleep of a singer of earth's beauties, lying so near to the blue sky and shrouded by the ancient pines in whose outstretched boughs the zephyrs seem to whisper a soft requiem.

According to the inscription, the tomb with the accessories was erected to commemorate the talents of the deceased by his followers and pupils. At the rear of this enclosure is a low deep

23. Stone Buddha at Jokomyo-ji. Photo by Takeshi Fujimori.

cave wherein are piled an abundance of small tombstones, suggesting that in former times a graveyard must have existed in this upland region. A track to the right can be followed across the hills and a descent to the road effected in another locality. However, should the same means of retreat be preferred, a broader and fairly easy path leads gradually downward from the Jizo, landing the pilgrim upon the level ground in the vicinity of a small shrine of Fudo.

Kuzuharagaoka Jinja

葛原ケ岡神社

❀

A SHORT DISTANCE beyond the railway bridge a track intersects the fields to the left. The characters cut upon a stone signpost convey the intimation that this path winds up to a small shrine called Kuzuharagaoka Jinja. This historic spot was the scene of a harrowing tragedy that occurred early in the fourteenth century. In commemoration, the shrine is dedicated to the memory of a celebrated scholar and patriot, Hino Toshimoto.

A high official at the court, and specially favored by the emperor Go-Daigo, Toshimoto, together with another Hino nobleman—his colleague Suketomo—was a prime mover in the plot to wrest the power from the shoguns at Kamakura and to restore the supremacy of the emperor. This scheme became known to the military authorities and, by order of the regent Takatoki, Toshimoto was seized and sent as a captive to Kamakura. Upon the site of this shrine he was met by the emissaries of the regent and executed. A brilliant member of a family long famed for their distinction in scholarship and literature, the unfortunate Toshimoto achieved such renown as a poet that his writings still remain as classics. A description of his long journey along the Tokaido from Kyoto to Kamakura is given in the *Taiheiki,* the famous and widely read history of the great events that occurred between the years 1318 and 1368.

The account of his capture runs thus:

> On the eleventh day of the seventh month he was arrested, taken to Rokuhara (the residence of the shogun's representative at Kyoto), and thence dispatched to the eastern provinces. He set out on his journey well knowing that the law allowed no pardon for a second offense of this kind, and that whatever might be pleaded in his defense, release was beyond hope. Either his doom would be accomplished during the journey or he would be executed at Kamakura. No other end was possible.

> But one night more and a strange lodging would be his,
> Far from Kadono, where in spring his steps had often
>   wandered in the snow of the fallen cherry-flowers;
> Far from Arashiyama, whence on an autumn eve he was
>   wont to return clad in the brocade of the red maple
>   leaves—
> Despondent, his mind could think of nothing but his home,
>   bound to him by strongest ties of love,
> And of his wife, and children, whose future was dark to him.
> "For the last time," he thought, as he looked back on the
>   nine-fold Imperial city,
> For many a year his wonted habitation.
> How sorrowful must have been his heart within him
> As he set out on this unlooked-for journey!

The scene of the execution is further described. Toshimoto, borne in a *kago,* at length arrived at the appointed place. Here he was received by the official deputized by the regent, and in the nearby upland field known as Kuzuharagaoka, a space was enclosed with a *maku,* or curtain, according to custom. The prisoner, with the utmost composure, knelt within the enclosure. Taking out a paper from his garment he wiped his neck ostensibly to prepare it for the fatal stroke, then upon the same paper inscribed his farewell poem. As he traced the final character and replaced his writing brush, the sword flashed from behind. The severed head fell upon the victim's knees and lodged between his arms presenting the uncanny spectacle of embracing his own head!

On February 22, 1885, the emperor Meiji promoted his rank in recognition of loyal and faithful services; four years later, the people of the neighborhood established this shrine—a small wooden structure approached through a large *torii*. The date of Toshimoto's death was May 20, 1329; here his remains were buried, his tomb being in the vicinity of the shrine.

Kaizō-ji

❀

THE MAIN PATH beyond the railway bridge is a cul-de-sac, terminating in the ancient temple of Kaizo-ji. The founder was a priest of great celebrity named Genno who, notwithstanding his piety and erudition, was still able to turn his attention to the practical side of life. To him is ascribed the invention of a tool (a species of hammer) that has been in use ever since, and to this day a *gennō*—as it is called in honor of its originator—is included in the outfit of all carpenters.

The name of this worthy priest is moreover linked with a weird legend famed in song and story, and also represented with great effect upon the stage. In the era of Koji (1142), many strange and bewildering occurrences took place in the court, all being at a loss to account for these successive manifestations. One evening the company were assembled at a banquet and the night grew late to strains of music and general revelry. Suddenly the palace quivered and shook to its foundations; all the lights were simultaneously extinguished, leaving the great hall enveloped in black darkness. The emperor was enthroned upon a raised dais, upon the lowest step of which was standing the prime favorite of His Majesty, a graceful and beautiful maiden known as the lady Tamamo (Flawless Jewel). To the horror and consternation of all

{ 190 }

the assembled guests, from her body radiated strange flames of golden light! At the same moment the emperor fell back in a faint and was moreover attacked by mysterious symptoms which the court physicians were at a loss to diagnose. A divine was hastily summoned, who at once ascribed the malady to the magic of the lady Tamamo. With a wild cry the sorceress assumed the form of a large fox and rushed from the palace, the animal eventually escaping for safety to the eastern provinces. When the influence of the witchcraft was removed, the emperor recovered and commanded three of his most valiant warriors to set out in pursuit of the fox.

The evil spirit was trapped and slain in the plain of Nasu, province of Shimotsuke (now Tochigi Prefecture), from whence it was supposed to have originally emanated. However, although the demon's body was killed, it still possessed the power of wreaking calamity, for its soul had petrified into a large stone known far and wide as the Sessho-seki (Deathstone). By occult powers it attracted any living thing that might be in the neighborhood—insects, birds, animals, or human beings—none could escape the curse; no sooner did they touch the stone than life became extinct and they perished with great suffering.

> The Deathstone stands on Nasu's moor
> Through winter snows and summer heat;
> The moss grows gray upon its sides,
> But the foul demon haunts it yet.
> Chill blows the blast; the owls' sad choir
> Hoots hoarsely through the moaning pines;
> Among the low chrysanthemums
> The skulking fox, the jackal whines,
> As o'er the moor the autumn light declines.
> (Translated by Basil Hall Chamberlain)

Some hundred years later the emperor Go-Fukakusa requested

the pious Genno, abbot of Kaizo-ji, to repair to this haunted place and attempt to exorcise the evil spirit from its prison. When he arrived at the dreadful spot, the priest found the Deathstone surrounded by piles of bleaching skeletons and bones of its victims.

However, offerings were made of pure water and meadow flowers, with the thin smoke of incense ascending to heaven. After long invocations and recital from sacred books, the holy man struck the fatal stone with his staff—lo, the spell was broken, it crumbled into a heap of ruins!

> Oh, horror! horror!
> The Deathstone's rent in twain.
> O'er moor and field
> A lurid glare burns fierce.
> There stands revealed a Fox—
> And yet again the phantom seems to wear
> The aspect of a maiden fair!
>
> (Chamberlain)

The same night the vision of a beautiful being appeared to the priest and expressed fervent thanks for delivering her soul from the evil incantation, whereby it was now liberated to escape to the realms of peace and bliss. This consummation naturally achieved high renown for the founder of Kaizo-ji. A memento of the event is still preserved at the temple in the shape of a fragment of the fatal stone engraved with a strange hieroglyphic, and which was supposed to possess an exorcising influence upon demented persons who were imagined by the superstitious to be possessed of a fox!

Kaizo-ji is a temple belonging to a branch of the Zen sect and is under the jurisdiction of Kencho-ji; it has a charming situation, encircled with rocks intersected by many interesting caves. Beside the steps leading up to the terrace is one of Kamakura's

24. Daibutsu, the Great Buddha at Kotoku-in. Photo by Kobin Yukawa.

25. Enoshima island. Photo by Teiichi Yamazaki.

26. Tomb of Minamoto no Yoritomo. Photo by Motoaki Sakamoto.

27. Mutsu family grave at Jufuku-ji. Photo by Taro Nakamura.

28. Nio, guardian deity at Sugimoto-dera. Photo by Fumio Sekiguchi.

29. Zen priests meditating at Engaku-ji. Photo by Masayuki Aramaki.

30. Zen priests leaving Engaku-ji. Photo by Masayuki Aramaki.

31. Snow on Jizo statues at Sugimoto-dera. Photo by Fumio Sekiguchi.

celebrated wells—the Sokonuke (bottomless) Well. It might be naturally inferred that so suggestive a title refers to the depth of water, but this is not the case.

In ancient times a pious nun was repairing to this temple to spend a vigil in *zazen*, or religious meditation. In those days of enthusiasm and fervor, it was the custom before any religious rite to purify the whole body with a shower of clear water—to symbolize detachment from the stains of earth—before entering the holy enclosure. During the nun's ablutions the base slipped from the vessel, and the silvery beams of the full moon were caught and reflected over her form in a diffusion of radiance suggesting a baptism of sacred fire. The cloistered visitant recorded this occurrence in a dainty and untranslatable poem of gossamer fancy. This little gem of thought has been preserved through the intervening centuries, and is inscribed upon a wooden panel beside the well.

The main temple contains a carved effigy of the founder in the center of the altar; all the other statues being enshrined in a small *butsuden*, or hall of images, on the left of the entrance gate. In this building a prominent object is a dark red-lacquered representation of Kobo Daishi. The great saint and teacher of the ninth century was associated with this part of Kamakura, and according to tradition hollowed sixteen excavations in the rocky floor of a nearby cave. With the water that percolated into these depressions Kobo Daishi is said to have worked many miracles in healing the sick and the blind. An adjoining path leads to this cave, which is widely known as the Juroku-ido, or Sixteen Pools.

The centerpiece of the high altar is a large statue of the Buddhist healer Yakushi Nyorai. On either side stands a gilded Kannon embellished with a green halo, while the walls are flanked by the twelve Shinsho that guard the healing divinity and are generally included with his effigy. This representation of Yakushi is a very ancient statue, concerning which there is a somewhat uncanny legend. In days of old, when Genno the founder was still living at Kaizo-ji, a strange wailing cry was constantly heard which seemed to proceed from a lonely part of a mountain behind the temple. After a time the priest determined to fathom the origin of this haunting sound, which seemed more suggestive of a weeping child than of an animal in pain. Investigation of that region revealed a small tomb from whence radiated a faint yellow light; also a strange and unknown fragrance appeared to emanate from this mysterious spot!

The wailing still being audible, the priest—reciting his prayers—advanced and laid upon the tomb his *kesa* (an outer garment of brocade worn over a priest's robes). Immediately the sound ceased and all became silent in that solitary and deserted place. When the day dawned, excavations beneath the little monument revealed the head of a statue of Yakushi Nyorai carved in wood—of a fresh and beautiful color and by no means injured or decayed by its sojourn in the damp earth. Whereupon the worthy Genno, interpreting this incident as an intimation from the divinity, caused a new statue of Yakushi Nyorai to be constructed, enclosing within its body the head that had appeared in so enigmatic a fashion. This figure is known as the Naki (weeping) Yakushi. It is stated that the cavity is opened and the mysterious head exhibited once in every sixty years; the *kesa* that was placed over the tomb is still said to be preserved in the temple as a sacred relic.

The Daibutsu
Sasuke Inari Shrine
Zeni-arai Benten

❁

THIS COLOSSAL statue of Amida—the pride and glory of Kamakura—is situated in a sequestered grove about a mile southwest of the railway station. The precincts are entered by a roofed gate, on either side of which the threatening figures of the Nio, or two Deva Kings, keep guard against demons and enemies of this sacred spot. Upon the entrance the following notice is affixed:

> Stranger, whosoever thou art, and whatsoever be thy creed, when thou enterest this sanctuary remember thou treadest upon ground hallowed by the worship of ages.
> This is the temple of Buddha and the gate of the Eternal, and should therefore be entered with reverence.

According to tradition, Yoritomo, with his consort Masako, repaired to Nara in 1195 to take part in certain religious festivities. The shogun was so impressed by the majestic proportions of the Daibutsu (Great Buddha) that he became desirous of erecting another gigantic figure in his own capital, but his death occurred before the scheme could assume any practical form. However, the pious and devoted Ita no Tsubone—who is said to have been a lady of Yoritomo's court—together with the priest Joko Shonin collected the funds for this purpose. Their efforts being crowned with such success that a large image was sculptured in wood, the construction of which, together with the temple wherein it was enshrined, occupying over five years—from March 1238 to June 1243.

This temple must have been a structure of great beauty and elaboration—but alas, the days of its glory were of short duration, for ten years later the whole fabric was ruined in a severe storm, the sacred figure also suffering great injury. From this catastrophe the Daibutsu in its present form originated, for it was resolved to create its successor in a more lasting form. The mass of metal necessary for casting a colossal image was collected and the work of constructing this triumph of Japanese art was achieved by the artist known as Ono Goroemon. The mighty figure bears the date of the fourth year of Kencho (1252), and consequently has reigned in solitary majesty over the little valley for between six and seven hundred years; where it has successfully resisted the havoc of storms and floods, and through the succeeding centuries has been the object of worship and admiration to countless streams of pilgrims and visitors from all corners of the globe.

Of the three huge historical effigies of Amida in Japan, the Kamakura figure alone survives intact and in its original form. The statue at Nara (which dates from the eighth century) has been twice repaired and recast; whereas the famous Kyoto Daibutsu was entirely destroyed—a small wooden substitute alone remaining to represent the gigantic figure set up by Hideyoshi, which towered to the height of 160 feet and the story of whose construction reads like a romance.

The measurements of the Kamakura Daibutsu may be roughly given as 50 feet in height by about 100 feet in circumference; the face being over 8 feet in length. The eyes (each some 4 feet across) are fashioned of pure gold and the silver boss (*byakugō*)—

representing the jewel from whence emanates the light that illumines the universe—is said to weigh 30 pounds. The weight of the statue is computed at 93 tons. Upon the head are 656 curls, a traditional characteristic of Amida.

When this valuable statue was completed, it was naturally enshrined within a splendid temple of suitable proportions; its mighty roof being supported by sixty-three massive pillars of *keyaki* wood, of which fifty of the circular stone bases still remain in evidence. However, this edifice was doomed to repeated calamities. It is recorded that in August 1335, during a civil war, an expedition was starting from Kamakura when suddenly a great storm arose, numbers of soldiers seeking shelter within the vast temple of the Daibutsu. During the night the building was wrecked by the violence of the wind, some five hundred of the unfortunate warriors perishing beneath the ruins. Again in September 1369, this ill-fated structure suffered heavy damage and was partially ruined by a typhoon.

In 1495, during another furious storm, a tidal wave rushed up the valley, completely annihilating the temple; since that time the great Buddha has remained unsheltered—a fact unlamented by its admirers, for however effective may have been the ornate environment and the "scented twilight of the gods," surely no artificial background could be more in accord with the dreamy meditation of this embodiment of eternal peace than the blue heaven with its shifting clouds, the sunshine, and the whispers of wind-stirred trees. The great divinity seems fraught with a special significance in the dark hours when the shadowy valley is flooded by the pure silver of the full moon, investing the lonely figure— its head bowed in sorrow for the sins and sufferings of the world—with a mysterious and unreal atmosphere that accentuates its austere majesty and utter aloofness from the unrest and turbulence of this human earth-life. Mortal forms may crawl and wander about its feet, but the great serene Daibutsu, oblivious and undistracted, will apparently sit enthroned upon his stony pedestal through all infinity, a symbol of repose and absolute detachment from the world.

Before the deity is an incense burner and two tall bronze lotus flowers, fifteen feet in height. From a small opening on the right side the interior of the statue can be entered, wherein are various effigies of Amida and inscriptions relating to the history of the Daibutsu. The statue of the Goddess of Mercy installed within the great cavity of the head was originally the chief image belonging to the private shrine of the second Tokugawa shogun. A steep ladder leads up to the shoulders, which are pierced by two windows. Immediately behind the Daibutsu is a large stone memorial before which fresh flowers and incense are constantly offered; this is in perpetual commemoration of Lady Ita no Tsubone, to whose efforts the origin of the great statue is partly due.

The hill at the rear is of easy access and commands a charming view, especially beautiful in spring, when the grove of cherry trees below embowers the mighty form in pale-pink clouds of bloom that seem to emphasize the contrast between the evanescent and the abiding. Many writers have given inspiring accounts of the sacred figure that seems to be the presiding genius of Kamakura. In Professor Chamberlain's article on metalwork he says:

> The grandest example of such colossal bronze-casting is the Daibutsu (Great Buddha) at Kamakura, which dates from the thirteenth century. He who has time should visit the Daibutsu repeatedly; for like St. Peter's and several other of the greatest works of art and nature, it fails to produce its full effect on a first, or even on a second visit; but the impression it produces grows on the beholder each time that he gazes afresh at the calm intellectual passionless face, which seems to concentrate in itself the whole philosophy of the Buddhist religion—the triumph of mind over sense,

32. Rear view of the Daibutsu.

of eternity over fleeting time, of the enduring majesty of Nirvana over the trivial prattle and the transitory agitations of mundane existence.

Lafcadio Hearn writes:

No matter how many photographs of the Colossus you may have already seen, this first vision of the reality is an astonishment. The gentleness, the dreamy passionlessness of those features—the immense repose of the whole figure—are full of beauty and charm. And, contrary to all expectation, the nearer you approach the giant Buddha, the greater this charm becomes. You look up into the solemnly beautiful face—into the half-closed eyes that seem to watch you through their eyelids of bronze as gently as those of a child, and you feel that the image typifies all that

{ 207 }

is tender and calm in the soul of the East. Yet you feel also that only Japanese thought could have created it. Its beauty, its dignity, its perfect repose, reflect the higher life of the race that imagined it; and though doubtless inspired by some Indian model, as the treatment of the hair and various symbolic marks reveal, the art is Japanese.

The path on the right behind the Daibutsu leads to an embryo park laid out as a memorial of the coronation of Emperor and Empress Taisho. For this purpose, land amounting to 20,000 *tsubo* was contributed by 121 owners, and many thousands of pine and cherry trees have been planted. If the hill at the northern end of the valley is scaled, it leads to the picturesque little Sasuke-Inari which lies below the crest and from whence a path leads back to Hase through the valley known as Sasukegayatsu. This foundation is of extreme antiquity, being mentioned in ancient records as belonging to the pre-Yoritomo days. Legend relates that during the early days of the first shogun, while he was still in seclusion at Hirugashima (Izu) the fox messenger of Inari appeared to Yoritomo, predicting that the scene of his future glory lay at Kamakura; hence the erection of this shrine .

On the hill behind the temple will be found a small rock cave beneath the roots of superb old trees and approached by numer-ous *torii*—the habitation of the mystic fox! Near the approach to this venerable temple is a stone landmark directing the pilgrim to the beautiful cave of Zeni-arai (coin-washing) Benten. This narrow track leads to a spacious cavern in the rock that has existed from ancient times. An image of Benten encircled by the serpent is installed within a niche; below the goddess the spring apparently wells out of the solid rock. According to tradition, if coins are washed in this deep pool it is an action of good omen, and they will increase in number, the pure water of the spring being associated with the god of wealth, wherein he is supposed to have washed the contents of his moneybags.

33. Cave at Zeni-arai Benten. Photo by Taro Nakamura.

Yugyō-ji (Fujisawa)

❀

THE MAIN ROAD to the left of the Daibutsu leads straight to Fujisawa, a town that was formerly of much more importance than at the present day. It is situated upon the main line some four miles from Kamakura, with which it is also connected by electric car. Fujisawa is noted for its Shojoko-ji, or Temple of Clear Light, popularly known as Yugyo-ji—the headquarters of the Jishu sect of Buddhism and which is moreover associated with an interesting and universally known legend of the fifteenth century. From ancient times the priests of this temple have been accredited with special powers of healing the sick. They travel all over the country during the course of their ministrations to the poor and the afflicted—the name Yugyo-ji signifying Temple of the Wanderer.

Dating from the year 1225, this foundation was originally of imposing proportions, but on more than one occasion havoc and desolation have been wrought by calamitous fires—the last of these catastrophes occurring as recently as 1880. However, thanks to the enthusiasm of faithful supporters, the temple has been resurrected from its ashes and the present building is well worth inspection—with its beautiful sweeping roof of elaborate gray tiles and its interior gay with a host of glittering decorations and colored carvings. The buildings on the left of the main temple, approached by a tiled gateway, are the guest rooms; these are of recent construction and are connected with the temple by a long covered passage. Various other vassal edifices are scattered around the precincts; the foreign-style building at the rear being a theological college for the training of priests.

Immediately behind the main temple is a graveyard containing circular monuments of vast size. This is the cemetery for the head priests of Yugyo-ji. Beneath these massive tombs the ashes of no fewer than sixty of those pious functionaries repose in peace. A path to the left leads up to an eminence beyond this graveyard. Here is found the small temple—so well known in popular history—that was formerly the Enmado, or hall dedicated to the judge of souls, wherein is enshrined the famous statue of Oguri Hangan, the hero of the legend. Beyond is the gate giving admittance to the enclosure wherein are the tombs of Oguri, surrounded by his ten followers; Terute Hime, his faithful wife; and also a monument marking the burial place of Onikage, the fierce horse that played a part in this thrilling drama.

According to tradition, during the reign of the emperor Go-Komatsu (1393–1433), Oguri was the lord of a district in Hitachi; a samurai of exalted qualities, famed for his great physical strength as well as for his brilliant powers of horsemanship. Through the treachery of an enemy, Lord Oguri became an object of suspicion to the shogun at Kamakura. He was falsely accused of attempting to raise a rebellion and an armed force was despatched to attack his castle. Summoning all the followers he could muster, Oguri and his little band made a brave resistance, but the enemy being strengthened by reinforcements and hopelessly outnumbering the defenders, the lord realized in time that discretion was the better part of valor. Assisted by ten of his loyal retainers they managed to secretly escape from the castle in the disguise of merchants and with the intention of taking refuge until the innocence of Oguri could be proved.

Toward nightfall the fugitives were crossing the province of Sagami in the vicinity of Fujisawa, and were compelled to request shelter at the best house they could find—a fatal choice, for this proved to be the headquarters of a notorious bandit chief named Yokoyama. The latter, scenting rich prey, welcomed the party cordially and feigned great hospitality, while in reality casting about in his mind for the easiest method of dispatching his guests and securing their possessions. In the yard of the robber's house, chained to an ancient cherry tree, was a majestic and beautiful stallion, but whose malignant and untamable disposition had given him the name of Onikage, or Demon Chestnut. Perceiving the interest that this fierce animal awakened in the Hangan, the robber chief thought here lay an easy means of compassing the doom of his victim—and with all politeness requested the newcomer to give an exhibition of his skill.

Oguri gladly assented. Unchaining the furious beast, whom none other dared approach, he performed marvelous feats of horsemanship—even compelling his wild steed to balance upon a chessboard! Yokoyama and his band, deeply impressed by the strength and bravery of the Hangan, deemed it inadvisable to attempt to exterminate the new arrivals by force—so another scheme was resolved upon. A banquet was prepared containing rare delicacies "with all strange flavors of mountain and sea"; dancing girls were summoned, and during the course of the entertainment the guests were to be served with wine mingled with a rank and deadly poison, brewed from the venom of the centipede and the blue lizard.

Now amongst the handmaidens in attendance at the banquet was one of exceeding beauty known as Terute. She was the daughter of a samurai who had long been without offspring, but in response to ardent and incessant prayers to the Goddess of Mercy this child had been granted them, and Terute was considered to be under the special protection of Kannon. However, this had not averted misfortune; her parents had passed away, leaving the poor child to battle with the world alone, and by degrees the samurai's daughter had drifted downward to the position of maid-servant in the bandit's house. Terute's heart was melted with pity at the doom that was hovering over this brave and splendid young lord and as the banquet proceeded she managed to secretly convey a warning. Oguri, feigning sudden sickness, refused to drink the toast at first, but on being pressed in an ominous manner he raised the cup to his lips in simulation, without touching the liquid. However, the fumes of the venom were so potent that his body was paralyzed; he fell to the ground unconscious and apparently lifeless. At the same moment the ten followers, who had responded to the toast without suspicion, all fell dead as a single man, blood gushing from their lips.

The evil heart of the robber was rejoiced at this dreadful scene. After seizing all the garments and property of his victims, he gave orders for the stripped corpses to be collected and cast into a waste moorland known as Uenogahara.

Now it happened that upon the night of the crime, the learned and pious Daiko Shonin, the fourteenth lord abbot of Yugyo-ji, was visited by a strange dream. In this vision a spectral messenger delivered to him a document sent by Enma, prince of the underworld, wherein the circumstances of the tragedy were related. The ten retainers had been foully slain and were beyond hope; but the lord Oguri was merely numbed, lying in death's semblance, and could yet be restored to the world of living men. Moreover, if escorted to the hot springs of Kumano (Province of Kishu), the far-famed healing properties of the water would render his recovery a certain fact.

The good priest awoke, and considering this dream of extraordinary significance, repaired without loss of time to the wilderness of Uenogahara—some two miles distant from the temple. In that desolate spot the pale light of dawn revealed the ghastly scene—the ground was strewn with corpses, with the wild dogs and ravens feasting upon their prey. However, the body of the

Hangan was untouched and his life was not yet extinct, as the fingers of one hand appeared to be slightly moving. The rescuer caused the unconscious form to be carried to the Enmado at Yugyo-ji, where all restoratives were applied: when the Lord Oguri was sufficiently revived the abbot caused a traveling vehicle to be constructed, by which means the sick man, under the care of two priests, was transported to the famous hot springs of Kumano, where in due time he was mercifully restored to health and strength.

Meanwhile, the maiden Terute experienced deep distress that her efforts to save the life of the brave and handsome Lord Oguri had proved all in vain. She managed to escape from the robbers' den in the hope of reaching Kanazawa in safety, but ill fortune again pursued her. She was caught by two ruffians who had been dispatched by Yokoyama to track the fugitive—ill-treated, stripped of her garments, and thrown for dead into a river. However, in these dire straits the child of Kannon earnestly besought the aid of her patron deity; veiled in celestial radiance the goddess from the nearby temple of Senko-ji appeared, and Terute was rescued. This miracle was witnessed by a fisherman living at Nojimasaki (Kanazawa), who, taking compassion upon the afflicted girl, took her to his own home, thinking she might render assistance in the household. But the worthy fisher had reckoned without the jealousy of his wife. In this world of misunderstood endeavors the best intentions have ever been productive of the worst results; the advent of this young and beautiful maiden aroused her worst instincts. The infuriated woman, a prey to degrading suspicions, resolved upon the death of her supposed rival. To that end, securing Terute to a tree, the old hag piled around her victim large boughs of burning pine, intending that she should be suffocated by the dense smoke. Again the divinity came to the rescue. A strong wind arose and in wafting the smoke in a contrary direction Terute was enabled to escape from death.

The old woman then resolved upon less drastic methods of

scattering the enemy, and managed to dispose of Terute to a trafficker in human beings, who carried off his unfortunate purchase to an establishment in Shinano. There, to his great wrath, she steadily refused to obey the commands of the wicked master of the house and so came to be employed as a serving maid to attend upon the other inmates. At first she was forced to work severely and experienced much harsh treatment. But again her guardian deity came to her assistance in the impossible tasks assigned to her, so the cruel master, realizing that Terute must be under divine protection and was no ordinary woman, began to treat her with more consideration.

Meanwhile the lord Oguri, having been completely restored to health, returned to his original destination of Mikawa. From there he issued an appeal to the emperor at Kyoto pleading that he had been falsely accused of treason by the Kamakura government. His case was investigated, his innocence established, and he returned in triumph to his castle at Hitachi. By order of Kyoto, on his return journey the Hangan captured and punished the evil bandit Yokoyama and his gang, afterward repairing to the temple of Yugyo-ji in order to express his gratitude to the benevolent Daiko Shonin for the preservation of his life. On that felicitous occasion, Oguri carved a wooden statue of himself, depositing it at the Enmado as a memorial of his return from death. This effigy, professing to be the identical image, is exhibited and venerated in the same spot today. On his return to the castle, the lord's first action was to send for the beautiful Terute, to whose timely warning he owed his life. Their union was celebrated with great rejoicing and utmost happiness ensued.

The death of Oguri Hangan took place on March 16, 1426. His son Sukeshige bore the remains to Yugyo-ji, and there beside the Hattoku-ike—or Pond of Eight Virtues—erected his parent's tomb, surrounded by the ten loyal retainers who had so treacherously met their fate while in the service of their master. The same year the faithful Terute cut her hair and became a nun; her name on entering religion being Chosho Bikuni. She built a small hut in close proximity to the Enmado, dedicating the remainder of her life to meditation and prayers for the welfare of her husband's soul. It is recorded that at daybreak she would seek in the meadows for wildflowers pearled with the dew of their morning freshness to offer at the tomb of her lord. Fourteen years later (October 14, 1440), her spirit tranquilly departed this life while in the attitude of prayer, facing the west. The little house she tenanted was after her death converted into a vassal temple of Yugyo-ji and is known as Chosei-in, in her memory.

Various versions are extant of this well-known and popular legend. One account of it represents the Lady Terute as the daughter of Yokoyama, the robber-chief. Oguri Hangan being allured by the spell of her beauty, the nuptials are secretly celebrated without the consent of her parent. Yokoyama's fury knows no bounds when he discovers what has happened, and he vows summary vengeance on the newly wedded pair. Meanwhile he dissembles. The great poisoning scene then takes place with great effect at the wedding banquet:

> Their bones burst asunder by reason of the violence of that poison, their lives passed from them quickly as dew in the morning from the grass.

The bridegroom and his party disposed of, the outraged parent turns his attention to his daughter. He commands two of his servants—brothers, with the suggestive names of Onio and Oniji*—to strip off her robes and tie her up in a package of rush matting. When it grows dark they must deposit their human freight in a boat, and rowing out into the Bay of Sagami cast the victim overboard into the deep waters. These malignant orders are carried out, but when the time is at hand to consign the

* *Onio:* Prince of Devils, *Oniji:* Second Devil.

piteous bride to the dark waves, compassion pierces the hearts of the rough brothers. In spite of their inauspicious names they are human. They deliberate, casting about for some means of averting her doom. At that moment the gleam of light shed by the vessel's lantern falls upon a small empty boat drifting toward them—presumably the agency of Kannon. Overjoyed at this solution the brothers carefully place their young mistress within it, and then return to report her death to Yokoyama. However, dangers still beset the path of the unhappy castaway. Terrible storms arise; the frail craft tosses on the billows for many a day and night. When at last a party of fishermen draws near, they manifest alarm, imagining the evil spirit of the tempest has assumed the guise of a young and beautiful maiden to lure them to their doom, they propose to dash her to pieces with their oars. But one amongst them was a kindhearted man who, being childless, had long desired to adopt a successor into his family. Entertaining the idea that this maiden might have been sent by the gods in answer to his prayer, he averted their evil intentions and took poor Terute to his home. But this shelter proved elusive: the wife's jealousy was aroused, and during the fisherman's absence she arranges to sell the maiden to a procurer whose vessel had just arrived in the bay. From that time on the harrowing account of the heroine's sufferings and distresses would fill a volume. She escapes from no fewer than seventy-five houses of ill-fame with purity unsullied, finally falling into the hands of a man named Chobei, the keeper of a notorious establishment in the province of Mino (Gifu Prefecture), where she is made to work as a maidservant and treated with great severity. However, when the agony has been sufficiently piled up, rescue is at hand from an unexpected source.

Although her lord Oguri had quaffed the cup of venom and his lifeless body had been cast away with his retainers, yet he was miraculously resuscitated in the following manner. One evening, as the worthy Daiko Shonin, lord abbot of the great temple of

Fujisawa, was returning from his ministrations in a distant part—he marveled to behold a grave in the wilderness of Uenogahara covered with myriad birds. Flitting about between them was a weird apparition, formless and featureless, hovering and fluttering amongst the dilapidated tombs in the rank grass and bushes of that deserted spot. At first the good priest was at a loss to explain the phantom; but he soon recalled a strange tradition, according to which certain souls cut off prematurely by violence from their earthly career were permitted to return to the world in the form of *gaki-ami,* a kind of ghost. Becoming convinced that for this reason the ghost had returned from purgatory, the benevolent abbot determined to render it all possible aid. He caused a little wheeled cart to be constructed for the *gaki-ami,* and placed within the vehicle a notice-board whereon the circumstances were recorded. All charitable persons were invited to assist in the good work by drawing the cart a short distance toward its destination, the famous hot springs of Kumano. The characters were as follows:

> Take pity upon this unfortunate being, and help it upon its journey to the hot springs of the temple of Kumano. Those who draw the cart even a little way, by pulling the rope attached to it, will be rewarded by great good fortune. To draw the cart one step shall be equal in merit to feeding one thousand priests, to draw it two steps shall be equal in merit to feeding ten thousand priests. And to draw it three steps shall be equal in merit to causing any dead relation—father, mother, or husband—to enter upon the way of Buddhahood.

Thus, by reason of this inscription many kindly wayfarers came forward to help the *gaki-ami* on its way, hoping by this act of charity to benefit the souls of their own relatives in the underworld. In due time the little vehicle reached the province of Mino and, as chance elected, was left standing in front of Chobei's house, where it attracted the notice of Terute.

All unknowing of her close connection with the phantom occupant, the unfortunate girl felt deep commiseration for its pitiful condition and perceiving in this a means of aiding the spirit of her lost husband, she managed to extract permission from her master Chobei to draw it for three days, leaving the cart in the town of Otsu, on Lake Biwa. There she bade farewell to the *gaki-ami* with much sorrow, for as it came from the land of shades she felt sure it must have seen her beloved lord in those dusky regions and great would have been her joy could she have questioned it regarding his condition. But that being impossible, she wrote upon the board a little note below the inscription, signed with the name she had assumed (Clover), and begging the *gaki-ami* when it should be restored to its former shape to visit the house of Chobei in Mino, where she would fain ask certain information in return for the service she had rendered.

By degrees the shape at last attained its destination. There, at the Spring of Healing, compassionate sick persons took pity on the wretched *gaki-ami;* after fourteen days the features and limbs had reappeared, a week later the transformed and resurrected Oguri Hangan appeared before them, valiant and imposing as in the days of yore! According to the virtue of this miracle achieved by the august god of Kumano, the young lord was restored to youth and health after having wandered as a formless specter for the space of three years. The emperor, taking interest in his wonderful case, granted a free pardon and moreover conferred upon Oguri Hangan the lordship of two more provinces in addition to his original domain of Hitachi—Sagami and Mino (now Ibaraki, Kanagawa, and Gifu prefectures).

It happened that while Oguri was making an official tour in his new dominion, he arrived at Mino and decided to take this opportunity of calling at the house of Chobei to express gratitude to his unknown deliverer, who had rendered such good service in his former unconscious state. Chobei was overwhelmed by the honor, entertaining the lord Oguri with all possible ceremony; but when the august visitor requested an interview with Kohagi (Clover), the proprietor of the house took exception to the indignity of introducing a poor servant maid to the honorable presence of such an exalted personage.

At the recital of Terute's woes the Hangan was justly enraged, and resolved to punish the cruel Chobei by death. However, he was spared at the intercession of Terute, who had vowed that owing to the permission of five days' absence to draw the *gaki-ami*, she would be willing to lay down her life for her master. But due vengeance was wreaked upon the perfidious robber and his band, while the brothers Onio and Oniji were appropriately rewarded for the humane part they had played in this harrowing drama. Robed in rich garments befitting her altered status, Terute Hime was escorted to the castle of her lord, and sorrow having thus been changed to happiness "their reunion was beautiful as the blossoming of spring."

Within the enclosure dedicated to these memories there exists a small museum containing various relics connected with the legend. These include the iron bit and stirrups that Oguri is supposed to have used in subduing the demon steed Onikage; a tinted effigy of the abbot of Yugyo-ji—Daiko Shonin, who played such an effective role in the rescue of Oguri; a statue of the Goddess of Mercy who so repeatedly saved Terute from death; her metal mirror; and a coin said to have been given Terute by her inhuman master Chobei, with the command to purchase seven times its value.

A personal link with both hero and heroine of this vivid tradition is preserved in two poems, traced with faded ink and alleged to have been inscribed with their own hands. The little verse written by Oguri runs as follows:

Uchi muko o
Kokoro no kagami
Kumorazuba
Geni Mikumano no
Kamiya mamoran

(If thou searchest the mirror of thy heart and clouds obscure it not, the august deity of Kumano will protect thee in safety.)

While Terute expresses herself thus:

Yono usa o
Minishi tsumazuba
Tsuini kono
Hotoke no michimo
Shirade suguran

(In this human life unless the cup of sorrow is drained to the dregs one may pass without knowing the path of the gods.)

Amanawa Jinja

❀

FROM THE MAIN street of Hase a turning leads up to this now insignificant temple, arched by a large stone *torii*. Dedicated to the sun goddess Amaterasu, the Amanawa Shinmei-gu is a branch of the parent temples at Ise. The date of the original shrine is unknown, but it is probably the most ancient foundation in Kamakura. A record of that era states that Yoritomo, his consort Masako, and his son Sanetomo (afterward third shogun) frequently worshipped at this shrine, the temple being held in high esteem by his government. According to the *Azuma Kagami*, when the political power of Yoritomo was firmly established, on January 2, 1186, the shogun repaired to Amanawa Jinja for his ceremonial New Year visit, thus proving the temple to have been in existence before his time. In October of the same year, Yoritomo gave orders for the reconstruction and improvement of the building.

This small structure is supposed to contain the effigy of an antique deity which was possessed by Yoshiie, the great ancestor of Yoritomo, and a statue of Yoshiie himself, but inspection being prohibited these facts are hard to verify. From the terrace upon which the shrine is situated a path winds up to the crest of the hill, with beautiful sea views between the boughs of the fine old trees.

Kōsoku-ji

❀

A FEW PACES before the gate of Hase Kannon, a path on the right leads to the little valley in which is situated the small but historic temple of Kosoku-ji, a locality held in high esteem by Nichiren worshippers for its connection with the saint and his disciples. This secluded and beautiful spot—enclosed on three sides by wooded heights—was in former times the abode of Mitsunori, a retainer of the regent Tokiyori, and who later entered priesthood under the name of Saishin. At the time that Nichiren was seized and sent to Katase to be beheaded, four of his disciples intended to offer up their lives with their master—Nichiro, Nisshin, and Shijo Kingo and his son. For safekeeping they were entrusted to Mitsunori, who confined his captives in a rocky cavern on the mountainside above his dwelling. However, the attempted execution of the saint and the miracle by which he was preserved from death made a profoundly deep impression upon the samurai, leading to his conversion whereupon he became an ardent disciple of Nichiren. A small hermitage was built on the grounds of his residence, which served as a place of worship until a suitable edifice could be erected. Thus originated the temple of Kosoku-ji—whose title is written with the same Chinese ideographs as the name of the founder—his former prisoner Nichiro being installed as the first priest.

Although of small dimensions the interior is fairly attractive, the centerpiece of the sanctuary being a statue of Nichiren that is alleged to have been carved by another of his disciples, Nikko. The garden possesses a venerable plum tree enclosed by a stone fence. This tree is an object of interest to the Nichiren pilgrims from the legend, duly recorded upon a notice-board, that the saint once hung his rosary upon one of its drooping boughs. An interesting tradition connected with this temple is that on his return from exile in the Island of Sado, Nichiren took up his abode upon this site and here he received Tokimune's famous charter, conferring full liberty upon the reformer to practice his religion free from molestation and opposition. An ascent on the right of this small valley leads up to the cave wherein the disciples were imprisoned and which contains a statue of Nichiro. Nearby is a spring of clear water known as the Well of the New Moon; its waters are said to have been used by Nichiren to moisten his inkstone in the composition of his essays during his sojourn in this locality.

Pictures of the imprisoned disciples are dispensed by the temple, together with the history of the cave; they were held in captivity from September 12, 1271, until April 1273—a period of some 18 months. Reprints are moreover furnished of the reprieve of Nichiren, also of the charter bestowed upon him by the shogunate three years later (May 2, 1227). The original of the latter document is asserted to be still in the possession of the temple.

Hase Kannon

A T THE END of the main street of Hase this ancient temple with its lofty thatched roof stands upon an elevated site on the hillside. From this terrace and also from the graveyard—which gradually rises to the summit of the eminence—a beautiful picture is gained of the green plain of Kamakura, framed by its ring of hills and the curving bay. This celebrated Hase-dera, enshrining the mighty golden figure of Kannon—the merciful goddess "who looketh down above the sound of prayer"—has been for many centuries the goal and destination of a ceaseless stream of worshippers, dating from the mists of antiquity. The original temple constructed upon this site is said to have been founded by the empress Gensho, who reigned from 715 to 724. However, the present building owes its existence to Yoshimasa, eighth Ashikaga shogun (1435–90), the great patron of art, under whose direction the famous Ginkaku-ji (Silver Pavilion) in Kyoto was constructed. The actual date of the Hase-dera of today is given as 1459, but some three and a half centuries ago it was thoroughly repaired under the auspices of the first Tokugawa shogun Ieyasu, in the year 1607.

In the lower courtyard, to the left of the entrance gate, stands a small temple wherein is installed a quaint figure of Daikoku, the popular god of riches and good luck. The divinity stands upon gilded bales of rice and is said to have been carved by Kobo Daishi (ninth century). This structure originally stood on the plateau above, beside the main temple, but about thirty years ago it was moved below, its former site becoming an orange-grove; the trees were planted at the instigation of the late Prince Ito.

Steps lead upward to another shrine tenanted by another deity of historic antiquity, a huge gilt figure of Amida. This statue is said to have been installed by Yoritomo and is worshipped especially for warding off calamities that may occur in the *yaku,* or unlucky ages. According to popular superstition, in the lives of human beings the *yakudoshi,* or periods especially prone to misfortune, occur twice: in men the ages of 25 and 42, and in women 19 and 33 respectively. Above this shrine stands the belfry containing an especially fine and well-constructed specimen, one of the three ancient large bells of Kamakura. Its rich melancholy boom may constantly be heard from afar, as a reminder to the soul of man that in her shrine upon the hill the merciful divinity "perceives the world sound" and is waiting to lead troubled spirits to "the holy path and the pure land." The inscription upon one of the panels of this bell is to the effect that when it is sounded all influences of ill omen disappear, all calamities cease, all prayers will be granted. Nevertheless a notice is affixed stating that to strike it is forbidden. An unusual feature of this inscription is that instead of being carved in the metal, it projects in relief. The name of the maker is inscribed as Mononobe Sueshige, and dated July 15, 1264.

In addition to the colossal figure enshrined in the dark chamber behind the sanctuary, this temple contains many other effigies of the Goddess of Mercy. The centerpiece of the altar is a large gilt statue* (eight feet in height) of Kannon ascribed to the

*This statue, the bell, and other treasures can be seen in the treasure hall to the left of the main temple.

celebrated priest Gyoki Bosatsu (eighth century). On either side are thirty-three carved wooden figures presented by the shogun Yoshimasa (1449–71), and representing the *keshin,* or incarnations—the different forms assumed by the divinity.

> When the love of Kannon is made concrete it expresses itself in various forms according to the needs of circumstance. In the *Pundarika Sutra,* Kannon is described as incarnating herself in many different personages. For instance, when she sees it most expedient to save a certain class of people through a certain mode of expression, she will assume the special mode and exercise all her influence in that capacity. She will be a philosopher, merchant, man of letters, person of low birth, or anything as required by the occasion, while her sole aim is to deliver all beings without exception from ignorance and selfishness. Therefore, wherever there is a heart groping in the dark, Kannon will not fail to extend her embracing arms.
>
> (Essay on Kannon by Shaku Soen, lord abbot of Engaku-ji)

Above the altar are two oblong panels whereon clouds are painted. The rows of small gilt figures are representations of the thirty-three statues of the Goddess of Mercy in the various temples of the western part of Japan, and which are visited by pilgrims in their prescribed order. The six bronze circular bas-reliefs of Kannon are valuable ancient relics, said to be of Indian origin. The panel over the entrance was inscribed with the words *Hase-dera* by the emperor Go-Tsuchimikado (1465); while the tablet suspended above the sanctuary was the autograph gift of another imperial patron, the emperor Kameyama—dated August 8, 1264, the characters signify "Worship and Prayer."

The left-hand aisle contains part of a petrified *kusunoki* (camphor tree) hollowed into a font for holy water, and presented to the temple by Yoshimasa in June 1450. Adjoining this relic is a beautiful bronze statue of Kannon, a thank-offering from an anonymous lady devotee. In the rear corridor is an image of Miroku Bosatsu said to have been an object of worship in the household shrine of Hatakeyama Shigetada—the most loyal of Yoritomo's retainers and who was treacherously assassinated in 1205 by Tokimasa (father of Masako) after the death of the first shogun. Miroku is the expected Messiah of Buddhism, who is supposed to appear several thousand years after the death of the Buddha to complete the salvation of mankind.

Beside this relic of the early days of Kamakura stands another ancient memorial—a colored effigy of the famous priest Tokudo, the first priest of the temple and whom tradition connects with the origin of the great Kannon. Of the remaining statues in the corridors, many are various representations of the patron deity. The gilt effigy at the back of the sanctuary is an eleven-faced Kannon by the famous Gyoki Bosatsu, to which unexpected attributes are accredited—petitions to this divinity being considered efficacious in exorcising the hindrances and obstacles that prevent the course of true love from running smooth! The picture of a large black horse is suspended on the outer wall of the sanctuary. The merciful goddess is held to be the divine protectress of horses (Bato Kannon). Consequently, when farmers are troubled with sickness or vicious tendencies in their animals they present to the temple a votive plaque (*ema*) with special prayers; this accounts for the effigies and representations of horses that are constantly in evidence wherever there is a temple dedicated to Kannon. The huge carved fish that hangs on the right side of the altar is a *mokugyo,* one of the temple instruments; when struck it emits a musical note and in former times was used during the services.

The famous statue of the Goddess of Mercy is preserved in the solitary obscurity of her chamber behind the altar; however, in the spring of every year for the space of one week (March 12–18), the doors above are thrown open and the golden face of the divinity is manifest by the light of day. But at less auspicious seasons, to obtain a glimpse of the mighty figure it is necessary to penetrate the gloom of her sanctuary and to view the goddess in sections by the dim light of glimmering candles.*

This process is thus described by Lafcadio Hearn:

> Then the old priest lights a lantern and leads the way through a low doorway on the left of the altar into the interior of the temple, into some very lofty darkness. I follow him cautiously while discerning nothing whatever but the flicker of the lantern; then we halt beside something which gleams. A moment, and my eyes, becoming more accustomed to the darkness, begin to distinguish outlines. The gleaming object defines itself gradually as a Foot, an immense golden Foot, and I perceive the hem of a golden robe undulating over the instep. Now the other foot appears; the figure is certainly standing. I can perceive that we are in a narrow, but also very lofty chamber, and that out of some mysterious blackness over head, ropes are dangling down into the circle of lantern light illuminating the golden feet. The priest lights two more lanterns, and suspends them upon hooks attached to a pair of pendent ropes about a yard apart; then he pulls up both together slowly. More of the golden robe is revealed as the lanterns ascend, swinging on their way, then the outlines of two mighty knees; then the curving of columnar thighs under chiseled drapery, and as with the still waving ascent of the lanterns the golden Vision towers ever higher through the gloom, expectation intensifies. There is no sound but the sound of the invisible pulleys overhead, which squeak like bats. Now above the golden girdle the suggestion of a

*Today, the chamber of the famous Kannon is brightly illuminated, permitting easier inspection of the statue.

bosom. Then the glowing of a golden hand uplifted in benediction. Then another golden hand holding a lotus. And at last a Face, golden, smiling with eternal youth and infinite tenderness, the face of Kannon.

So revealed out of the consecrated darkness, this ideal of divine femininity, creation of a forgotten art and time—is more than impressive. I can scarcely call the emotion which it produces admiration; it is rather reverence.

But the lanterns, which paused awhile at the level of the beautiful face, now ascend still higher with a fresh squeaking of pulleys. And lo! The tiara of the divinity appears, with strangest symbolism. It is a pyramid of faces—charming faces of maidens, miniature faces of Kannon herself.

For this is the Kannon of the Eleven Faces—Juichimen Kannon.

The origin of this famous figure is shrouded in the mysteries of tradition. By command of the emperor Uda, a detailed account was written of the legend by the famous scholar and statesman Sugawara no Michizane, and which bears the date February 10, 896. A condensed version of this work is issued by the temple and may be briefly summarized as follows:

Many centuries ago, in the reign of the empress Gensho (715–24), there lived a holy priest in the province of Yamato (Nara) known as Tokudo Shonin. This worthy was not only famed for his piety and learning, but was also considered to be the reincarnation of a great saint of former times, Hoki Bosatsu, who had been reborn into this world for the salvation of souls. It happened that one night Tokudo Shonin was passing through a valley in Yamato, and there he beheld upon the ground the fallen trunk of a mighty camphor tree over one hundred feet in length. From the tree a soft radiance, suggesting a halo, was diffused; moreover, the air was filled with a strange unearthly fragrance. Convinced by these manifestations that this tree was designed for some holy purpose, the priest fell upon his knees, reciting the scriptures and praying that the sacred wood might be consecrated and immortalized in the form of the Goddess of Mercy.

Suddenly there appeared two mysterious venerable figures who averred they had come to execute his desire and the holy tree should be fashioned into the likeness of Kannon. For three days Tokudo Shonin continued to fast and pray, and for the space of that time the strangers labored without ceasing. The mighty trunk was hewn in twain, and at the end of the third day it was transformed into two majestic statues of Kannon, the beloved Goddess of Compassion and Mercy.

Aware that this marvel had not been achieved by mere human agency, the priest besought these aged visitants to reveal their origin. They replied that they were the gods Tensho-Daijin and Kasuga-Myojin, who had thus assumed earthly forms in order to execute the pious aspiration of Tokudo and carve these representations of the Merciful One, which would be of great and special benefit in answering the prayers and saving the souls of mankind. Their labors ended, the mystic deities disappeared in a cloud and were seen no more. It is recorded that this event took place in March 721, a report thereof being laid before the empress. An imperial messenger was promptly despatched to Yamato to do reverence and to present offerings to the divinities that had originated in so mysterious a manner; moreover, the holy priest Gyoki Bosatsu was requested to preside at the consecration ceremony. The temple for their reception was duly constructed at Hase, Yamato, and the dedication was celebrated amidst great rejoicings. When the ceremonies were ended, Gyoki Bosatsu solemnly addressed the newly consecrated figures, decreeing that the statue framed from the base of the tree should dwell within its shrine at Hase for all eternity. But the twin form, that had been carved from the upper half of the sacred camphor tree, he commanded to be reverently committed to the ocean, that the waves might bear the goddess to whatever spot that destiny might decide and where its influence might be most potent in rescuing the souls of men from destruction.

For sixteen long years nothing was heard of the fate of the statue. However, one summer night (June 18, 736) the fisherfolk of Kamakura received the tidings that in the Bay of Sagami a strange object was floating in the deep, from which gleams of light were radiated: the long-lost goddess had arrived! With profound demonstrations of joy the sacred image was conveyed to the shore and found a temporary shelter within a shed of straw and rushes, where all the neighborhood thronged to worship and to acclaim with offerings the newly arrived divinity from the sea. From this circumstance that spot received the name that it bears even to the present day of Kariyagasaki, or Promontory of the Temporary Shed.

This intelligence soon reached the imperial ear; again a messenger was despatched with instructions that a suitable temple should be constructed for the reception of the mighty image. This edifice received the name of Shin (new) Hase-dera after the original temple of Kannon in Yamato; it also bears the title of Kaiko-San, or Temple of the Radiance of the Sea. According to imperial desire, the holy Tokudo Shonin became the first priest to preside over the new foundation. From that remote age this famous statue of mystic origin has been worshipped and hallowed by the devotion of myriads of the faithful, who have derived manifold benefits and preservation from malign influences, from the compassion and charity of this merciful goddess—the incarnation of lovingkindness who is said to have renounced the joys of paradise in order "to guide the feet of countless weary pilgrims to the Heaven of eternal peace in Nirvana."

O thou Pure One, whose radiance is without stain, whose
knowledge is without shadow—
O thou forever shining like that sun whose glory no power
may dim—
Thou sun-like in the course of thy mercy pourest light upon
the world!

(Invocation to Kannon, Hokke Sutra)

Gongorō Jinja

❁

A FEW STEPS beyond the southern gate of Hase-dera a path leads to an adjoining small temple, proved by ancient records to have been in existence in the pre-Yoritomo days. The dedication is to Gongoro Kagemasa, a hero possessed of exceptional valor and strength. At the age of sixteen, in a fight waged by Yoritomo's ancestors he took part in an expeditionary force under Minamoto no Yoshiie (1091). Ancient popular history states that during a fierce battle Kagemasa was shot by an arrow in the right eye. Without stopping to draw out the weapon the valiant youth rushed upon his antagonist and dispatched him with a fatal wound. Hence this shrine is credited by the superstitious with the power of healing eye diseases. The date of its foundation is unknown, but in recent years it has been restored and rebuilt—the former building being still preserved in the lower courtyard.

On the right of the temple an enclosure contains two large circular stones; according to tradition the deified hero played at ball with the smaller one, while the large stone he brought back from the north in his *tamoto,* or sleeve! Behind this memorial to the physical feats of the departed warrior, *torii* lead to a small shrine supposed to be possessed of curative qualities; the ancient stone at the rear was taken from the sea at Yuigahama by fishermen. Facing the temple, the barren trunk of what was once a venerable tree is protected by a roof; legend asserts that Kagemasa supported his bow against this almost fossilized survival.

Every year in July and September, quite an elaborate festival is celebrated in connection with the shrine of Gongoro Jinja, when the neighborhood is gaily adorned and many curious old customs are revived. The buildings on the left of the temple enclose the *mikoshi,* or decorated sacred palanquins that are used on this occasion.

The Road to
Enoshima

❀

江
ノ
島
へ
向
っ
て

THE ROAD to Enoshima abounds in beautiful scenery and spots of historic interest. The main route passes through Gokuraku-ji Kiridoshi, or Pass. Immediately before the hill is ascended the famous Hoshi no Ido, or Well of Stars, is passed on the right. This well is frequently referred to in ancient literature relating to Kamakura. According to tradition its waters were of crystal purity and possessed the mystic faculty of always reflecting the stars in its depths, even in broad daylight. However, a kitchen maid from the neighborhood came to draw water and heedlessly let fall a knife into the starry depths below: the spell was broken—since that hour of profanation the magic reflection was no longer visible.

The little shrine upon the hill above is the Kokuzo-do, and was also known as Temple of the Star-Well. Legend relates that in the reign of the emperor Shomu (eighth century) strange luminous gleams were observed radiating from the well. This phenomenon arousing the curiosity of the villagers, an investigation was made which revealed an effigy of Kokuzo—a saint typifying infinite benevolence and wisdom, and generally represented with a sword and jewel in either hand. These circumstances becoming known to the emperor, he commanded the priest

Gyoki to carve a statue representing the newly-acquired deity, and which was duly installed as the chief object of · ·ship. As this small shrine was falling into decay, restoration and redecoration has recently been effected by popular subscription. It is under the jurisdiction of Shoju-in, a temple situated on the lower slope of Reisangasaki, and entered from the top of the pass. Shoju-in was founded by Yasutoki, third Hojo regent (1224–42). It is recorded that in the ninth century the saint Kobo Daishi, on the occasion of a visit to Enoshima, made a sojourn on this site to perform the rite of *goma,* or invocation by holy fire.

This road intersecting the hills was constructed by a famous priest—Ryokan, (also known as Ninsho), first head of Gokuraku-ji—who thus furnished a main approach to the temple from Kamakura. At the time of Nitta Yoshisada's invasion (July 5, 1333), the great general attempted to pour his troops down into Kamakura from this route. But the resistance experienced from the soldiers of the regency was so powerful, and the pass had been so strongly fortified with stakes, fences, and other works, that the loyalist army was unable to advance.

Adjoining the temple of Shoju-in, and almost opposite the six crude representations of Jizo, is an entrance on the left with a notice-board to the effect that this path ascends to the Koch monument. The scenery upon this promontory is delightful— the summit commanding far distant views of great beauty in all directions. The height is known as Reisangasaki; recently, owing to the generosity of an inhabitant of Kamakura, it has been converted into a public park. In the "sun-embroidered green gloom" beneath the shade of lofty trees, rest houses and rustic seats lure the wanderer to repose and exorcise the city's toil and dust in communion with this wide symphony of azure, green, and golden sunbeams, his meditations lulled by the music of the long curved breakers upon the rocks below—"the thunder chant of the sea which echoes round the world, eternal yet ever new."

Upon the southern crest of the hill stands the stone monument recording the fact that this beautiful spot was the favorite retreat of the eminent bacteriologist Dr. Robert Koch during his sojourn in Kamakura. Nearby stands a fenced-in camphor tree, planted when a small sapling by the doctor's own hands as an emblem of his gratification. The town, with its forest of roofs and pines, lies beneath, stretching away across the hill-surrounded plain. The sandy crescent of beach curves around to the rocks and cliffs of the little fishing hamlet of Iijima; beyond lies another fishing village, Kotsubo—the green hill of Zushi—Hayama—and the peninsula of Miura, which sweeps out seaward toward the east and culminates in the town of Misaki—forming the eastern barrier of the Sagami Bay and also the lower entrance gate to the Gulf of Tokyo. All around glitters the immensity of sapphire water. Oshima's volcanic cone is silhouetted upon the horizon on the southeast; from the western side glimpses of Enoshima appear between the tall pines and cryptomeria, backed by distant ranges and crowned with Mount Fuji's "ivory altar to the dawn" soaring above the Hakone peaks into the "luminous mystery of the blue." To the north, the gray-green figure of the mighty Daibutsu can be plainly discerned, enthroned in solitary grandeur amidst the dark foliage of his sacred grove.

On the northern side of the summit of Reisangasaki are many ancient tombs collected within a small enclosure. These, with various coins and other antique relics, were unearthed a few years ago when excavations were made to level this part of the hill, evidence that in the bygone centuries this lovely spot sheltered a vanished and forgotten garden of the dead. In those remote days this part of Reisangasaki belonged to the temple of Gokuraku-ji; it is recorded that the first abbot Ryokan used a vassal temple called Buppo-ji (Teaching of Buddha) that was situated upon this height for his own residence. The same record states that from here the famous priest employed his mystic ritual in the prayers for rain. Nichiren also invoked the compassion of the gods to terminate a severe drought from this commanding site; upon that occasion the saint moreover is said to have inscribed texts of scripture upon slips of wood and cast them into the sea below—these were eagerly rescued by fishermen and treasured as holy relics.

On the lower slope is a small but historic pool lying in the shadow of lofty trees; this is known as the Amagoi-ike or "Pond of the Rain-Prayers." A notice-board records the following statement:

> In the eighth year of Bun'ei (1271) there occurred over one hundred days of drought and distress was rife in the land. Consequently the regent Tokimune commanded the head priest of Gokuraku-ji, Ryokan, to offer prayers for rain. This functionary, accompanied by many other priests, erected an altar upon the mountain beside this pond, where the gods were earnestly besought to alleviate the peoples' suffering.

Two or three somewhat precipitous paths (near the Koch monument) descend upon the western slope, joining the main road in the neighborhood of Inamuragasaki; however should the same exit be preferred, there are numerous means of regaining the lower level. From the high road of the pass a short distance westward brings the pilgrim to the ancient temple of Gokuraku-ji, with the railway line encroaching upon its grounds and passing immediately before its doors.

Gokuraku-ji

❀

A THATCHED GATE and a long paved approach leads to Gokuraku-ji, or the Temple of Paradise; this small building roofed with moldering thatch being the solitary remnant of the vast and flourishing foundation of past centuries.

Gokuraku-ji was established by Hojo Shigetoki (a grandson of the great Tokimasa), who died in 1261 at the age of 64. His residence was in the vicinity of the temple, which derives its name from the nom de plume of its founder. Early records state that in 1257 an aged priest formed the project of building the first edifice in this locality; he installed a statue of Amida in a temporary shrine as the chief object of worship—but died before his design could be realized. Two years later, Shigetoki—in consultation with the famous priest Ryokan—removed an erection from elsewhere to this site. Shigetoki also died soon afterward, and his beautiful tomb is preserved at the rear of the temple grounds. However, the project was carried out on an extensive scale by his sons Nagatoki and Naritoki; an imposing fabric was constructed, comprising the large number of about fifty various buildings. Gokuraku-ji was dedicated to the Shingon, or True Word tenets, founded by Kobo Daishi in the ninth century, and whose mystic creed is said to bear more resemblance to Christianity than any other of the Buddhist sects. It obtained a great hold upon the people and at the present day there are many millions of adherents of the Shingonshu in Japan, with over 12,000 temples.

Ryokan, first abbot of Gokuraku-ji and the most noted philanthropist of his day, was a man of noble character; much is written concerning his abilities, his benevolence, and his generosity. He lived the self-denying and ascetic life of a saint, being known far and wide for his fatherly protection of the poor and the distressed, and especially as the savior and refuge of the lowest outcasts of civilization—those afflicted with leprosy. It is recorded that during the twenty years of his administration in this temple, the hospitals of Gokuraku-ji cured no fewer than 46,800 of these miserable beings, the total number that received treatment amounting to 57,250. In addition to the hospitals within the temple enclosure, this charitable priest established eighteen separate institutions in different parts of Kamakura. Nor were the activities of Ryokan confined to his spiritual ministrations and to the alleviation of distress. As an example of his public spirit it is specified that during his long lifetime he erected and repaired 83 temples; constructed 189 bridges, 71 roads, and excavated 33 wells; also establishing numerous public bathhouses, hospitals, and homes for the sick and poor.

Records further narrate that in his sixty-fifth year, Ryokan was commanded by the regent Tokimune to offer special prayers for the discomfiture of the enemy at the time of the Mongolian invasion. Moreover, his intercessions were considered of such efficacy that upon some twenty different occasions he conducted the service of prayers for rain in time of drought, and for cessation in time of flood. Another quaint chronicle states that in 1298, at the age of eighty-two, this humane priest built a hospital for horses in the compound of the temple. He constantly visited the stables and offered special prayers for the recovery of his four-footed friends, while in severe cases he would inscribe texts of scripture upon *ofuda,* or slips of wood, suspending them round the patients' necks. Shortly before the death of Ryokan, a severe drought caused great distress. The special services had been repeatedly resorted to, but with no avail; so beside the waterfall (that still exists some distance behind the temple) the aged priest supplicated the gods with greatest fervency to take compassion upon the suffering people, offering his own life as a hostage. During his petition it is stated that a small snake appeared from the bushes, listening attentively to the proceedings; shortly afterward rain fell in abundance. Ordained priest at the early age of sixteen (he entered religion upon the death of his mother), this famous philanthropist and benefactor died in 1303 at the advanced age of eighty-seven, having been a member of the priesthood for the long period of seventy-one years, surely a record! It may be here mentioned that serpents and *ryū*— "dragons" as they are not very happily translated—were considered in an occult and supernatural light. In China the dragon was held as a lofty and sublime manifestation dwelling in celestial regions above the clouds, and this shape was often supposed to be assumed by the gods when they deigned to appear upon the earth. Hence carvings and representations of dragons frequently occur in the decoration of shrines and temples, the goddess Benten being especially associated with a serpent attendant which is supposed to be sacred to her and to minister to her desires.

In March 1275, Gokuraku-ji was destroyed by fire. However, under the direction of Ryokan it was rebuilt and all the former prosperity was restored. But in 1425 another conflagration occurred, and a few years later (1433) a severe earthquake wrought heavy damage. The great temple proved unable to recover from these repeated catastrophes—from that time it gradually declined to the single insignificant building of the present day. The grounds contain five gaunt and hoary cherry trees of great antiquity which are said to have been planted by Hojo Tokimune (sixth regent 1270–84). The blossoms are of a curious and exceptional formation, bearing both single and double flowers combined upon the same stalk; these patriarchal trees are protected by the government, being frequently submitted to official inspection.

Before the temple two ancient stone vessels will be observed, relics of those early days when Gokuraku-ji was a literal paradise to the afflicted. These receptacles were formerly in the dispensary and are said to have been used as mortars in the preparation of certain drugs and medicines for the benefit of the numerous hospitals and homes. The ancient chart still in possession of the temple shows that in addition to the forty-nine edifices of this extensive foundation, the auxiliary buildings of the enclosure amounted to more than double that number, including a medical bathhouse for patients, schools, and many institutions devoted to the special care of lepers. So famous did the good works of this presiding genius become, that at his death the emperor Go-Daigo conferred upon him the title of *bosatsu*—a term implying the highest virtue, and only applied to a saint who has attained to a state of enlightenment one degree below Buddhahood.

In 1261 the temple of Gokuraku-ji was promoted by imperial order and specially authorized to pray for the welfare of the imperial family; the tablet conferring this honor in the emperor Go-Uda's own handwriting being still preserved. The interior of the temple is more attractive than the exterior of the building would suggest. The chief object of veneration—a statue of the Buddha ascribed to Kosho, second head of the temple—is enclosed within the sanctuary above the main altar and flanked upon either side by large dark figures of ten of the disciples. On the right of the altar is a curious effigy of Fudo (god of wisdom), surrounded by his background of flames; this quaint image is said to have been brought from China by Kobo Daishi in the year 807.

It was formerly enshrined elsewhere, but on the destruction of that temple in the early days of the Meiji era, it was entrusted to Gokuraku-ji for safekeeping. However, in order to provide this venerable divinity with an independent environment, the temple authorities issued an appeal requesting one hundred thousand benevolent souls to subscribe the small sum of five *sen* apiece—in which case the amount realized would suffice to construct a separate shrine for its reception.

On the opposite side stands the old *jindaiko,* or war drum, stated to have been used by Nitta Yoshisada—together with the lacquered saddle ornamented with mother-of-pearl, and the heavy iron stirrups used by Nitta's general, Odate Muneuji, in those martial days. Three unusual paintings on silk are suspended at the back of the altar. These are ascribed to the efforts of Ryokan, each picture containing one thousand representations of Amida. Upon every successive day the worthy priest is said to have traced a new representation of the deity, consequently nine years were needed for the completion of this laborious task.

Around the walls are exhibited, in a sort of museum, a collection of antiquities that are said to have been retrieved from the various vicissitudes of the temple. Amongst these, items of interest include a well-preserved painting of the *nehan,* or death of Buddha—according to the label, the gift of Masako; a faded and ghostly material that was originally a banner presented by Tokimune; a letter inscribed by Ryokan; a statue of Buddha that was possessed by Sanetomo (third shogun, 1203); and a remarkable carving ascribed to Kobo Daishi—the thousand Jizo. This work consists of a central figure of the divinity about one inch in height, surrounded in tiers by what were originally a thousand microscopic images, each about the size of a grain of rice. At the present time the ranks of the diminutive saints are reduced to some two or three hundred.

The compartments at the back are occupied by statues. The

right and left respectively contain striking effigies of the first and second priests of this temple, the figure of Ryokan being especially realistic, a testimony to the upright and noble character of this great man. The central niche enshrines a National Treasure—a fine statue (by Zenkei) of the Buddha with uplifted hands, represented while delivering a discourse; also a beautiful figure of Monju Bosatsu, holding a sword and scroll. The statue on the right is stated to have been a former possession of Tokiyori (fifth Hojo regent, 1246) and represents the god of healing, Yakushi Nyorai. This felicitous gift was originally presented by Tokiyori to one of the hospitals of Gokuraku-ji.

The remaining case contains various other antique objects, amongst others a three-faced Daikoku, the popular god of riches: a curious group with the goddess Benten seated upon a throne surrounded by various quaint figures—this carving is said to have occupied a place in Mochiuji's (fourth Ashikaga shogun, died 1439) private shrine, the tablet originally inscribed with the emperor Go-Uda's own hand, but from which time has obliterated the characters; also another imperial gift—"Pictures of Paradise." The appropriate presentation is studded with myriad saints and was bestowed upon the temple by the emperor Go-Fukakusa (accession 1247). Two interesting possessions—preserved elsewhere and produced on request—are the ancient colored chart depicting all the innumerable buildings originally included in the enclosure of Gokuraku-ji; also three rolls of manuscript ascribed to Sugawara no Michizane, the great literary genius who died in the year 903 and was subsequently deified as Tenjin.* Originally ten rolls of these essays were in existence, of which some have disappeared, the residue being in possession elsewhere. The handwriting is exquisite, miniature, and wonderfully distinct. Although the width of the manuscript is less than

*Many of the treasures referred to above can be seen in the treasure hall on the temple grounds.

three inches, each line contains twenty-five characters, the rolls being of a uniform length of some 36 feet.

Gokuraku-ji possesses, even in the present degenerate days, quite an extensive area of land, a large extent of which is under cultivation; peaches, pears, and grapes are grown for the market—some 300,000 peaches being produced annually. The small shrine on the right of the temple is dedicated to Kobo Daishi, and contains a lacquered statue of the saint.

The path intersecting the peach orchard culminates in a thicket of tall cedars with a fine old *ichō* guarding the entrance. In the midst of this solitary green space stands a truly regal monument, the tomb of Ryokan, the benefactor of all who needed help and who so effectively laid the spiritual foundations of Gokuraku-ji. According to the cicerone's proud assertion, this tomb enjoys the distinction of being the largest in Eastern Japan. Its graceful shape and majestic proportions seem emphasized by the remoteness of this somber grove. The mighty stones bear neither Sanskrit characters nor any sort of inscription traced upon their rugged surfaces, their sole ornament being the film woven by Nature of heavy moss—so rich of hue it seems to glow and radiate the intense green kindled by the few sunbeams that pierce the sheltering veil of the surrounding foliage. The beautiful old tomb on the left of this enclosure symbolizes the resting place of Hojo Shigetoki, who established the temple upon its present site.

Inamuragasaki

稲村ヶ崎

❁

FROM GOKURAKU-JI to Inamuragasaki is but a short distance. This historic cliff—so universally celebrated as the scene of the immortal drama of Nitta Yoshisada and the sword—appears to have received its name because the formation of the eminence somewhat resembles a rice stack like those seen at harvest time. At the present day the base of this steep promontory always lies in deep water, but from ancient writings it appears that in the Kamakura period a narrow strip of sand was left bare at low tide. The *Azuma Kagami* records that on September 21, 1191, Yoritomo and his suite repaired to Inamuragasaki in order to witness an archery tournament that took place on the beach.

A version of Nitta Yoshisada's invasion is given in the *Taiheiki*—the celebrated classical history containing an account of the emperor Go-Daigo's attempts to overthrow the ascendancy of the Eastern usurpers, and may be translated as follows:

> During the night preceding the attack, Nitta ascended to the summit of the cliff, and in the moonlight watched the enemy's encampment. The silvery beams, paling in the

light of dawn, revealed the dangers and difficulties with which the undertaking was beset. As far as the *kiridōshi* (pass) on the northern side, the mountain was high and the pass was steep and bristling with defenses. A fortress had been constructed, and hostile warriors, numbering many tens of thousands, were lying in wait. To the south, although so scanty was the strip of sand below the cliff, yet it was blocked with timber and obstacles to impede their progress; moreover, the sea-approach was guarded by hundreds of war ships stationed near the shore, and manned with archers all in readiness to pour their darts upon the foe. Nitta Yoshisada dismounted from his horse; from the edge of the towering cliff he fixed his gaze beyond the waiting craft and uttering a fervid appeal to the sea-god he cast his sword into the deep. Lo, a miracle! The tide—that had never before receded thus—obeyed the summons and slowly rolled back its waves to the distance of twenty *chō* (over one mile); sweeping the threatening boats away upon the retreating flood, and leaving broad sands for the attacking host to fall upon their prey.

The tiny bay to the west of Inamuragasaki is known as Sode no Ura (Sleeve Inlet) as it is supposed to resemble the shape of a sleeve. The seashore, extending from this point to Koshigoe is called Shichirigahama (literally Seven Ri Beach, six *chō* comprising one *ri* in the old Chinese system of measurement). This was the site of an ancient battleground; a record of over 200 years ago states that even at that time skeletons, bones, and broken weapons were constantly unearthed. The same chronicle describes the sand of this shore as being of black iron, dark as lacquer, and very fine—glittering like jewels in the sunlight and considered highly efficacious in polishing swords and weapons. Unlike the Kamakura beach, the wild and rocky shore of Shichirigahama is in the present day almost destitute of shells. However, according to the same authority, in those days it was noted for the discovery of a beautiful pale pink variety called the *hanagai,* or flower shell, which was much used by girls in the construction of artificial flowers.

A few paces beyond Inamuragasaki a little brook flows into the sea; beside the bridge spanning this stream is a small cascade falling over the rocks in three tiers. This is the Otonashi, or Soundless Fall, the water being supposed to descend upon beds of sand that muffle the sound. On the main road, a short distance before reaching this bridge, is an ancient pine with long drooping branches. Nichiren was said to have hung his *kesa* (part of his priest's robe) upon one of the boughs as he halted beneath its shade on his way to the execution ground at Katase, thus causing the tree to become a sacred landmark. The road continues with beautiful views to the Yukiaibashi, or Bridge of Meeting—the spot so famous in connection with the attempted execution of Nichiren; the messenger hastening to report the miraculous delivery to Kamakura met at this little stream the emissary of Tokiyori bringing the reprieve from the regency.

Another interesting association with Nichiren exists in this neighborhood and enjoys great popularity with his numerous devotees; this is known as the Amagoi-ike, the lake from which the saint successfully prayed for rain. To the right of the bridge a path intersects the valley, its entrance being marked by a tall gray stone inscribed with scarlet characters and informing the faithful that this road leads to the holy ground sanctified by the intercession of Nichiren. Several of these monuments stand by the wayside to indicate the route—after a short distance a turn to the left brings into view this famous hill.

In former times a large lake called Tanabe no Ike existed below the small eminence—its shape, outlined by high banks, can be plainly distinguished, but the waters have been drained and the site converted into ricefields. It is said that the project has been discussed of restoring the lake and converting the historic scene to its pristine aspect—a charming addition to the landscape should this be accomplished. The little height is ascended by a rustic path; at the entrance is a well whose waters are used by the more ardent believers to purify themselves before mounting to the hallowed spot. The path leads to a huge pine of curious formation—gnarled and hoary, enclosed within a small fence and encircled with a *shimenawa,* or tasseled rope, used to indicate an object of veneration. Beneath these far-spreading twisted boughs tradition asserts the saint knelt to supplicate the gods to banish the dread specter of famine and grant the longed-for rain. According to the legend, while the saint was wrestling in prayer for the alleviation of the general distress, a *ryū,* or dragon, appeared beside him and then ascended into the clear blue heavens. Soon afterward dark clouds rolled up from the horizon and the drought was at an end.

Near the ancient tree stands a monument roofed with a wooden canopy; this is dedicated to the holy messenger that assumed the guise of the dragon, and commands much attention from the numerous pilgrims that visit this place. On the western side, facing these memorials, a small commemorative temple has been erected and through the efforts of the faithful a celebrated contemporary sculptor (Takeuchi Kyuichi) was requested to carve a statue of Nichiren to be installed therein. While the artist was considering what material would be best suited to his subject, a destructive storm occurred in Kamakura, during which a large bough of the consecrated pine crashed to the ground. This was forwarded to the sculptor and he converted it into the desired effigy of the saint. This statue is duly enshrined within the sanctuary and is considered a striking work of art. The detached shrine on the left contains a large statue of Jogyo Bosatsu—one of Buddha's immediate disciples and of whom Nichiren is believed by his followers to be a reincarnation. This small building is also newly erected, and results from the enthusiasm of a guild of Yokohama devotees.

The Shichirigahama beach culminates in a beautiful pine-crowned rock—nearby lies Enoshima, the fairy islet; beyond, the gleaming shape of Mount Fuji hovers in the "unshadowed calms of over-curving sky" with indescribable effect. Many poems have been inspired by the romantic beauty of this scene. Katase, the village on the mainland opposite Enoshima, is also celebrated in history as the spot where the Mongolian ambassadors sent by Kublai Khan (1275 and 1279), on their mission of attempting to induce the regency to pay tribute to China, met their doom. Both embassies met with the same drastic reception: the leaders of the former expedition were arrested upon their arrival by order of Tokimune, and escorted to the execution ground at Kamakura; the latter were beheaded upon the Katase beach, their heads being pilloried as a warning.

The eastern part of Katase is known as Koshigoe, famous in history from its association with the popular Yoshitsune, ill-fated younger brother of Yoritomo. The story is well known. Yoritomo's mind had been poisoned against his brother, and after his brilliant victories over the Taira, when Yoshitsune was on his way to Kamakura to deliver his prisoners and to give an account of his triumphs—in which he had rendered powerful assistance to Yoritomo—he was intercepted at Koshigoe and a document was given to him by Hojo Tokimasa prohibiting his entry to Kamakura. Yoshitsune remained at Koshigoe some twenty days while vainly attempting to allay Yoritomo's suspicions. During this period he stayed at the small temple of Manpuku-ji in close proximity to the beach. Many relics of Yoshitsune and his giant follower Benkei are still preserved; the venerable tree in front of the little building is said to have been planted by Yoshitsune's own hands. On the right is a charming landscape garden backed by high rocky cliffs. "Benkei's stone" is pointed out, which tradition states he used as a seat; moreover, this lake is known as Suzuri no Ike, as Benkei is said to have used its waters to moisten the ink in inditing Yoshitsune's celebrated appeal to his implacable brother.

Here am I, weeping crimson tears in vain at thy displeasure. Well was it said that good medicine tastes bitter in the mouth, and true words ring harshly in the ear. This is why the slanders that men speak of me remain unproved, why I am kept out of Kamakura unable to lay bare my heart.

These many days have I lain here and could not gaze upon my brother's face. The bond of our blood-brotherhood is sundered . . . But a short season after I was born, my honored sire passed to another world, and I was left fatherless. Clasped in my mother's bosom I was carried down to Yamato and since that day I have not known a moment free from care and danger. Though it was but to drag out a useless life, we wandered round the capital suffering hardships, hid in all manner of rustic spots, dwelt in remote and distant provinces, whose rough inhabitants did treat us with contumely. But at last I was summoned to assist in overthrowing the house of Taira, and in this conflict I first laid Kiso Yoshinaka low. Then so that I might demolish the Taira men, I spurred my steed on frowning precipices. Careless of death in the face of the foe, I braved the dangers of wind and wave, not recking that my body might sink to the bottom of the sea and be devoured by monsters of the deep. My pillow was my harness, arms my trade . . .

(Translated by William George Aston)

The original draft of this famous document is said to be still preserved at Manpuku-ji, and it was to this temple that Yoshitsune's head was supposed to have been sent for identification after his death in 1188. It is recorded that the latter grim relic of the brilliant young hero was dispatched to Yoritomo in a lacquered "headbox"; it arrived during the festivities that marked the triumphant completion of the temple of Hachiman.

A short distance beyond this small shrine of memories lies the large and important temple of Ryuko-ji.

Ryūkō-ji (Katase)

竜口寺（片瀬）

❀

THIS TEMPLE, situated in a part known as Tatsunokuchi, or Mouth of the Dragon, is the pride and glory of the village of Katase. The picturesque grounds—upon an extensive and parklike scale—extend over the surrounding hills and are intersected by a labyrinth of winding shady paths which command a feast of beauty and color. The green heights of Enoshima lie like a jewel in the rich blue ocean below, spangled with the sails of countless white-winged ships and boats plying the waves; the distant mountains, with an uninterrupted view of Mount Fuji, blend into a serene picture justly famed for its romantic character.

But the wide celebrity of Ryuko-ji does not emanate from scenic attractions, but from its association with the thrilling episode in the life of the most popular saint Nichiren. In commemoration of his miraculous deliverance from the sword in 1271, the temple was erected by his disciples in the year 1337 in order to preserve the sanctity of this historic spot. When the precincts are entered by the main gate, a short distance to the left is a small green pond enclosed with ornamental stones adjoining which is a grassy hillock crowned with an antique monument of beautiful shape—this marks the site of the *keijō,* or execution ground; a large stone nearby is engraved with a record of the circumstances. This part was used for the public execution of criminals from the year 723. In those days, and also in Nichiren's time, the sea appears to have been in close proximity, and must have receded considerably during the succeeding centuries. In ancient times the small pond was quite a large lake; the fact that its shape was considered suggestive of a dragon's mouth gave the name to this locality.

According to tradition, its waters were inhabited by a poisonous seven-headed serpent who was the scourge of the neighborhood and whose habit it was to prey upon and devour the terrified inhabitants of those regions. This monster was subjugated by the goddess Benten, who descended from heaven upon the adjacent island of Enoshima in order to rescue the distressed villagers from the dragon in the year 552. The flight of steps behind the monument leads up to a venerable shrine which, according to ancient chronicles, was originally established in the year 516 to propitiate the serpent, who was considered an evil spirit and was consecrated as a *myōjin,* or deity.

From the main gate below, steps lead up to the *sanmon,* or tower-gate, beneath whose thatched roof the beams and panels are decorated with fine carvings of scenes in which hermits and patriarchs are the chief figures. From this gate the upper courtyard is entered. On the left is a small temple containing elaborate decorations; the central statue is the founder of the sect, surrounded by figures representing his chief disciples. Before this building is a pine enclosed by a small fence—this is the Hikari-matsu, or Glittering Pine. According to the legend, the goddess Myoken Bosatsu upon one occasion descended into the tree enveloped in a dazzling effulgence of light. A stone monument stands nearby recording this event; also a shrine, gay with artificial flowers and other emblems, is erected in honor of the goddess. However, although the site is identical, this is not the actual pine that was thus honored by the deity. According to the aged custodian of the little shrine, the present is the grandchild of the original Hikari-matsu!

On the rocky slope to the left are two caves. The lower contains a large statue of the founder carved in wood; the upper cavern was the historic prison wherein Nichiren was confined whilst awaiting his execution.

The main temple occupies a commanding site upon the upper plateau. The timbers are ornamented with many carvings of dragons, birds, pines, and various animals. Outside the entrance stands a green copper incense burner of quaint shape—the carved inscription stating it to be the gift of a merchant of Edo. Near this emblem a curious object is attached to a pillar, containing one hundred movable slips of wood enclosed within a frame. It constantly happens that pious persons—in fulfillment of a vow, or as a penance, or perhaps merely to emphasize their petitions—undertake to make one hundred circuits of the broad gallery surrounding the temple, while incessantly repeating the formula of their religion. This is called the *hyakudo,* or hundred rounds, and is considered of great efficacy in prayer; each time the frame is passed the suppliant turns back one slip of wood to mark the number of his revolutions. In times of war the number of devotees making the *hyakudo* would greatly increase—the relatives hoping by their intercession to preserve their loved ones from the perils of the battlefield.

Like all Nichiren temples, the interior abounds in color and gorgeous decorations. In front of the altar—surmounted by an angel in bright robes playing the flute—is suspended a *tengai,* or canopy, from which float long pendants; hosts of lanterns, flowers, banners; and a paraphernalia of other adornments present a gay and somewhat garish ensemble, in strong contrast to the subdued and mysterious twilight atmosphere of the Zen interiors. Upon the floor rest numbers of small vermilion lacquer stands, carved with gilt lotus flowers and bearing red-and-gilt cases containing the scriptures. The coffered ceiling is painted with designs of Nichiren's crest, the citron, in blue, red, and gold. The inner sanctuary is elaborately carved and hung with a rich curtain of scarlet and gold brocade.

Within the left-hand chamber is preserved a revered possession of the temple; upon a high carved stand of dark red lacquer, with cushions of glittering brocade, reposes the stone upon which the saint is said to have been kneeling at the time the divine thunderbolt paralyzed the hand of the executioner. On the great anniversary festival of September 12, this highly venerated memento is displayed from the greater height of the sanctuary above the main altar. Another curious memorial of their founder is also exhibited upon these occasions, in the shape of the wooden lid of a cooking vessel. Legend asserts that when the priest was taken captive and was on his way to Tatsunokuchi to be beheaded, the little band passed the lake known as Tanabe no Ike—in the backwoods behind the Shichirigahama beach. An old woman, whose heart was melted by compassion for the unfortunate captive, bestowed upon him her own repast of *bota-mochi*—a cake made of sweetened riceflour. Having no plate whereon to place her offering, she utilized the circular lid of her *nabe* —or small cooking pot. The saint, touched by the kind action of his aged sympathizer, inscribed upon the wooden lid a text of the scriptures.

On the wall near the memorable stone hangs a large picture painted in colors and vividly representing the execution scene at the moment of the thunderbolt. The large vestibule abounds with countless *ema*—votive plaques of all shapes and sizes presented by worshippers as a mark of gratitude for answers to prayer, or for some benefit obtained and ascribed to the saint's influence. Many of these represent harrowing calamities in which rescue was effected through the intervention of Nichiren.

Further ascents behind the temple conduct the pilgrim to an upper terrace whereon stands another small temple of fabulously ancient foundation. This dates back to the days of legend—the Shichimen-do, or Shrine of the Seven Heads, whose object was to exorcise the evil qualities from the dragon tenant of the lake below. Nearby tower the picturesque roofs of a fine five-storied pagoda; this memorial to the founder of the sect is of recent construction, having been erected by devotees in 1910. The lowest story is a repository for the statue of Nichiren, surrounded by many glittering figures of saints.

A sloping path on the western side of this terrace leads to a space upon the height above that is well known for its inspiring panorama, this particular aspect of Mount Fuji's sacred crest floating into the crystal blue of space above ridge upon ridge of purple mountains being justly famed for its vision of ethereal loveliness. The scene is at its best upon a clear day in the colder seasons of the year. The intervening plain is rich with every tone of green; the river below, gay with flitting sails, winds into the horizon toward Fujisawa, while beneath the broken line of peaks the sweep of blue bay curves in a complete semicircle, fringed with its rolling line of snowy breakers.

Nichiren Shōnin

THE NAME OF Nichiren stands out as the most picturesque and striking figure in the history of Japanese Buddhism. The son of a fisherman of Kominato, province of Awa, this boy—who was destined to take his place in the ranks of the immortals—was born in 1222. In his youthful days he gave proof of extraordinary intelligence, astonishing all by his sagacity and mature powers of reasoning. At the age of eleven he entered as a pupil the monastery of Seisho-ji near his home, where he remained studying his religion until four years later, when he took the tonsure and assumed the name of Rencho (Lotus Eternal). The next year the boy-priest came to Kamakura, continuing a course of studies under the distinguished divines of the capital for four years; then revisiting his native place, in the solitary mountains adjoining the temple of Seisho-ji this voluminous writer composed his first essays.

Shortly after returning to Kamakura he encountered a renowned priest from Kyoto, whom he accompanied to Hieizan—the Buddhist stronghold overlooking Lake Biwa—remaining there for eleven years absorbed in study and in contact with the most erudite ecclesiastics of the time, including the famous Chinese priest Doryu, who some five years later, at the request of the regent Tokiyori, became lord abbot of the great Kamakura monastery, Kencho-ji. All these years the young reformer profoundly devoted himself to the study of his religion, and the fame of his scholarship and spiritual asceticism began to be spread abroad.

Now the time of probation was at an end; Nichiren—or Rencho, as he was still called—was ready to enter the arena as teacher, proselytizer, and founder of the new sect. At the age of thirty-one (1253), he returned to his original temple of Seisho-ji and there in the silence and the seclusion of the mountain, entered into a state of profound fasting, meditation, and prayer. At daybreak on the morning of the eighth day the first rays of the rising sun pierced the mists of dawn, gilding with its radiance the lonely figure kneeling in spiritual ecstasy upon the woodland peak. The saint arose and saluted the flood of golden light illuminating the world as the symbol of his creed—in triumph crying out with passionate fervor the formula and watchword of his sect, that has been since repeated by countless millions of souls:

> *Namu myōhō renge kyō*
> (All adoration to the lotus of truth)

This dramatic moment was the birth of the Hokke-shu, or Nichiren sect. From that time the saint went forth to wrestle with the souls of men, and to expound his doctrines as Nichiren, or Lotus of the Sun.

At once starting upon his career as reformer, his listeners construed his impassioned discourse as the ravings of a madman, Nichiren barely escaping from their attacks without serious injury. However, he was enabled to flee from his assailants and again repaired to Kamakura—at that time the most important city of the empire—where he took up his abode in a straw hut in the part called Matsubagayatsu (Valley of Pine Needles). Hence-

34. Nichiren Shonin Tsujiseppo-ato.

forth he devoted the evenings to study and to the composition of his essays. During the daytime he emerged to preach his doctrines in the public thoroughfares, proclaiming himself with intense conviction as the only true exponent of the law and a divine messenger sent to bring salvation to mankind.

At that time the city of Kamakura was experiencing a succession of calamities—earthquakes, tempests, inundation, pestilence, and a famine so severe that human beings, as well as horses and animals, were dying of hunger wholesale, their bodies lying unburied by the roadside. Nichiren attributed this dreadful condition to the moral shortcomings of the panic-stricken inhabitants, discovering in the scriptures prophecies of the woes that would overtake those who degraded the true religion by their evil deeds and superstitions. This stormy priest was the first in the land to practice sectarian aggression—until then the attitude of the various rival sects of Buddhism in Japan had been one of gentle tolerance. He was likewise the first to make use of this dramatic method of promulgating his doctrines in public, and which he warmly defended when rebuked that street propaganda was derogatory to the priesthood. He retorted that it was necessary for the soldier upon the field of battle to take his food standing; all criticisms were silenced before his ready eloquence. The site occupied by Nichiren for his sermons by the wayside is situated in the street running parallel to Tsurugaoka Hachiman Shrine and is carefully preserved. Enclosed with a granite fence, the central object (*tsujiseppō-ato*) is said to be the identical stone upon which the reformer rested during his discourses.

The doctrine so fiercely promulgated was based upon the mysterious Law of the White Lotus which was the final teaching of Buddha; and which, he asserted, contained the fundamental essence and culmination of all the former instructions classified under three heads—worship, law, and morals. Fierce intolerance and denunciation of all the former sects of Buddhism was a salient feature of Nichiren's teachings. To the remonstrance that all the other sects could not be false and heretical he retorted that the scaffolding merely availed until the temple was built— "Know ye that the Jodo is the road to Hell; the Zen, the teaching of infernal hosts; the Shingon, a heresy that will destroy the nation; the Ritsu, a deadly enemy of the land!"

Meanwhile Nichiren was reaping a steady harvest of followers and supporters, not only commoners, but men of high education, even distinguished samurai, were converted to his doctrines. One of his earliest believers was the samurai Shijo Kingo, "the beloved disciple," an ardent and faithful adherent who did his utmost to support and succor the saint during his persecutions, even at the risk of his own life. The residence of this devoted man subsequently became a small temple and still exists (near the Hase station) as a memorial to his fidelity.

Obviously Nichiren's sentiments did not enhance his popularity with the other sects. Moreover, the sequence of severe calamities that befell the city of Kamakura was attributed by popular superstition to Nichiren's agency, thereby incurring the general odium and more than ever intensifying the unpopularity of his doctrines. During his discourses he was not only insulted by word, but was constantly attacked by the mob, returning to his dwelling covered with blood and wounds. But persecution little availed to daunt this heroic spirit; it is recorded that he appeared to welcome ill usage and cruel treatment, and in an ecstasy would give thanks to the Almighty that he was deemed worthy to suffer a baptism of blood in the cause of the All Highest. Indeed, several of his disciples died a martyr's death while protecting their beloved master from the fury of his assailants.

In the year 1260, Nichiren had the temerity to present to the regent Tokiyori (an ardent follower of the Zen sect) his celebrated *Risshō Ankoku Ron* (Treatise upon Peace and Righteousness), wherein plain language was used regarding the perilous condition of the people and the futile attempts of their rulers to save them; it moreover contained the prophecy that a foreign invasion was near at hand. In this essay the other sects of Buddhism and their priests are severely condemned:

> Woe unto them! They have missed the entrance into the gate that leads to the true Buddhism, and have fallen into the prison-house of the false teachings. They are fettered, entangled, bewildered. Whither will their blind wanderings lead them?

This treatise not unnaturally had the effect of stirring up wrath and indignation on all sides—the political powers, as well as the ecclesiastical faction, becoming open enemies of the new reformer. His hermitage was attacked and set fire to in the night, but Nichiren was again successful in eluding his foes, escaping on this occasion to the province of Shimousa (now Chiba–Ibaraki prefectures). However, the next year he was captured by command of the regent, and as a disturber of the public peace was banished to Ito in the province of Izu. A signpost still stands upon the sand dunes of the Kamakura beach recording the fact that this famous priest started into exile from that spot. During the period of banishment his activities continued unabated, the number of his followers were steadily increasing and many books and essays were written. Sheltered in the hut of a poor fisherman—of whose kindness he always cherished grateful memories—Nichiren remained in Izu for some two years; when released he returned to Kamakura to resume his propaganda. The next few years were spent in missionary journeys around the neighboring provinces, including a visit to his native place—where the prophet was again furiously attacked and again escaped from death by almost a miracle. It is recorded that during these wanderings, in his forty-eighth year, the saint ascended the snowy heights of Mount Fuji and buried upon the sacred mountain the Hokke scriptures, copied by his own hand.

In 1271 Nichiren was again seized as an offender against the public peace—this time at the instigation of the various other sects of Buddhism—and sentenced to be executed at Katase, the village upon the mainland opposite the island of Enoshima. As an example, the prisoner was mounted upon a horse and carried around the streets of Kamakura by his guards before proceeding to the place of execution, arriving at Katase in the dead of night. Many of his sorrowful disciples and converts assembled, weeping by the roadside to take a last farewell. The devoted Kingo, with his brothers, led the horse's bridle and accompanied their beloved master into the valley of death with every expectation of laying down their own lives at the same time.

According to the well-known popular tradition the scene that followed was dramatic in the extreme. Nichiren, incessantly repeating the scriptures, knelt upon the rope mat and bared his neck to receive the fatal stroke. At the moment the executioner brandished his sword on high, a sudden crash of thunder shook the earth; the sky was lit up, and from the black clouds a hissing ball of fire shattered the uplifted sword into three pieces, paralyzing the arm of the executioner, who fell to the ground. This miraculous demonstration being naturally construed as a mark of divine wrath, a messenger hastened at full speed to report to Kamakura what occurred. However, the previous night a heavenly being had appeared to the regent in a dream, warning him not to slay the captive priest: a reprieve had already been dispatched, the two messengers meeting at a small stream that flows into the sea on the Shichirigahama beach and which to this day bears the name Yukiaigawa, or River of Meeting.

An important and interesting temple was erected at Katase in close proximity to the site of the execution ground, wherein various relics of the saint are preserved: this is Ryuko-ji, or Temple of the Dragon's Mouth. Nearby is the small dark cave wherein Nichiren was imprisoned while awaiting his doom. These events took place September 12, 1271. Every year as the anniversary recurs the temple precincts are thronged by crowds of devotees, who arrive the previous day in large parties and gaily decorated processions from far and near to commemorate the miraculous deliverance of their beloved saint and spend the whole night in a state of religious fervor worthy of their founder— loudly vociferating the formula (which has been translated "All glory to the scripture of the Lotus of Good Law") to the incessant accompaniment of hand drums, a process absolutely deafening to those who prefer milder methods of attaining salvation.

The regent Tokimune on this occasion transmuted Nichiren's sentence to banishment in the distant island of Sado, where after a long and perilous journey he arrived at the beginning of

December 1271. His only shelter was a dilapidated hut situated in a bleak graveyard, where he experienced severe hardships. Barely sufficient of the poorest food was obtainable to sustain life, moreover, his thin monk's habit of coarse hemp afforded but meager protection to the deep snows and icy winds of that rigorous climate. Harsh treatment and attacks from his enemies accentuated his forlorn and abandoned condition, and however the dauntless spirit of the saint might soar above all trials and persecutions, he must surely have perished from cold and starvation during the long winter months had not rescue been forthcoming from an unexpected quarter.

One night one of his opponents, armed with a sword, approached the isolated hut with the intention of killing "the devil-priest." Nichiren, kneeling upon the bare earth, was reciting the scriptures. The intense sincerity and magnetic quality of his voice arrested and affected his intending slayer to such an extent that the man experienced a complete change of heart, becoming a faithful convert. Together with his wife the devoted couple did all in their power to succor and ameliorate the pitiful condition of the castaway. Many other converts were won by his impassioned oratory; even in that wild and distant spot Nichiren was able to write many essays and to hold communication with his disciples.

Three years later the exile was released and permitted to return to Kamakura. There he was accorded an interview with the regent, to whom he expounded his doctrines, again warning him of the impending attack on Japan by outsiders, which he prophesied would occur not later than the same year. This prediction was verified, for a few months later (October 1274) the first Mongolian attack occurred, when the islands of Tsushima and Iki were much devastated by the enemy and large numbers of Japanese soldiers fell in battle. Thereupon Nichiren's status underwent a complete change. Thousands embraced the Hokke-shu (Sect of the Lotus Flower), and the reformer's triumph was complete, a charter being conferred by the regent granting him full liberty in the promulgation of his doctrines. Moreover, he was offered by Tokimune a temple and lands in Kamakura, but earthly glory held no attractions for this lofty soul, and now Nichiren's real greatness becomes evident. The world lay at his feet, but he renounced it and with a small band of followers retired into the seclusion of a wild mountain—Minobu-san. There, in a hut of the most austere simplicity, he dedicated his remaining days to study of the scriptures and to the instruction of his disciples.

Around this dominant figure are entwined countless legends and traditions. It is said that on the morning of his birth (January 1222), the farmers, going to their labor in the fields on that cold winter's daybreak, marveled to behold the glory of the lotus flowers that rose from the mud and tangle of last year's withered leaves, opening their pure glistening chalices in the frosty atmosphere to herald the advent of the saint. Moreover, at the same time a spring of crystal water suddenly gushed from the earth in close proximity to the cottage wherein his parents dwelt—a manifestation that was held to symbolize the purity and truth of his teachings. It is impossible for devotees and admirers of Nichiren to make pilgrimages to the place of his birth, for the actual site whereon the fisherman's cottage stood has long disappeared and lies beneath the blue ripples upon the ocean bed, this part of the seacoast having been washed away by the fierce storms and tidal waves of succeeding centuries. A universally known legend records that at the time his enemies determined to compass the destruction of Nichiren by setting fire to his hermitage, a celestial messenger, disguised as a beautiful monkey with long snow white fur, mysteriously appeared and guided the saint to a place of safety. The cave that afforded him a refuge on that occasion is supposed to be on a hill in the backwoods of Zushi, and is easily accessible from Kamakura. At the entrance of the cave hangs a representation of Nichiren attended by his little rescuer. A picturesque mountain temple built in the rock adjoins this interesting spot, that was erected in commemoration of this incident and is known as Sarubatake, or Garden of the Monkey.

Nichiren remained in his retreat at Minobu until the age of sixty—a haven of peace and rest after the vicissitudes and persecutions of a tempestuous career extending over forty years. This mountain was included in the territory of a distinguished samurai named Hagii, who was also a devoted adherent of Nichiren. The former naturally wished to make life easier and to reduce the privations of the saint in his wild retreat, but Nichiren's ascetic nature could not change; he would accept no favor. However, an exception was made in the gift of a horse from Lord Hagii—to which animal he was deeply attached—and later, shortly before his death he consented to the construction of an assembly hall for the instruction of his followers.

The master, with his seven disciples, lived a life of utmost austerity; one of the little band would now and again descend to the valley below in quest of fresh water and the meager supply of fresh vegetables upon which they subsisted. The cold of winter was rigorous in the extreme, and must have recalled the saint's earlier sufferings during his exile in Sado. He writes that although the height of his hut was but seven feet, snow lay on the ground to the depth of ten feet. "Ice makes up the walls and the icicles are like the beads of garlands decorating shrines." The spring flowers of that lofty region did not bloom until summer and the fruits only ripened at the approach of winter, the sole human beings that ever appeared being an occasional woodcutter, and at rare intervals a comrade in religion, braving the dangers of the lonely mountain passes to visit the hermit in his retirement. Their life and the beauty of its setting is graphically described by Nichiren in his letters—the fantastic shapes of the great rocks; the dense forest; the roar of the torrent in the valley; the distant views, and the surrounding rugged peaks. At night the silence of that desolate region was broken by the cry of the wolves and the wild monkeys, and occasionally the melancholy whining call of the stag to his mate.

After some eight years of this isolated existence, Nichiren was attacked by illness. At this period he writes:

> During these eight years illness and age have brought me severe suffering, both body and mind seem crumbling into ruin—my weakness daily increases. For ten days I have taken no food and my suffering is increased by the bitter cold—my body is like a stone!
>
> (Translated by Masaharu Anesaki)

After a time he was persuaded to repair to the curative hot springs of Hitachi in the hope of ameliorating his condition.

On September 9, 1282, the little procession set forth on the last journey from the mountain home so dear to the master's heart and to which he was destined never to return. Of this retreat he wrote, "Here at last, thanks to the protection of Lord Hagii am I able to study the scriptures in peace, without fear of attack." The saint, in his emaciated condition, traveled slowly upon his trusty horse, supported by four of his disciples; also the son of Lord Hagii, with twenty of his retainers, escorted the failing priest upon the long and arduous journey. However, after nine days of travel Nichiren, in his enfeebled condition, felt himself unable to proceed. They had now reached the plain of Musashi (now Saitama–Tokyo–Kanagawa prefectures), so he decided to rest awhile and break the journey in the mansion of another important samurai and faithful adherent called Ikegami Munenaka, whose residence was near Omori on the outskirts of the capital. Here the little band arrived on September 18; but the master grew steadily weaker, and it was evident that his end was approaching. His intrepid spirit never failed: large numbers of followers and devotees flocked around the dying saint, whom he exhorted and instructed until the last moments.

From his deathbed Nichiren indited several letters, one being affectionately concerned with the welfare of his faithful friend the horse, who, with the groom, he had entrusted to a friend for safekeeping and to protect him from rough treatment after his master should have passed away. On October 13 this great saint and reformer breathed his last; to the fervent reiteration of the formula *Namu myōhō renge kyō,* mingled with the tears and lamentations of all the multitude assembled, Nichiren ended his stormy career upon this earth and in his sixty-first year passed to the higher enlightenment.

According to his own desire the sacred ashes were sent to Minobu—of which the saint had written that his soul would haunt that paradise upon earth for all eternity. A relic was retained at Ikegami to become the object of special veneration at the commemorative temple that was erected upon this hallowed spot by the faithful samurai and disciple Lord Ikegami, from whom that district takes its name. This celebrated and most popular temple is known as Honmon-ji (the Main Gate)—one of the headquarters of the sect and Mecca of the faithful. Every year upon the anniversary of the death-day of their beloved founder, the whole neighborhood is thronged with worshippers and the scene constitutes a remarkable tribute to his memory. A special sanctuary encloses the actual spot whereupon Nichiren breathed his last, with the pillar (now draped in silk) against which the master leaned during his last hours upon earth—affecting memorials that are venerated with utmost devotion by the faithful. A temple had originally been erected upon Minobu-san to commemorate the tomb. This was succeeded some two centuries later (1474) by elaborate and more imposing edifices. Although devastated by fire upon seven different occasions, they have always been rebuilt—being known by the original name of Minobu-san Kuon-ji. The scene becomes most impressive upon the anniversaries of the great requiem festival of October 13, when large numbers of pilgrims and worshippers repair to this remote mountain to do homage before the tomb of the great departed.

The Nichiren is essentially a democratic sect, making an especially strong appeal to the lower classes. The abstruse study of the *Hokekyō* being attainable only to the initiated, to the ordinary believer the sole requirement deemed essential to the attainment of enlightenment consists in the reverent ejaculation of the formula *Namu myōhō renge kyō* chanted to a vigorous accompaniment of drums—and to which full justice is done by the inexhaustible enthusiasm of his pious followers.

In common with the great leaders of men of every age and clime Nichiren has his traducers, by whom he has been scoffed at—and even denounced as a charlatan and mountebank—for what they are pleased to describe as his theatrical and Salvation Army methods; but whatever may have been temperamental and intellectual errors of this great man, none can gainsay that he was passionately true to his convictions, passionately brave, honest, and sincere. Moreover, his teachings have borne abundant fruit, for at the present day in Japan thousands of temples are dedicated to the Nichiren doctrines, his devoted adherents numbering many million souls.

When you fall into an abyss and someone has lowered a rope to pull you out, should you hesitate to grasp the rope because you doubt the power of the helper? Has not Buddha declared 'I alone am the Protector and Savior?' There is the power! Is it not taught that faith is the only entrance (to salvation)? There is the rope! One who hesitates to seize it, and will not utter the Sacred Truth, will never be able to climb the precipice of *bodhi* (enlightenment) ... Our hearts ache and our sleeves are wet (with tears) until we see face to face the tender figure of the one who says to us 'I am thy father.' At this thought our hearts beat, even as when we behold the brilliant clouds in the

evening sky, or the pale moonlight of the fast-falling night .
. . Should any season be passed without thinking of the
compassionate promise "Constantly I am thinking of you"?
Should any month or day be spent without revering the
teaching that there is none who cannot attain Buddhahood? Devote yourself with your whole heart to the "Adoration to the Lotus of the Perfect Truth," and utter it yourself
as well as admonish others to do the same. Such is your task
in this human life.

Nichiren (Anesaki)

Myōhon-ji

❀

THIS PICTURESQUE and beautiful old temple is the largest of the Nichiren sect in Kamakura; it is also famed for its historic associations and the tragedy that was enacted upon its site. The long approach begins from the Ebisudo Bridge spanning the Nameri River. After some distance mossy steps ascend to the Niomon—or Gate of the Kings—lying in the deep shadows of noble cryptomeria, whose dark foliage lends a note of solemn and dignified remoteness to this valley so thickly enclosed with forest trees and known as Hikigayatsu. The name originated from the fact that here lived the woman who tended Yoritomo from his infancy, and who came of a family belonging to the district of Hiki in the province of Musashi. The great shogun naturally cherished the associations of his old nurse and it is recorded that he frequently repaired to this spot, accompanied by Masako, to visit the family.

The nurse was known as Hiki no Ama, or the Nun of Hiki; here she resided with her adopted son Yoshikazu and his offspring. This Yoshikazu was a samurai of high renown and a special favorite with Yoritomo; he was also a member of the council of illustrious men that was formed after Yoritomo's death to discuss the affairs of the *bakufu,* or military government, but whose deliberations were subject to the endorsement of Masako and her father Hojo Tokimasa. Yoshikazu's daughter, known in history as Wakasa no Tsubone, was the mistress of Yoriie, eldest son of Yoritomo; she became the mother of Ichiman, Yoriie's eldest son and also a girl babe, who is known as Take no Gosho from the name of her residence.

The loyalty of Yoshikazu to his master led him to organize a scheme that aimed at the destruction of his enemies the Hojo, whose power was rapidly increasing, and whose aim was to destroy all the Minamoto, replacing them with Hojo—a state of affairs that was speedily consummated. The knowledge of this plot soon reached Tokimasa's ears, with the result that Yoshikazu was assassinated, a large number of valiant soldiers and partisans also perishing at the same time. This tragedy took place September 2, 1203.

On the left of the Niomon is an enclosure with stone lanterns, etc., within which is a small monument. This is the tomb of Ichiman, the baby son of Yoriie, who was only three years of age when the extermination of the Hiki family took place; certain of the kinsmen of Yoshikazu were slain at Nagoe, Tokimasa's residence, the site of which is in the vicinity of Myohon-ji. The remaining members assembled at the abode of Ichiman at Yukinoshita (another part of Kamakura), but all perished in the attack, including the little heir. On the following day, amongst the ashes was discovered the sleeve of the child's robe. This relic, together with some bones, was buried here and the tomb was erected, which is universally known as the Sodezuka, or Sleeve-tomb. Within the small enclosure a memorial stone tablet was erected in 1904 to commemorate the 700th anniversary of the death of Ichiman, grandson of Yoritomo, and bearing an account of these historical facts engraved upon its surface.

At the time these events took place, the youngest son of Yoshikazu, Daigaku Saburo, happened to be in charge of a relative elsewhere and so escaped the general annihilation. He was taken to Kyoto for greater safety, and there educated, achieving high distinction for his scholarship and the lofty character of his mind. When the emperor Juntoku (1211—22) was exiled to the island of Sado he was accompanied by Saburo, who served and attended his imperial master with great devotion during the period of his banishment. Meanwhile, circumstances in the military capital had undergone considerable change; when liberty was restored to the remaining member of the unfortunate house of Hiki, he was able to return to Kamakura. This was the time when Nichiren's activities were at their height. Daigaku Saburo became an enthusiastic convert and layman pupil of the saint, assuming the religious name of Nichigaku. The temple is said to have received its name from Nichiren himself, *Myōhon* being the posthumous title of Yoshikazu's wife. On the hill behind the present site Daigaku Saburo built a small place of worship in the year 1260—the Hokke-do—in memory of Take no Gosho, daughter of Yoriie and Wakasa, who had escaped the general slaughter when an infant, eventually becoming the wife of Yoritsune—kinsman of Yoritomo and successor to the shogunate upon the death of Sanetomo. At the beginning of the Meiji era, this Hokke-do was removed below to the site where it still exists near the lake, and was re-named the Shaka-do, a valuable statue of the Buddha being enshrined therein. The original wooden pillars are said to remain intact and still support the little building.

Upon the island in the lake stands a moss-encrusted stone pagoda. According to tradition this was erected in remote times by a wealthy man of Yui (the district adjoining the seashore), to commemorate the tragic fate of his baby girl, who was carried away by an eagle. The bereaved parent is said to have established several of these memorial stones in various parts of Kamakura.

Behind the tomb of Ichiman is a fireproof building containing the temple's most important treasures. These include an ancient statue of the Buddha said to have been carved by the famous

Chinese sculptor-priest Chinwakei; a picture of Buddha painted by Nichiren; and various other prized objects. The building near the residence of the priests is a large guest hall, containing a high altar and attractively decorated.

On the left-hand side of the Gate of the Kings steps lead up to the temple graveyard, wherein are divers mossed and ancient tombs. However, the central monument of polished marble marks the passing of a modern hero (1916), and is reared above the ashes of Admiral Kamimura—the distinguished commander who played an effective role in the Russo-Japanese War (1904–5) and who was a devoted adherent of the Nichiren doctrines.

A short distance beyond the first tiled gate of this foundation a path ascends to a space in the hillside, enshrouded by trees and dedicated to the days of legend. Beside the green waters of a small deep lake stands a little temple—Jakushi Myojin, or Shrine to Allay the Sufferings of the Serpent.

On the fatal day of September 2, 1203, the despairing Wakasa no Tsubone is said to have drowned herself in this pond, when her spirit assumed the guise of a dragon. Moreover, according to ancient chronicles, the ghostly inhabitant of its depths entered the young daughter of Hojo Masamura—causing the possessed girl deep anguish. At the request of Wakasa's brother, Daigaku Saburo, Nichiren recited the scriptures and prayed for the lost soul on the banks of this lake. The demon was exorcised. In the watches of the night Wakasa appeared to the saint in joy and gratitude that by virtue of his intercession her spirit was liberated from its tortures to ascend to the regions of the blessed. The apparition averred that for all eternity her ghost would hover around this sacred spot, to protect the temple from malign influences—hence the redeemed soul came to be deified as Jakushi Myojin.

Near the lake (Jagyo no Ike, or Pond of the Dragon) is a spring of extreme antiquity, sheltered by a roof: this is the Dragon's Well (Jagyo no Ido), so-called from the following tradition. In the course of a civil war that was being waged in the Oei era (1394–1427), for protective purposes a priest of the temple—Nichigyo by name—is said to have concealed beneath its waters a holy figure that had been bestowed by the deified Wakasa. During this period if any person ventured to approach the well with the intention of drawing water, the dragon appeared—putting the alarmed intruder to flight; moreover, evil befell them.

On either side of the main temple are the famous *kaidō* (*Pyrus spectabilis*)—the right-hand specimen being a veritable giant of its species, which as a rule does not attain to large proportions. Toward mid-April, when these great bushes are in full bloom, numerous visitors assemble to admire the enchanting effect of the billowing masses of pale pink and crimson blossom that transforms the austere dignity of this usually solitary courtyard into a vision of fairyland.* A track on the right ascends somewhat steeply to the summit of the hills above the temple, which are intersected with paths and command views on all sides of quite exceptional beauty, through the boles and drooping boughs of the magnificent old pines. In November the numerous scarlet maples invest the landscape with a brilliant note of color. An easy and picturesque descent on the eastern side leads down into the valley of Matsubagayatsu, rendering it unnecessary to return by the same route.

*Although both of these bushes have long since perished, a young *kaidō* now stands in place of the former great one.

Hongaku-ji and Myōryū-ji

本
覚
寺
・
妙
隆
寺

❀

F ACING THE Myohon-ji entrance, upon the opposite side
of the Ebisudo Bridge, is another Nichiren temple of
ancient foundation. This is Hongaku-ji, an edifice professing to possess a relic of the saint in the shape of one of his
bones and which apparently enjoys great popularity, judging
from the incessant sound of drums that resounds throughout the
neighborhood. The building was originally in charge of Nichiren's
disciple Nisshutsu; he was succeeded by his well-known pupil
Nissho, who subsequently became the eleventh head of Minobu,
dwelling in that remote mountain for the long space of forty
years.

Prayers offered in this temple are credited with special efficacy
in the cure of eye diseases, and the pugilistic occupants of the
two-storied gate are thickly bespattered with paper pellets adher-
ing to their huge forms—a sign that the petitions have been
received with favor. Behind the building is a group of beautiful
ancient tombs, but the passing of their dusty occupants has long
fallen into oblivion with the ebbing centuries, their names being
forgotten and unknown. On the left, lying in the heavy shadows
of a spreading tree, is a small monument of celebrity—sacred to
the memory of Masamune, the famous maker of sword blades

{ 277 }

who died in the thirteenth century; the date upon the tomb is given as January 11, 1288.

A short distance to the north of Hongaku-ji, a few steps beyond Nichiren's preaching site, is another old temple, Myoryu-ji, founded by another disciple of the saint—Nichiei.

He was succeeded by Nisshin "the persecuted," who was also known as Nabe-Kanmuri—or Crowned-with-a-Cooking-Vessel! This unusual title was acquired through the severe persecutions Nisshin was subjected to during his mission. The hostile listeners to his doctrines were in the habit of emphasizing their disagreement with the propaganda by hurling stones, tiles, or any missile that lay at hand at the head of the unfortunate exponent. Hence Nisshin was driven to protecting himself from his assailants by wearing a large iron cooking pot as a helmet! Within the temple are preserved three paintings illustrating in a graphic manner the horrible tortures to which the priest was subjected during the period of his ministry.

Another relic of early days is the beautiful pine, whose great boughs droop before the moldy old temple as though to protect what is left of it from the blighting influences of the outer world. Near this pine is a pond of walled-in curious shape, somewhat resembling an arena. It is said that upon this site Nisshin was in the habit of practicing austerities. At the rear is a statue of the saint protected by a roof, the monument on the right being his tomb. Blood-curdling accounts are recorded of the merciless discipline and tortures this heroic priest inflicted upon himself. It is chronicled that upon one occasion of special prayer and mortification, for ten succeeding days he plucked the nails from each of his fingers, beseeching Heaven that if his petitions were heard with favor, new nails might grow within one hundred days as a sign and token. With the blood that flowed from his lacerated flesh this agonized martyr painted a mandala, or representation of the joys of the blessed, which trophy was known as the Tsume-kiri no Mandala, or Nail-cut Picture of Paradise.

Hōkai-ji

❀

A SHORT DISTANCE to the north beyond Hongaku-ji lies the temple of Hokai-ji. Although the building has shrunk to melancholy proportions, this spot is famed as the scene of the culminating tragedy of the Hojo; the mansion occupied by the nine generations of the Hojo regents stood near the site of the present small survival. When the imperialist troops under Nitta Yoshisada took Kamakura by storm, turning the city into a holocaust of flame, the ninth and last Hojo regent Takatoki, realizing the end was at hand, assembled his family in the ancestral temple of Tosho-ji. There, with some 870 of his officers and loyal retainers, all drank the farewell cups and "died the death of fidelity," displaying extraordinary heroism. Takatoki himself, as of the most exalted rank, was the last to fall upon his sword, and with him perished the line of the Hojo rulers. Later, it is recorded that the first Ashikaga shogun, Takauji, requested permission of the emperor Go-Daigo to remove Tosho-ji to the present site, together with all the bones and skeletons of the Hojo—this was duly effected, and the name changed to Hokai-ji. The newly-established temple was presided over by the priest Enkan, on whose demise Takauji's second son, Jigen, succeeded to the office.

It was commonly rumored that after this dreadful scene of carnage was enacted, the neighborhood was haunted by the ghosts of the Hojo martyrs; so a shrine called Tokuso Gongen was erected to pacify the troubled spirits—(the Hojo estate was known as Tokuso). This small structure is still in existence on the left of the main entrance. Upon the altar of Hokai-ji are installed three large figures—Jizo, Benten, and Teishaku respectively; according to the temple record this divine trio was brought to these shores by a Chinese ship in 1335. Another small shrine on the left of the main entrance is dedicated to Shotoku Taishi, son of the emperor Yomei, whose influence was so potent in establishing Buddhism in Japan. The central object is a quaint colored statue of this famous prince of the seventh century. A short distance behind the temple of Hokai-ji on the hillside is the Harakiri-yagura—the cave containing the tomb of Takatoki. A wooden pillar is inscribed with the facts concerning the orgy of suicide that took place upon this spot, dyeing the earth with rivers of blood and wiping out the powerful family that ruled Japan from 1203 to 1333.

Enmei-ji

❁

I N THE neighborhood of the station is a bridge known as Enmei-ji-bashi. Beside this bridge stands an unpretentious temple of modest proportions—Enmei-ji, but the possessor of a remarkable statue to which a remarkable legend is attached.

An ancient history of Kamakura records that in the remote ages a certain nobleman upon one occasion was playing *sugoroku* (a game of chance, played on a board with dice) with a lady opponent. After several contests, and becoming wearied of the ordinary stakes, he insisted that the next game should be played with the condition that the loser should discard all clothing, and stand disrobed upon the board. The lady lost! In confusion and consternation at such prospect she closed her eyes and fervently prayed to the compassionate Jizo for rescue. Immediately a vision of the divinity appeared upon the board; his garments falling away, the form of a woman was disclosed.

The present statue of the Jizo was carved in illustration and commemoration of this incident, being known and celebrated as the Hadaka (naked) Jizo—the unique specimen of its kind in Japan. The Hadaka Jizo is enshrined within a curtained niche on the left of the altar, it is of life size and realistically tinted in natural colors. Arrayed in the silken robes of a priest and holding the customary emblems, the statue gives no suggestion of its unusual form—but when the vestments are removed the body is revealed to be of feminine shape. In conformity with the legend the feet of the divinity are resting upon a *sugoroku* board. The temple guardian asserts that formerly the latter was constructed of beautiful and valuable wood—but owing to the cupidity of a priest this trophy has disappeared, at the present time the Jizo being reduced to an ordinary board for his pedestal.

The original temple of Enmei-ji was founded in 1332, and was of imposing proportions. However, at the beginning of the Meiji era the building had become so decayed that its destruction was considered advisable. At the same time the Kyo-do, or Hall of the Scriptures, belonging to Komyo-ji was also done away with; so the timbers of the latter were procured wherewith to reconstruct Enmei-ji, the present small structure being the result. Upon the altar are several statues of great antiquity, the centerpiece being a venerable image of Amida. At one time a son of Okajima Yasoemon (one of the Forty-seven Ronin) was a priest of Enmei-ji and formerly the temple was in possession of a valuable painting of the immortal Forty-seven, but alas, like the *sugoroku* board this has also become "the evidence of things unseen."

Fudaraku-ji

❀

I N THE MAIN street of Zaimokuza an old stone monument records that in close proximity stood the celebrated temple of Fudaraku-ji, to which Yoritomo frequently repaired for worship, the first priest being the famous Mongaku. A few steps to the north is the diminutive building that represents the former foundation of Fudaraku-ji and serves as a shelter for the few remnants of the treasures of bygone centuries. The original temple was established on a scale of great magnificence by Yoritomo in the year 1181 as an act of gratitude for the benefit of Mongaku, who in earlier times had befriended the great shogun.

It is recorded that this edifice having fallen into decay, the temple was repaired and reestablished in the fourteenth century under the auspices of another important priest, Raiki (died 1352). This restoration lasted until 1874, when the entire temple of Fudaraku-ji was destroyed by fire. After that catastrophe for many years all that remained was a small hut, hastily constructed upon the same site for the purpose of enclosing the few temple treasures that had been rescued from the disaster. Nearly fifty years ago subscriptions were levied in the neighborhood which resulted in the present microscopic structure, the former hut remaining in the capacity of kitchen to the establishment.

Certain of the relics are of historic interest and of extreme antiquity, descriptions of them existing in ancient records of Kamakura. These included:

- A large dark figure of Fudo carved by the priest Chisho, and which is said to have been the identical image by whose powers the Taira were finally subjugated!
- A Yakushi Sanzon, or statue of the healing Buddha, with his two satellites Nikko and Gekko Bosatsu—the sun and moon deities; these are attributed to Unkei. Formerly the set was completed by the Juni Shinsho, or twelve guardian ministers, but in the vicissitudes of the temple these have disappeared.
- A celebrated effigy of Yoritomo, representing him at the age of forty-two, and garbed in official uniform.
- The *ihai* (memorial-tablet) of Yoritomo.
- A threadbare embroidered altar cloth, said to have been the gift of Yoritomo.
- Another venerable memorial of the same epoch is a piece of crumbling material which was originally a scarlet ensign of the Taira, and may possibly be the sole remaining specimen in existence of that famous standard.

Until recent years the temple possessed a nude statue of Mongaku, the spiritual founder, but this trophy has been removed to a temple in Hongo, Tokyo.

Mongaku was a man with an extraordinary history and had played a lurid role in a love tragedy that is universally known in Japan, and lends itself to effective representation upon the stage. Originally a warrior of Kyoto known as Endo Morito, he conceived a passionate and consuming affection for the wife of a brother officer named Wataru—a beautiful woman known as Kesa Gozen, and one of the undying heroines of early romance. Loyal and faithful as she was fair to the outward eye, Kesa Gozen indignantly repudiated all advances of her would-be lover, but rejection merely produced the customary effect of fanning the flame and strengthening Morito's determination to gain possession of the coveted beauty. As a last resort he swore a solemn oath that if Kesa continued deaf to his blandishments the life of her mother should pay the penalty of her decision. In desperation the unfortunate girl feigned to connive at his plot, which was to cut off Wataru's head under cover of the night, thus leaving the coast clear for Morito's marriage with his widow. All details were arranged. Kesa's part was to see that Wataru had quaffed a sufficiency of wine to ensure his sleeping heavily, then, as a sign, she would damp her lord's knot of hair so that in the darkness the assassin could make no mistake in his victim. The fateful night arrived. Kesa wrote a farewell message to her beloved spouse explaining the situation, then, dressing her own hair according to male fashion, she saturated it with water, reclining in the bed her husband was accustomed to occupy. At midnight the murderer crept into the room. With one stroke the head of the beautiful Kesa was severed and carrying it with him wrapped in a cloth he escaped into the darkness.

When Morito examined his trophy and realized what had taken place, his horror and remorse were overpowering. He rushed to the unfortunate husband, confessing his guilt and imploring the injured Wataru to slay him with the same sword in expiation of the dreadful deed. But Wataru, seeing the proud soldier lying so grief-stricken and humbled in the dust, forbore to strike and bade him live to purify his guilt with long years of sorrow and repentance. He moreover proposed they should both renounce the vanities of the world and embracing religion should devote the remainder of their lives to good works and prayers for the welfare of the departed spirit. On entering the priesthood, Morito assumed the name of Mongaku, and various acts of merciless penance were attributed to him. It is said that at the severest season of the year he stood for twenty-one days beneath a waterfall, with the icy torrent descending upon his nude body.

The circumstances that brought this priest into association

with Yoritomo were as follows. His temple in Kyoto having fallen into dilapidation, Mongaku set about collecting subscriptions for its renovation; for that purpose he repaired to the palace to seek an interview with the emperor Go-Shirakawa. However, a protracted banquet being in process, the priest was left unannounced for such a long space of time that he grew incensed and roughly assaulted one of the officers of the court. By this impetuous action the imperial wrath was incurred: Mongaku first underwent a term of imprisonment and was subsequently exiled to Izu. At that time the young Yoritomo was sojourning in the same region, and formed a most favorable impression of Mongaku's abilities. The latter rendered the future shogun valuable assistance—moreover, after his pardon was obtained the priest was able to secure from the emperor an important document authorizing the exiled Minamoto to raise an army. For these services Yoritomo was duly grateful and later on, as a practical form of his appreciation, the large temple of Fudaraku-ji was erected for the benefit of Mongaku.

Nichiren Temples
(Ankokuron-ji, Myōhō-ji, and Chōshō-ji)

❈

IN THE DISTRICT of Kamakura known as Matsubagayatsu (Valley of Pine Needles) are three temples of the Nichiren sect in close proximity of each other—Ankokuron-ji, Myoho-ji, and Chosho-ji. These are well worth inspection for their picturesque environment and the charming views commanded from the enclosing hills. For centuries these three foundations have been contesting in rivalry as to which is of the first importance in their association with the master. According to the opinion of various of the Nichiren devotees, the small temple of Ankokuron-ji is supposed to be the identical site of the founder's hermitage wherein he found a shelter from the year 1253, during the stormy time of persecution. Here the saint is said to have meditated for four years before publishing his famous *Treatise upon Peace and Righteousness*, which resulted in his attempted execution and ultimate banishment to the island of Sado. This essay is said to have been actually written in the cave to the right on entering the gate, wherein is a monument to Nichiren, protected from falling rocks by a wooden canopy.

Beside the entrance to Ankokuron-ji stands a noble pine tree of curious and unique shape, its huge trunk encircled by the *shimenawa*, or sacred rope. This veteran is possibly one of

Kamakura's most ancient pines; but alas, its dignity and beauty suffered grievously in the severe typhoon of October 1917, which proved so devastating to many of these ancient survivals— numbers of the venerable trees in the Tsurugaoka Hachiman approach being uprooted and destroyed upon that fatal night. In the vicinity of the historic cave an ascent leads to a beautiful spot above, fringed with great pines and affording a wide prospect of sea and distant landscape between their far-spreading boughs. This path winds along the crest of the hill, and if continued in a westerly direction gradually descends through the emerald shadows of a bamboo grove to the graveyard of the temple—especially appealing in early spring when the numerous plum trees are in bloom, perfuming the air with their delicate fragrance. Above the bamboo thicket is another cave associated with the meditations of Nichiren and containing a statue of the saint with his little friend of the legend—the white monkey guiding him by the long sleeve of his robe, and piloting the master to a haven of refuge from his assailants.

The temple of Ankokuron-ji was first built during Nichiren's lifetime in the year 1274, to commemorate his association with this historic site; two buildings alone have survived to the present day—the Hondo, or Main Temple, and a small offshoot dedicated to Inari, god of the harvest, behind which is the famous cave.

A noticeable feature of the main altar is an enormous head of the Buddha. This unexpected object originally belonged to the temple of Zuirin-ji, near Ueno, Tokyo. A venerable priest of that foundation cherished the intention of fashioning a huge effigy of Shaka, but only lived to complete the head. Superstition credits this head with efficacy in the cure of disease.

The beautiful and interesting old temple of Myoho-ji is situated on the hillside a few paces westward of Ankokuron-ji. According to the temple record, Nichiren first came to make his home upon this site in 1253; after his return from exile in the province of Izu, the saint dwelt in this part for nineteen years and from here he retired to Minobu in May 1272. The building originally erected upon the present site was known as Honkoku-ji; at the time of Nichiren's death in October 1282, the saint is said to have specially committed the care of this temple to his disciple Nichiro. In early days various personages of distinction presided over the destiny of Myoho-ji. The fourth priest was Nichiro, uncle of the first Ashikaga shogun, Takauji. A famous pupil and disciple of this dignitary was said to have been a scion of the imperial house, a natural son of the martyred Prince Morinaga and who assumed the name of Nichiei on entering the priesthood.

During the prince's imprisonment in the cave at Daitonomiya, he was attended by a court lady named Minami no Kata; after the assassination she is said to have borne a son to the royal captive, who was known as Ryogon Shinno until he took the tonsure. Myoho-ji was rebuilt upon the original site in 1357 under the auspices of Nichiei, who presided over it himself until his death occurred in 1397, at the age of sixty-four. Upon the summit of the hill behind the temple he constructed a *kuyōtō,* or memorial, to the spirit of his father Prince Morinaga, where he daily offered prayers and burnt incense in memory of his murdered parent. Another monument also exists as the memorial of Minami no Kata.

The temple was falling into a condition of dilapidation, but some hundred years ago was completely renovated and reconstructed by a *daimyō* of Kyushu, Lord Hosokawa, to commemorate the death of his beautiful young daughter. The interior is unexpectedly attractive, being lavishly ornamented with paintings—even those omnipresent emblems of the Nichiren sect: the big drums bearing a design of lotus flowers, now considerably impaired by the enthusiasm of the faithful. The *fusuma,* or sliding doors, are decorated with various scenes and figures—also sprays of blossom, storks, peacocks, and angels playing instruments; while the ceiling is gay with clusters of flowers painted in caissons with charming effect. The altar glitters with numerous gilt figures of the saints and divinities, the centerpiece being a large effigy of Nichiren, his head draped with a silken covering. The ceiling above the sanctuary is decorated with a quaint design of waves and clouds.

Upon the altar of a side chamber (on the left) various treasures of the temple are deposited, amongst which is an elaborate antique reliquary enclosing a small piece of bone, said to be a sacred relic of Nichiren. The corresponding chamber on the right contains a venerable effigy of Prince Morinaga; also an ornate case enshrines a large black statue of his posthumous son, Nichiei, clad in his priest's robes of ancient silk, and which, it is averred, are the identical vestments worn by the defunct ecclesiastic during his lifetime.

Above the Gate of the Kings the rock is pierced by two deep caves, one containing a large representation of Nichiren rudely hewn of granite, the other a mausoleum wherein repose many of the departed priests of Myoho-ji. The large temple upon the upper level is the Hokke-do, or Hall of the Scriptures, whose altar is embellished with a magnificent gilt sanctuary enclosing another ancient statue of Nichiren. The large figure carved in wood and tinted in natural hues; on the right is another representation of the founder arrayed in his priestly vestments. Facing the steps is a white building—the Shakado, or Hall of the Buddha, wherein is a large statue only visible upon special occasions. The ornamental cluster of ancient *sotetsu* (*Cycas revoluta,* or unrolled cocoa palm) constitutes a link to the early days and is said to have been planted by Nichiei.

Adjoining the belfry, with its fine old bell of green copper, another long ascent of mossy and somewhat dilapidated steps guides the wanderer to the crest of the hill above, from whence a romantic prospect is unfolded. The track on the right leads to the ancient memorial to Prince Morinaga, erected by his son. A notice-board records the fact that, at the time his hermitage was attacked, this was the path by which Nichiren escaped when escorted by his celestial guide in the guise of the white monkey to the shelter of the cave in the backwoods beyond. The path bearing to the left of the ascent culminates in a secluded and beautiful spot encircled with great pines, and wherein is a group of ancient gray monuments, heavily mossed. One of these lichened stones bears an inscription to the effect that this grove was a favorite retreat of Nichiren during his sojourn in the hut below, and doubtless the solitude and peace of this woodland sanctuary—with its vision of the changing ocean, the distant mountain-ranges and the pure snows of Mount Fuji—would make a strong appeal to the saint, who was at that time at the height of the persecutions and perils of his stormy career, striving in deadly earnest to win the souls of men amidst oft-recurring scenes of turbulence and conflict.

The third of this group lies opposite Ankokuron-ji to the south, just beyond the railway lines. Chosho-ji was originally an offshoot of Myoho-ji and established by a disciple of Nichiren called Nichisai, who died in 1299. Later it was re-erected by another disciple, Nichiryu, a native of Nichiren's birthplace, Kominato, Boshu (now Chiba), and a missionary to the central provinces of Japan (1385–1464). This old temple is romantically situated at the foot of the hills and is embowered with flowering trees. The footpath at the rear, beside a row of ancient monuments, leads to the uplands above; a descent can be effected from this beautiful spot by another route leading to Zaimokuza. The building on the right of the Hondo is the Hall of Prayer.

Various personal relics and writings ascribed to Nichiren are preserved at this temple, which assumes a very gay and crowded aspect on festivals connected with the saint. Within the courtyard is an ancient maple whose gnarled and twisted boughs are protected by a fence. It is asserted that this tree, as a dwarf plant, was tended by Nichiren himself. Although obviously of great age, its feathery foliage is still luxuriant, in late spring the new leaves assuming a delicate rose pink hue that turns to green with the advance of summer. Near the roofed gate of Chosho-ji a spring of exceptionally pure water gushes from the earth within a stone enclosure; this is known as the Nichiren-sui (Spring of Nichiren), and is famed as the spot where miracles are said to have been performed by the saint.

Kōmyō-ji

SITUATED IN Zaimokuza and one of Kamakura's five largest temples, Komyo-ji is still an edifice of imposing proportions and the only one of any importance that stands in close proximity to the sea. In its setting of dark foliage beneath irregular wooded hills, the beautiful curved gray roofs are visible from a long distance and form a distinguishing feature of the eastern part of the bay. This ancient foundation was established in the year 1243 by the fourth Hojo ruler Tsunetoki, elder brother of Tokiyori and regent of Kamakura (1242–46). Its original site was in the valley of Sasukegayatsu. In this early phase of existence the building was known as Renge-ji, or Temple of the Lotus; however, according to instructions received from the powers above in a dream, Tsunetoki re-christened it as Komyo-ji, or Temple of Shining Light. Soon afterward this edifice, together with its various offshoots and vassal buildings, was removed to its present beautiful site adjoining the shore, where the splash and murmur of waves form a rhythmical accompaniment to the devotions of the faithful with their incessant chant of the holy formula *Namu Amida Butsu.*

Good fortune appears to have smiled upon these metamorphoses, for so far Komyo-ji has escaped the dread enemy that proved fatal to so many of Kamakura's survivals from the remote past; although worn and storm-beaten to the extent of approaching dilapidation, the main temple stands today in practically its original condition. The structure viewed from the rear bears ample evidence of the centuries it has weathered, the ancient timber has assumed the spectral hues belonging to "the weirdness of decay," and is literally so bleached and time-whitened that it appears on the verge of becoming fossilized.

From its earliest days, Komyo-ji has enjoyed the support of patrons of exalted rank. Several of the emperors were interested in the Jodo doctrines and bestowed marks of their favor upon the temple; while from certain of the Ashikaga shoguns, also from Hideyoshi, Ieyasu, etc., various gifts of land were received, the original documents confirming these endowments being still preserved amongst the temple treasures. Komyo-ji moreover possesses the distinction of being the sole headquarters of the Jodo sect in Eastern Japan—this fact is recorded upon a large stone monument standing beside the first entrance gate. The Jodo (Pure Land) sect of Buddhism was founded by Honen Shonin in 1224. Its doctrines teach that the path of salvation is attained by absolute faith in the power of the Amida Buddha, great merit being attached to frequent appeals to the Holy Name and fervent reiteration of the formula *Namu Amida Butsu*.

The spiritual foundations of Komyo-ji were laid by the first lord abbot Ryochu—also known by his posthumous name of Kishu Zenji, conferred by the emperor. This famous divine was a distinguished pupil of Honen Shonin's disciple Shoko, by whom he was greatly valued and beloved—indeed the master affectionately described his favorite as his other self, and confidently advised his other disciples to consult Ryochu for advice in their difficulties, spiritual or otherwise. After presiding over the affairs of Komyo-ji for the lengthy period of over forty years, he died in the year 1287, and was buried on the hillside behind the temple in the peaceful and beautiful graveyard of the priests.

Entering the first tiled gate, a stone monument in the court-yard on the right records the fact that this part is called Zendozuka (Hill of Zendo), and concerning which the following legend is related. Zendo was a Chinese priest famed for his saintly quali-ties. Once upon a time a ship sailed to Japan from China bearing the statue of this great divine, which had miraculously become endowed with life and bore the semblance of an ordinary priest, the vessel duly arriving at Kyushu, in the province of Chikuzen. At that time Shoko, the disciple of Honen Shonin, in a dream received the tidings that the great teacher Zendo had arrived in Japan and was counseled by the celestial informant to repair to Hakozaki, Kyushu, in order to welcome the distinguished guest. In accordance with these instructions, Shoko discovered the arrival of the effigy (which had resumed its inanimate form on reaching land) and there constructed a temporary shrine for its veneration; but later on the figure was removed to the temple in Kyushu known as Zendo-ji, and placed in charge of Shoko. Now upon the occasion of the visit of Ryochu to this temple, Shoko entrusted the statue to his famous pupil, but the future lord abbot of Komyo-ji being at that time on an extended missionary pilgrimage through mountainous and wild regions of the coun-try, he resolved to commit the effigy of the saint to the deep, in order that heaven might guide the sacred figure in the most auspicious direction. Later on, when Ryochu was installed at his post in Kamakura, strange rumors were reported by the fisher-men concerning supernatural gleams of light that were mani-fested in the ocean. For seven days and seven nights these luminous demonstrations were beheld, heralding the arrival of the holy image, which finally landed of its own accord and was duly installed within the temple of Komyo-ji, where it is still revered by the faithful at the present day. Hence the name Zendozuka. Behind the stone monument is a building contain-ing a large copper representation of the Chinese saint: this is a copy of the original figure, which is enshrined elsewhere.

On the left of the Zendo repository is a stone resembling a tomb and bearing the enigmatic inscription of Kami no To, or Monument of Hair. The explanation is that in bygone days when embryo priests and monks had served the term of their novitiate, on taking the tonsure their heads were shaved during a special ceremony. According to the custom of the period, the hair of laymen was allowed to grow long and bushy, being confined with cords into a coiffure of various forms according to their rank and station. Hence, after the consecration rites, these emblems of their severance from the material world were interred at this spot beneath the Kami no To.

The *sanmon*, or tower-gate, is well worth braving the steep and somewhat gymnastic stairway; the wide prospect from the balcony is always beautiful—in early morning, when the sun gilds the gleaming shape of the great white mountain directly opposite; but more especially in the hour before the twilight, when the waves are embroidered with the "gems that the sunset sheds" and the world is transfigured in a glory of luminous crimson and gold. An imperial tribute is suspended below the eaves, a tablet that was inscribed by the emperor Go-Hanazono (1308–48); the characters signify Tenshozan, or Hill of Divine Enlightenment. According to an inscription affixed to a pillar of the building, the present tower-gate was re-erected in November 1533. The interior of the upper story contains an altar that is enriched with numerous large and finely executed statues. The centerpiece is an impressive representation of Shaka Sanzon (The Three Saints), and which includes Monju and Fugen Bosatsu mounted upon their quaint beasts. The warlike figures at each corner are the Shi Tenno—the Four Heavenly Kings who guard the world from evil by keeping watch at each corner of the horizon. These divinities are also known as the Deva Kings, or Gods of the Four Directions. Their apparition is described in one of the sutras and is somewhat reminiscent of the adoration of the Magi in the New Testament:

On a beautiful night the Four Great Kings entered the holy grove, filling all the place with light, and having reverently saluted the Blessed One they stood in the four directions like four mighty fire-brands.

This central group is flanked on either side by an imposing set of the Sixteen Disciples of Buddha. In China there existed a temple called Shoin-ji possessing a famous set of pictures of the Sixteen Disciples (Rakan), painted by Sengetsu Taishi, a priest of great celebrity; upon these originals the present effigies are said to be faithfully modeled. The countenances of these saintly men are distinctly more whimsical and savoring of things mundane than might be expected in beings of such exalted sanctity; however, apparently they had their lighter phases, and the artist elected to seize one of these off-moments.

Regarding the small vassal temple on the right of the tower-gate, Renjo-in, ancient records state that the first priest Ryochu abode here during the removal and reconstruction of Komyo-ji upon its present site. In the courtyard, leaning toward the main temple, is another link to the remote days of its foundation in the shape of a ghostly and ancient specimen of a Chinese juniper, which is said to have been planted by the first lord abbot. Fortified against possible catastrophe by two sturdy supports, its gnarled and twisted trunk seems the typification of antiquity; yet the dark feathery foliage defies the passing centuries, remaining still fresh and apparently flourishing.

The main temple is on a large scale, with a vast sharply sloping copper roof. Along the ridge pole at the summit the imperial crest is in evidence, symbolizing the various patrons of royal blood that have evinced interest in the fortunes of Komyo-ji. The effect of the salt breezes upon the metal ornaments has caused them to assume a vivid hue of beautiful peacock blue, an addition of high decorative value in contrast to the somber sweep of dark copper. Within, a gay and exhilarating note prevails, with much ornamentation, carvings of angels, flowers, etc., colored in bright tints. Above the inner entrance hangs a tablet painted in animated hues of scarlet, green, and gold, and bearing the inscription Kishu Zenji, the posthumous title conferred upon the first priest by the emperor Go-Uda (1274–87), whose imperial hand traced these characters. The sanctuary upon the main altar enshrines a statue of the first lord abbot which is said to have been carved by himself; this revered relic is shrouded from vulgar intrusion behind locked doors, being revealed to the faithful only upon the anniversary of his death, July 6.

To the right of the high altar is a chamber known as the Nenbutsudo, or Hall of Prayer. Here another imperial tablet is in evidence whereupon the characters *kitō,* or prayer, were inscribed by the emperor Go-Tsuchimikado (1465–1500). The chief objects of veneration are a large antique representation of Amida, which tradition attributes to Prince Shotoku (died 621); an effigy of the founder of the Jodo sect Honen Shonin; and several painted figures of the various head priests of Komyo-ji. In the corresponding chamber on the left are two quaint and interesting statues of the second and third priests of the temple: crowned with mysterious black headgear, the robes of these ancient divines are elaborately painted in various colors with a charming design of flowers and gilding. The large figure on the left is another representation of Honen Shonin.

A passage connects the main temple with the Hall of Amida. This divinity occupying the center of the altar is described as a masterpiece of Unkei and is also said to serve as a reliquary, enclosing a small bone of the famous sculptor; on either side are cases containing valuable antique statues ascribed to the Kamakura period. This hall is connected by another corridor with the guest chambers. These apartments are on a spacious scale, the doors and panels being decorated with paintings by Kano Tanshin, an artist who died in 1718—son of a Kyoto painter of great distinction, Kano Tan'yu. An inner chamber specially ornamented and bearing the imperial crest in gold is for the reception of guests of exalted rank. Within the sanctum is yet another gilt statue of Amida, behind which, forming a rich background, is a large and elaborate painting of a mandala, the stylized depiction of the Buddhist paradise.* Amongst other relics preserved here is the original *geba*, or wood notice-board, that in ancient times stood at the entrance of the temple precincts prohibiting the entrance of horses or vehicles.

A large recess on the left constitutes a sort of mortuary chapel of the Naito family, wherein in solemn array repose numbers of *ihai*, beautiful and richly decorated memorial tablets bearing the posthumous names of the departed. The lord Naito Tadaoki was the first *daimyō* of Sanuki. A valiant warrior, he fought in the last decisive battles of Osaka (1614–15), when Hideyori (son of Hideyoshi) perished, and Ieyasu was established as the first of the Tokugawa line of rulers. This important *daimyō* was an ardent devotee of the Jodo sect, and a special admirer of the teachings of Ryochu. Since that time his descendants have been enthusiastic supporters of Komyo-ji, the beautiful and well-known family graveyard being situated within the temple grounds. In the center of this dusky chamber is an ancient statue of the first lord of Naito, clad in the towering headgear and flowing garments that represent the ceremonial robes of state in that picturesque era.

An appealing feature on the northern side of this vast guest hall is the charming effect presented by the landscape garden: tier upon tier of curiously trained trees and bushes rise from the green lake below, the picture closing in with the great pines upon the heights above; a veritable Old World study of blended hues of verdure that seems to convey an inexpressible sensation of tranquillity and repose. The corresponding section on the southern side is decorated with paintings and also contains an ancient

---

*The mandala and other treasures are now on display at the Kokuhokan.

colored chart, representing the aspect of the temple in bygone centuries.

Emerging from the main entrance to the guest-hall one is confronted with the *shōrō*, or belfry, upon the opposite side of the courtyard—a fine and massive structure ornamented with carvings of flowers and fabulous beasts around the huge timbers; the great bell of green copper was constructed in July 1647. An inscription states that this belfry was erected by a native of the Shizuoka district named Yui Matsubei, in memory of the adventurous samurai Yui Shosetsu, so well known in Japanese history. In the days of the fourth Tokugawa shogun (Ietsuna) a revolutionary plot was instigated by Yui Shosetsu with the intention of overthrowing the military rule. The castle of the shogun was to be seized and the city of Edo set on fire, but before this program could be carried out the conspiracy was discovered, and its leader committed suicide in 1651.

Near the belfry, beneath the branches of a venerable oak, stands a stone figure of extreme antiquity representing the Healing Buddha, Yakushi Nyorai, and credited by the superstitious with the power of exorcising disease. This relic is said to have been established in the thirteenth century by the first priest of Komyo-ji. The head of the deity is decorated with ears of stupendous size, a characteristic frequently apparent in representations of divinities—these strangely elongated features apparently being considered attributes of sanctity, in striking opposition to the Western association of ideas.

A path bearing in a westerly direction leads to the Nisondo, or Hall of the Two Saints. The most conspicuous feature is a large and gaily adorned effigy of the Enoshima deity, Benten. In strong contrast to this hilarious representation of the goddess—who appears in her lightest and most festive mood—is the somber and imposing image of the Chinese sage Zendo; which is, according to tradition, the veritable statue of the saint carved by his own hands that floated upon the waves to its present haven. A lofty and dignified figure with oblique gleaming eyes, it is recorded that at the time of his arrival from the sea texts from the scriptures were inscribed upon his garments in letters of gold; however, time has left no trace of these characters. The incarnation of austerity, he stands beside his smiling companion in dark and unenlivened gloom.

Concerning this effigy of Benten—patroness of music and the fine arts, as well as the dispenser of good luck—tradition also ascribes a legend. It is written that in days of old, Kamakura was visited by a terrible storm; great winds hissed fury and defiance, while the dark waves reared their angry crests mountains high above the fretted surface of the bay. When the tempest was at its height, the figure of a goddess was discovered floating upon the billows; the mysterious visitant proving to be the presiding deity of Enoshima, she was restored to her shrine upon that island. But again and again the apparition was beheld, upon each occasion in the vicinity of Komyo-ji. Hence, after resorting to the test of divination, the populace arrived at the conclusion that the goddess was thus manifesting her desire; the present statue of Benten was constructed, after which the apparition was beheld no more and since that time the two sacred figures have jointly reigned in the Hall of the Two Saints, within sound of the "mystic hymn-chant of the waves" that safely guided them to their destination. Apropos of this incident it may be mentioned that during the typhoon of October 1917, the grounds of Komyo-ji were again inundated, the mighty deep on this occasion depositing before the temple doors neither a goddess nor a saint, but a trophy more in accordance with the commercial spirit of the times in the shape of an enormous fish, still living, and which was identified as a well-developed specimen of the porpoise tribe! Below the statue of Zendo is an antique and crumbling wooden *usu*, or mortar; this, it is asserted, was originally used as the stand or pedestal upon which the holy image was placed upon its arrival.

The white building south of the Nisondo is the Kyodo, the place where the rolls of the scriptures are preserved. This repository is guarded by three Chinese gods—Fu-Daishi and his two sons, Fuwaku and Fukon, who are considered to exercise a protective influence over the sacred writings. The central deity, of unmistakably Chinese origin, reposes in a large ecclesiastical chair in the attitude of benediction, supported on either side by the smaller figures—which are also known as the Laughing Buddha (Warai-botoke), and appear to be of a high order of workmanship.* These quaint effigies are usually found in the vicinity of libraries of the Buddhist scriptures and according to popular opinion Fu-Daishi—a deified Chinese priest of the sixth century—was the originator of the prayer wheel, or scriptures revolving on a pivot, with its convenient theory that whoever sets the wheel in motion with pious intent acquires the same merit as though he had read through the entire volumes of Holy Writ, 6,771 in number!

The path beside the Nisondo leads to the cemetery of the Naito family, enclosing the noble and dignified old tombs, stone lanterns, and various figures of beautiful shape, all lavishly adorned with filmy traceries of silvery and gray-green lichen. Indeed the figures of saints—some of which, alas, have suffered damage from the fierce storms to which this part of the coast is specially exposed—appear to be clad in veritable garments of this exquisite texture, woven of Nature's mystic shuttle.

In the rocky walls of the hill behind this graveyard are two caves. At the back of the larger one a huge and curious image of Benten seated in a boat is rudely cut in relief. The adjoining cave, from which a long tunnel-like arm extends, is known as the Ryugu Kutsu. According to Japanese mythology the name Ryugu

---

*The smaller buildings, such as the Nisondo and Kyodo, collapsed in the great Tokyo Earthquake of 1923. The effigies of Benten and Zendo are kept in the main temple now.

is given to a mystic and imaginary kingdom presided over by the beautiful sea goddess Otohime, and concerning which many charming stories and legends are related. It is recorded that a certain abbot of Komyo-ji, Giyo Shonin by name, was a priest of great learning, so much so that the rumor of his talents and virtues apparently penetrated to the depths of the sea. Hence the denizens of the fairy kingdom sent a deputation—presumably of fishes—inviting the holy and pious Giyo Shonin to deliver certain of his famous discourses in Ryugu. The priest lending a favorable ear to their proposals, this cave became the starting point of the expedition!

At the rear of the main temple on the right, a path ascends the hill to a plateau whereon seats of a somewhat precarious nature are provided for visitors of light weight, and command a delightful view. The large cave contains an antique statue of Jizo—said to have been carved by Kobo Daishi.* The path on the western side of the main temple intersects the corridor leading to the Hall of Amida and crosses the hills behind the little fishing village of Kotsubo, forming one of the numerous routes to Zushi. A flight of stone steps immediately behind the temple leads up to a pair of small shrines of almost fabulous foundation, known as the Shinmei-gu; one is dedicated to the sun goddess Amaterasu, the other to Kasuga and Hachiman the war god. A path rising immediately on the right of these twin shrines ascends to a beautiful spot on the crest of the hill above—perhaps the most romantic of all Komyo-ji's various coigns of vantage for distant views—also well known for the legend connected with the great pine, whose gaunt boughs stretch forth, weird and spectral, and to which is affixed the inscription Ryuto no Matsu, or Pine of the Dragon's Lantern. According to tradition, in ancient days the neighborhood was mystified by the sparkles and gleams of light that were observed to flash from the tree after nightfall. This

*This Jizo now stands in the front yard of the temple.

phenomenon was discovered to originate from a *ryū*, or dragon, who was in the habit of emerging from the sea in the darkness in order to worship and offer lights to the gods from the branches of this pine. It is unnecessary to return by the same route as the track continues in an easterly direction, curving around to a descent into the road to Kotsubo, and from which the temple is of easy access.

On the left of the twin shrines a wooden *torii* spans an ascent winding up to another plateau on the summit of another eminence—the Hill of Autumn Leaves. Surrounded by stately old pines, this terrace also commands a wide vista and possesses a shrine known as Akiha Jinja, or Shrine of Autumn Leaves. This small building is of very ancient origin, being dedicated to the second abbot of Komyo-ji; this worthy priest was supposed to have assumed the form of a *tengu* (goblin) after his demise, revisiting the scene of his earthly ministrations under this somewhat unattractive guise. The shrine is clean and well kept, containing various mysterious objects that are possibly connected with the habits of the intangible *tengu*. The ceiling is gay with paintings of birds and sprays of flowers upon a blue ground, while before the altar is a *gomadan*, or large square receptacle wherein the sacred fire of invocation is kindled upon special occasions. As in the case of the Dragon's Lantern, it is also practicable to effect an exodus from the Hill of Autumn Leaves via the western slope, without retracing one's steps. But should the latter route be preferred and the main path regained, a few paces toward the north brings the wanderer to stone steps heavily coated with luminous green moss and apparently seldom desecrated by the foot of man. Upon the tall monument that stands sentinel below, the formula of the Jodo sect is deeply graven: *Namu Amida Butsu*.

This ascent leads to a little grove of hallowed memories appropriately framed in solemn cryptomeria, the graveyard of the priests—wherein is interred the line of ancient divines that presided over the affairs of Komyo-ji. The centerpiece—a mighty circular monument of imposing proportions—marks the resting place of the spiritual founder Ryochu, while the beautiful gray tomb in a separate grove on the left memorializes the dignitary to whom the temple of Komyo-ji owes its existence, the fourth Hojo regent Tsunetoki.

An interesting festival known as the Juya, or Ten Nights of Prayer, is annually held at this temple, the opening day being October 13. This celebration originated some five centuries ago in the reign of the emperor Go-Tsuchimikado, when the fame of the ninth abbot of Komyo-ji, Yushu Shonin, afterward known as Jikaku Taishi, attracted the attention of the court. The emperor, himself an enthusiastic believer of the Jodo sect, summoned Yushu to Kyoto, where many special services and protracted discussions of religious topics took place. High honors were bestowed upon the priest and to commemorate this event it was decreed that from henceforth the ten nights of prayer and religious instruction should become one of the established rites of the Jodo sect.

In the present material days of dwindling faith and piety the ten nights have shrunk to the measure of barely three, but whatever the occasion may lack in length it amply atones for in enthusiasm. Each year as the thirteenth day of October duly recurs, all ways apparently lead to Komyo-ji, and the streets of Zaimokuza assume their most festive aspect. Throngs of villagers from villages and hamlets near and afar swarm to the spot clad in gala attire; whole families turning out en bloc, and many types rarely encountered on ordinary occasions are in evidence at the Juya, which is probably the great outing of the year to many of these rustic participants. An avenue of booths line the streets, wherein every need of humanity is catered to and every imaginable product is on sale. The precincts of Komyo-ji are so thronged that at times it is almost impossible to wedge oneself into the dense flood of human beings, all intent upon combining piety with pleasure. Here within the great temple courts are not only booths vending all descriptions of commodity, but an abundance of portable and highly popular restaurants under canvas (*yatai*), whose location is heralded by a variety of odors, savory and otherwise. Moreover, a number of entertainment tents and erections, some upon quite an elaborate scale and conducted by itinerant showmen, awaken liveliest interest in the younger members of the community. Moving pictures—with a brass band aloft—are exhibited in a tall structure decked with oil paintings of a lurid and blood-curdling description; wrestlers; fortune-tellers; peep-shows; trained bears; wire-walkers; acrobats; conjurers; performing dogs; ball-dancers; freaks of nature; stuffed monstrosities—fishy of form and suggestive of Caliban; snake charmers; and the ever-attractive *saru-shibai*—theaters wherein thrilling dramas are enacted, the actors consisting of a troupe of trained monkeys and dogs equipped with appropriate wigs and wardrobes—these constitute a few of the joys of the Ten Nights of Prayer that may be indulged in at a very modest expenditure. The interior of the temple, specially adorned, also presents a scene of uncommon animation. The spacious main building and also the adjoining Hall of Amida is filled to overflowing with enthusiastic worshippers. Fervent families equipped with their bundles of necessities encamp upon the mats and profitably spend the entire night in prayer and participation in the services, which occur at intervals and consist of sermons, religious instruction, chanting the scriptures, etc. Large reinforcements of priests officiate upon these occasions, and the rich hues of their vestments—blending in the dim interior with rainbow effect—add effectively to the picturesque nature of the scene, which is of distinctly impressive character. Every beautiful tint seems to be included in these ecclesiastical robes of flowing silk: bright coral and scarlet, flame red, lovely tones of blue, emerald greens, royal purples, mysterious yellows, varied shades of amethyst and heliotrope—all blend into a kaleidoscopic riot of color that seems to recall the stained windows of old cathedrals. An effective finishing touch is afforded by the *kesa*—the Buddhist small outer vestment, which is composed of gold and silver brocade. This decorative appendage is supposed to correspond to the stole of worship, and has been not very felicitously described as the "priests' scarf."

At certain of the services the *chigo* take part in the capacity of attendants, or pages, with charming effect; these are little maidens who stand in long lines below the altar, clad in robes of bright scarlet silk and equipped with long sprays of flowers, while their dark coiffures are crowned with glittering ornaments. As it grows dusky, innumerable candles are lighted that silhouette the worshippers with flickering shadows; clouds of incense fill the air with the fragrance of its thin blue smoke. The group of priests kneeling before the altar intone in unison from the sacred books. At regular intervals certain of their number strike a silvery and plaintive note upon a small bell-like object held in the hollow of the left hand, whilst others revolve with weird effect a strange metallic whirring instrument, the multitude occasionally responding in a deep and sonorous wave of sound that fills the vast building with their call upon the holy name—*Namu Amida Butsu.*

Exhausted by their long vigil, the next day finds numbers of these jaded devotees recruiting for the next batch of religious exercises. Many slumber heavily at their posts, with heads pillowed upon their bundles; others stimulate themselves with various forms of refreshment, in which oranges play an effective part— while the ever-ubiquitous children scramble about and play subdued little games around the forms of their recumbent elders.

The excitement of the Juya, although protracted, soon comes to an end. Within three days the participants have ebbed away, leaving, alas, the gray old temple and its courtyards distinctly the worse for wear. Bottles, papers—every description of unneeded article absolutely paves the neighborhood and forms a depressing aftermath. However, thanks to the valiant efforts of a little band of blue-clad and smiling functionaries—who grapple with the situation armed with bamboo rakes and gigantic receptacles for garbage—all traces of the fray vanish into the limbo of dead joys and for another year the ancient courts resume their normal atmosphere of aloofness and peaceful seclusion.

As might be expected, Komyo-ji possesses a formidable collection of treasures. These emerge from their cases and wrappings and are accessible to the admiration of the interested visitor on the occasion of the annual airing, which takes place in early autumn. Numbers of these objects are of great value and extreme antiquity, including many imperial gifts; numerous writings, vestments, and personal relics of the first lord abbot Ryochu; fine old pictures; and writings of various famous divines. The following articles are specially described in ancient records: the writing box of somewhat vague origin, but which is said to have belonged either to Michizane or to Masako; a roll of the scriptures inscribed by Shoko Shonin (master of Ryochu); an antique statue of the Sun Goddess carved by the emperor Ojin (third century!); and also a description of the early days of Komyo-ji temple illustrated by the famous painter Tosa Mitsuoki.

Jinmu-ji
and Kanazawa

❀

THE ANCIENT TEMPLE of Jinmu-ji is situated upon the rocky eminence known as Konodake, high up in the hills behind Zushi. A pilgrimage to the peace and solitude of this lovely spot constitutes one of the most delightful walks from Kamakura. Somewhat over a mile in the direction of Taura a tall stone carved with the temple's name stands beside a roofed gate. From this point a long path ascends "through verdurous glooms and winding mossy ways" to the sequestered space enclosed by rocks wherein is situated the main edifice of Jinmu-ji. Belonging to the Tendai sect of Buddhism, this foundation owes its existence to the celebrated priest of the eighth century, Gyoki Bosatsu. It is chronicled that later it was repaired and restored under the direction of another famous divine, Jikaku, who died in 864. An appealing feature that especially lingers in the memory in connection with this remote mountain-temple is its intense greenness. Every shade of verdure blends into an inexpressibly restful and harmonious ensemble; from the deep tones of ancient forest trees to the pale hues of the jungle of ferns, and the rich luminous emerald that glows from the heavy film of moss clinging to the huge boulders, and lavishly carpeting these leafy aisles and corridors, that:

{ 309 }

Strange tapestry by Nature spun
On viewless looms aloof from sun,
And spread through lonely nooks and grots
Where shadows reign and leafy rest.

Steps cut in the solid rock lead up past the belfry, past the six Jizo in their placid niches, to a higher level entered by a two-storied gate from which the protective presence of the kings has disappeared. The building opposite is the famous Yakushi-do described in early records, dedicated to the Healing Buddha and containing a venerable image said to have been carved by the priest Gyoki himself. A smaller shrine nearby contains the Anzan Jizo, to whom expectant mothers have recourse, prayers to this divinity being considered efficacious in securing a safe journey into the world for the impending scion. Amongst the noble old trees a great pine is conspicuous, whose trunk measures ten feet in diameter. This is described in ancient books as the Tengu no Koshikake-Matsu, or the pine upon whose boughs a *tengu* was in the habit of reclining.

The path to the summit ascends from the left of the Yakushi-do. After a short climb the track forks to the right, where a relic of past days will be observed in the shape of a notice carved in stone whereon members of the female sex are prohibited from desecrating the sacred mountain by proceeding beyond that point! A beautiful monument of green stone records the visit of the emperor Taisho, when Crown Prince, to the heights of Jinmu-ji. The narrow path winds up to the summit of this chain of hills, along which enchanting views are commanded in all directions—the peninsula lying beneath like a map in relief. It is asserted that when the atmosphere is clear the peak of Nantai-san, above Chuzen-ji (Nikko), is plainly visible. To the south, the vast Pacific glitters in the sunshine, while on the northern side is outlined the indented shores and irregular promontories of the bay of Tokyo; nearby lies Yokosuka, the great naval port, with its wide harbor and grim vessels of war; the blue inlet of Taura; and beyond, the pine-clad islets and jagged coast of Kanazawa.

This latter resort is six miles from Kamakura along the high road, and was first discovered by a Chinese priest of the Ming dynasty, who detected a resemblance between the celebrated Hsi-hu, or Western Lake in China, and the lovely and imaginative scenery of Kanazawa, beloved of poets and painters and widely famed for its Hakkei, or Eight Views. The latter are named from the Chinese originals:

> Sunlight dispersing the mists of Susaki,
> Descending wild geese of Hirakata,
> The twilight bell of Shomyo-ji,
> The evening snow of Uchikawa,
> Returning sails of Otsutomo,
> The sunset glow of Nojima,
> The autumn moon of Seto,
> The evening showers of Koizumi.

In this instance the "wild geese" are represented by the people of the district gathering shells in the lagoon at low tide; viewed from a distance they present a similar effect to the birds of the Chinese scene. The names refer to various spots of scenic beauty in the immediate neighborhood. Noken-do—a small temple on the hillside above—and also a height outside the village are considered the best coigns of vantage for admiring the poetic effects of the Eight Views.

In the days of the Kamakura period, Kanazawa was a town of considerable importance and possessed a celebrated library of Japanese and Chinese books—the Kanazawa Bunko first established by Hojo Sanetoki, a grandson of the second regent. This collection of valuable works having somewhat declined, it was restored under the auspices of a member of the Uesugi family, Norizane; however, toward the end of the sixteenth century the library practically disappeared. A remnant still exists in the shape of certain of the books and documents preserved in Kanazawa's most important temple, Shomyo-ji, also founded by Sanetoki. The late Prince Ito, who possessed a villa at Kanazawa, contributed over three hundred books to the latter collection, which were used as works of reference at the time the Constitution of Japan was compiled. The name of this romantic spot is derived from the fact that in the Hojo days it was the stronghold of Sanetoki, another name of whom was Kanazawa; the site of his castle remains to the present day.

The picturesque old temple of Tainei-ji enshrines an ancient figure known as the Heso Yakushi from its legend. Long, long ago, a very poor thread-spinner lived in the village; her poverty was so extreme that on the death-day of her parents she was unable to make the customary offerings. In despair she wove all her thread into a number of *heso*, or round cotton balls—but no one needed them, and none would buy. At last a beautiful youth appeared and purchased all her stock. Overjoyed, the poor woman at last was able to make her offerings. Lo, in front of the compassionate Yakushi lay a pile of the cotton balls—the deity himself had come to the rescue and personated her deliverer!

Tradition also associates this temple with Yoritomo's unfortunate brother Noriyori. Five hundred soldiers led by Kajiwara Kagetoki were sent to attack him during his exile at Shuzen-ji, province of Izu, but Noriyori set fire to his place of residence and then committed suicide. His charred head was found and despatched to Yoritomo at Kamakura; subsequently this relic was buried in the temple of Tainei-ji.

The Cave of Taya
(Taya no Dōkutsu)

❀

A BOUT FIVE miles from Kamakura in a northwesterly direction (one mile beyond Ofuna Station) lies the little hamlet of Taya, whose claim to celebrity centers in its great cavern piercing a hill within the precincts of the temple of Josen-ji. The latter is of such ancient origin that all records of its foundation have merged into obscurity; but the famous cave is of comparatively recent construction, its present form having been inaugurated about a century ago.

As the water supply from the ordinary wells of the hamlet proved inadequate for irrigating the fields, an enterprising resident of the neighborhood—Sato Shichizaemon by name—initiated his undertaking with the primary object of utilizing the waters of the underground springs; however, his labors were extended over a period of thirty years, and resulted in the excavation of a species of imperishable subterranean temple—ceilings and walls of the numerous corridors and chambers being decorated with the large number of 350 figures. These carvings were executed by amateur artists from the vicinity of this little village, and include numerous animals, dragons, turtles, birds, angels, and historical personages in addition to the multitude of disciples, saints, and Buddhist divinities.

{ 313 }

Within the dark and ghostly chambers of this winding labyrinth, two special altars hewn in the eternal rock enshrine the goddesses Benten and Kannon respectively—their sanctuaries adorned with sprays of living flowers that are silhouetted with pallid and spectral effect in the heavy gloom, but dimly illumined by the flickering lamps. The faint scent of incense and the clamorous roar of hidden waters accentuate the illusion of lost souls wandering in the purgatorial shadows beyond the Styx.

According to another record preserved in the temple, the cave appears to have been in existence in medieval days—probably on a considerably smaller scale—and is supposed to have originated about the time Kamakura was devastated by Nitta Yoshisada's army (1333) for purposes of refuge and concealment.

The rock has been penetrated to the depth of 1260 feet, the corridors vary in width from 4 to 12 feet, while the height averages from 6 to 21 feet—certain of the chambers being the size of a 10-tatami-mat room (1 tatami mat being 3 by 6 feet).

The grounds of Josen-ji are especially picturesque in April, when the fine old cherry trees are in bloom, forming a landmark from afar. The small temple moreover possesses a somewhat unique treasure in the shape of a figure of the Buddha that was brought from Siam (Thailand) some years ago by a priest named Shaku Konen; the Master reclines in a recumbent position and is represented as delivering his last discourse upon earth before the *nehan* took place, when his soul was translated to the peace and bliss of Nirvana.

> Then the Blessed One, perceiving that death was near, uttered these words: "He who gives away shall have real gain. He who subdues himself shall be free of passions. The righteous man casts off sin; and by rooting out lust, bitterness, and illusion, do we reach Nirvana . . . . Decay is inherent in all component things, but the truth will remain forever. Work out your Salvation with diligence!"

This was the last word of the Tathâgata. Then the Tathâgata fell into a deep meditation, and having passed through the four dhyânas,* entered Nirvana.

(Translated by Paul Carus)

*Dhyâna: beatific vision, ecstasy.

Enoshima

❀

T HE LITTLE ISLE of Enoshima—the sacred island dedicated to the sea goddess Benten, whose name is a talisman conjuring ineffaceable visions of beauty to the memory of the pilgrim—rises from the blue ocean some quarter of a mile from the mainland at Katase.

This small town, although apparently of no great significance, possesses more than one claim to distinction. Upon its shores the drama of the Mongolian ambassadors was enacted in 1275 and 1279—the second party of envoys having been actually beheaded upon the beach; the nearby temple of Ryuko-ji is immortalized and has ever been the unceasing goal of the devout by its association with the saint Nichiren, who so barely escaped martyrdom by the intervention of the celestial thunderbolt within its precincts (1271); moreover, this delectable spot forms the mainland link, and principal approach to the "mystic island, so full of strange gods and strange presences, so wrapped in the web of story and so little a part of the life of today that one almost expects to see it float out to sea and melt into cloud upon the horizon!"

The best route for a pilgrimage to the lovely islet is the main road from Kamakura, which leads through Gokuraku-ji across the "velvety, soundless, brown stretch of sand" known as Shichirigahama (Seven-Ri Beach), where a turn in the path suddenly reveals a panorama that is beyond description. Before one, glittering in the sunlight, lie the vast waters of Sagami Bay, whose western barrier of the Hakone peaks—culminating in purple Amagi-san and crowned by the snows of the Queen of Mountains high in the blue vaults of heaven—forms the setting of the "dusky embowered mass floating in haze and sunshine out at sea, the island of the tortoise, Enoshima." The wayfarer would be ill advised to explore the island—at any rate upon an initial visit—in gray and cloudy weather, for although beautiful at all times and seasons—especially at the sunset hour in winter, and also when flooded by the glamour of the full moon—the mountainous surroundings vanish in the mists and it would be a loss indeed to forgo the coloring of this gleaming expanse of sapphire and forget-me-not flecked with white sails, which is verily "a revelation of the riches and beauties of the world of water that laps around our world of earth."

Like Mont St. Michel in Normandy, and its namesake St. Michel's Mount in Cornwall, Enoshima is only completely surrounded by the waves at high tide; when the waters abate, a stretch of sand is revealed, rendering it possible to cross to the island dryshod. However, as the pine-clad promontory of Katase is approached, it becomes apparent that a more permanent link with the mainland is formed by a long bridge of planks swaying with the waves and of such light construction that in the many tempests that attack this wild coast, it is a frequent occurrence that more or less of this frail causeway suffers damage and is washed away by the fury of the storm.

The march of progress, that is so fatal to Old World romance, scattering the fabled gods with the clang of its iron-shod feet, is already threatening the abode of Benten. Rumor whispers that the problem is afloat concerning the realizing of a new approach, wrought of steel and concrete, permanent, storm-defying, and capable of hurling defiance at Neptune in his most ominous moods—an electric car depositing the pilgrims at the very portals of the shrine of the sea goddess! Apropos of which, it may be of interest to mention that the number of visitors to Enoshima (i.e., those who paid the bridge toll of 3 *sen*) during the year 1920 amounted to the large figure of 400,000.

In bygone centuries Enoshima seems to have been completely isolated from the coast. According to an ancient record (*Azuma Kagami*, compiled 1180–1266) on the 15th day in the first month of Kenpo (1216), in accordance with a manifestation of the goddess, the ocean receded upon either side, leaving a dry path from the island to the mainland and rendering it possible for worshippers to proceed on foot. This fact excited great interest in the neighborhood; vast multitudes of people—including a special emissary from the shogun Sanetomo at Kamakura—hastened to the spot to verify the fact and inspect the wonderful causeway for themselves.

Another chronicle of great antiquity (*Taiheiki*, a narrative of events that occurred 1318–68) records that upon a certain occasion the famous Hojo Tokimasa (father-in-law and chief adviser of Yoritomo) repaired to Enoshima to worship and propitiate the deity in order to make special intercession for the prosperity of his descendants. On the night of the third week of the prayer and fasting period, the vision of a heavenly being appeared to Tokimasa, informing him that as in a former existence he had been a priest of Hakone famed for his great piety, as a reward he had been reborn into this world and his descendants would become rulers of the land. This prophecy was amply fulfilled, Tokimasa becoming founder of the Hojo dynasty that ruled Japan for a period of over 130 years (1199–1333). After these words, the celestial apparition assumed the shape of a huge dragon and disappeared into the sea, leaving behind her, as a sign and token, three scales, which became the well-known crest of the house of Hojo!

As Enoshima is approached from the long bridge "the details of the little town define delightfully through the faint sea haze, curved bluish sweeps of fantastic roofs, angles of airy balconies, high-peaked curious gables, all above a fluttering of queerly shaped banners covered with mysterious lettering." The great bronze *torii,* ornamented with quaint carvings of waves and tortoises, forms the island gate—the "ever-open portal of the Sea City"—from whence begins the ascent that culminates in the ancient temple of Benten, a path trodden and sanctified by the feet of a myriad stream of pilgrims and worshippers for such countless centuries—a procession extending beyond the earliest annals of recorded eras into the vague mists of antiquity.

The one narrow street of this miniature sea-city, climbing steeply to the groves above, is thickly lined on either side with hostelries and diminutive shops—above which wave the picturesque line of blue banner-shaped advertisements, giving the impression of an avenue of fluttering blue wings, "fanned by the lifting pinions of the wind." These emporiums bear a strong family likeness to each other, and abound with every description of article that can be carried away as an *omiyage,* or souvenir, of the island; and which the visitor is entreated to purchase and bear off in triumph to the expectant circle of relatives and friends at home. Beads of all colors; paperweights and balls of tinted stones; every species of toy for the little one; the ever-popular hair ornaments; rings, pins, necklaces, brooches, all the varied embellishments devised by man's ingenuity for the adornment of the human race abound on every side and are mostly constructed of shells. Moreover, the dimly lighted shop interiors are opalescent with things nacreous, and multitudes of small objects gleam with a soft iridescence of rainbow hues from the receptacles and shelves; these are representations of divers shapes and forms— storks, crabs, combs, pipes, lanterns, figures of gods, doves, bees, beetles, frogs, whole schools of fish, turtles, foxes, rabbits, monkeys, badgers— indeed manifold specimens of beasts, birds and fishes, as well as of the reptile and insect kingdoms, are skillfully carved in mother-of-pearl and sold for an infinitesimal price. For Enoshima, as well as being the domain of shells—befitting to its sea goddess—is also the "City of Mother-of-Pearl."

Shells abound everywhere, of every color, size, and shape:

> They lie heaped on doorstep and window and wall—shells as white and lustrous as bridal moons; shells dazzling and whorled as the snow-queen's crown; shells rosy, thick, thousands upon thousands, like shed petals piled together, as if all the cherry blossoms of the spring had been blown out to Enoshima on the saving breeze, and touched to immortality, as they fell on the brown stand of Benten's magic island. Here at my feet are deep, huge nautilus shells like hollow pearls fitted with moonlight; solemn conch shells that have slept under brown seaweed in autumn starlight, and have caught the rhymed chant of the waves on the shore; open shells of green and gray mother-of-pearl, with shifting crimson gleams on the vigorous edge turned in like an ear, where five round holes pierce through in mystic symmetry, as if the sea-king's daughter had been trying her earrings there; and little shells in myriads, thick as the Empress' cherry blossoms in spring; there are showers of spun glass, as sharp and silvery as moonbeams on ice—the glass ropes of the beautiful Hyalonema sponges; there are huge tortoise shields, measuring four and five feet across; there are sprays of shells like lilies-of-the-valley dipped in milk, sea-foam lilies—born of a kiss where the sun met the wave.*

This quaint street of shells and trophies of the deep culminates at another of the chain of *torii* that extends through

---

*This charming description of the shells of Enoshima was written by Mrs. Hugh Fraser.

Katase—this "gateway of the silent gods" being of green moss-stained stone. From this point the irregular rock-hewn ascents rise to the summit of the island. Immediately facing the *torii,* broad flights of steep stone steps give access to the lowest of the three temples of the sea goddess wherein Benten reigns, supreme but invisible. Lying one above another upon lofty terraces in the pillared solemnity of ancient forest trees, this threefold shrine impresses the pilgrim with a sense of sadness and desolation. No statue of the beauteous deity appears, to greet her worshippers with kindly smiles—bare and melancholy are her altars. All decoration, images, and gay adornment have been banished by the depressing hand of the iconoclast; all that is visible being the austere symbols of the Shinto faith—the mirror, typifying the human soul, and the clusters of pure white *gohei* gently rustling in the sea breezes that penetrate the thick screen of foliage and whisper around the shrine "like sighs from ghosts of perished hours." What magic can lurk within the mysteries of the mirror to inspire travelers along the highways and byways of life with hope and confidence in the future, or solace in the present? "The face of the Buddha is as the face of a friend—serene, merciful, gracious to poor humanity; but in the mirror of Shinto, man finds only his own travel-stained reflection—the picture of that self which must be left behind before he can enter into peace."

According to an early record, upon April 5, 1180, the famous priest, friend, and counselor of Yoritomo, Mongaku Shonin, proceeded to Enoshima in order to spend three weeks in prayer and fasting and the performance of austerities. The holy man was accompanied by Yoritomo and upon that occasion mystical rites in honor of Benten took place. However, popular tradition associates the deity with her island fastness from considerably earlier times. Legend avers that in the year 552 this part of the coast was shaken by a series of great earthquakes, when the beautiful goddess Benten descended from heaven in clouds of celestial radiance to dwell upon an islet that had suddenly appeared in the sea; the ostensible reason for this apparition being the subjugation of the poisonous dragon who was preying upon the unfortunate in habitants of Katase, and who made his lair within the depths of the mighty cavern below.

Poised upon the edge of the cliff upon either side of this lowest sanctuary are two stones of fabulous antiquity and described in ancient records. The weird mass crowning the abyss upon the left is known as the Gamaishi, or the Toadstone. According to the legend, an Old World priest was engaged in prayer upon that spot, when a large toad appeared, disturbing his devotions; so by virtue of his supplication the intruding reptile was petrified into a block of stone and remains as a warning to those who would trifle with matters sacred to the other world. It is supposed to bear a resemblance to a giant frog, but in former years the head of the monster became loosened, and disappeared.

Surrounded by a grove of bushes upon the opposite bank stands the Fukuishi, or Stone of Good Luck, and whoever may be fortunate enough to find any article lying in its vicinity may take it as a sign that he will become the possessor of wealth! It is said that the blind man Sugiyama Kengyo—celebrated as the originator of a school of *hari* (acupuncture)—in his student days, while still poor and obscure and discouraged at his lack of success, made a pilgrimage to the holy island of Enoshima for a period of fasting and prayer. When his austerities were terminated the blind student stumbled against the stone, to discover—for his sight was momentarily restored by miraculous means—a needle glittering in the sand; then darkness again descended upon him. In after years this man became famous as the founder of a school of *hari* which still exists at the present day. Moreover, he was honored by a summons to the sick bed of the highest in the land, the reigning shogun, and is said to have relieved his sufferings by skilled application of the same needle so mysteriously revealed to him at the Fukuishi. When the ruler, in gratitude, desired to reward Sugiyama for his ministrations, the blind man requested that a donation should be bestowed upon the temple of Benten at Enoshima, as from thence had emanated all his good luck. A large tablet of ornamental stone in the vicinity of the Fukuishi is inscribed with Chinese characters and bears a detailed history of the career of Sugiyama Kengyo.

From the *torii* below, two ways are available to ascend over the crest to the Dragon's Cave, which penetrates the sheer rocky precipice upon the southern flank of the island. The western path is the more beautiful, the woodland grove remaining as in happier days unprofaned by the despoiling hand of man, and leading beneath the heavy shade of over arching trees—with visions of the gentian blue wavelets dancing between the leaves—to a junction with the eastern footway, from whence one ascends to the eminence whereon the third and chief shrine is situated. The same atmosphere of desertion and aloofness pervades the present-day aspect of each of the Benten temples. The same stone lanterns and graven monuments, darkened by time and velveted with moss, lie in the dusky shadows and green dimness of solemn forest trees. However, in this uppermost shrine an unexpected and desolating feature has appeared in the shape of a row of invading souvenir shops, which boldly encroach upon the very courts of "Benten's desecrated home."

Facing the temple steps is a small *haiden,* or place of prayer, where the pilgrims make their offerings and bow their heads in supplication to the deity. The ceiling is arranged in caissons, the center being decorated with an ancient and curious painting of a large tortoise (by the celebrated artist Hoitsu) which is said to look in eight directions—another name for the Benten temple being Kinkisan, or Hill of the Golden Tortoise. Legend relates that at one time the cave below was inhabited by a giant turtle; it is moreover chronicled that in bygone centuries the great cavern was known as the Golden Cave, from whence gold and copper ores seem to have been obtained—the process of separation from sand and alloy being effected upon the mainland at the spot known as Kane-arai-sawa, or Metal-washing Pond. Hence this may, in fact, indicate the possible origin of the legend of the Golden Tortoise.

Upon a rock to the right of the temple, is the seated figure of a man—a bronze statue that has been decorated by the salt breezes with an aesthetic hue of green. This work of art represents Yamada Kengyo, the originator of a school of music (*koto*) in Japan. The effigy was erected to his memory by a group of followers and musical adherents in 1916, to celebrate the centenary of his death.

In close proximity to the temple, a teahouse is perched above the precipice, open to the sea and sun and from thence flights of worn, uneven, and somewhat perilous steps steeply descend to the rocks below. The view from this inn, which hangs like a sea-bird's nest high on the face of the cliff, is enchanting. "What a sea! The breadth and the blue of it! From this lofty place the horizon is so distant that it almost ceases to be; the world is a sapphire globe endomed in sunshot crystal; earth seems an accident, Enoshima a seaweed freak that has come up to breathe!" An appealing feature of this far-flung sea picture is the whirring of the winged denizens of the Dragon's Cave—the flocks of tame doves which nest in the glooms of the great cavern nearby and gaily circle and hover in the soft blue atmosphere—their iridescent plumage flashing in the sunlight like the gems of the sea kingdom's princess. Lured by a promise of plenty from the inn, these "small almoners of Heaven" find coigns of vantage in the boughs of the great surrounding pine trees—serenading with soft music and watching their opportunity with alert and eager eye, alight to daintily refresh themselves with any stray remnants unneeded by the teahouse guests.

By carefully negotiating the hazardous descent cut in the sheer face of the cliff, one lands upon the region of rocks and weedy pools below; and to those mortals who are under the sway of the sea spell, this rocky floor of Enoshima is a never-ceasing wonder and delight.

Ancient dealers in magic and the arts of necromancy aver that there exists a secret road to the soul in all the sons of men—an elemental affinity which is the veiled door to the inner life; some are children of air, some of fire, some of earth, others of water. And to those of us who at birth, or in former eons, were dowered by the fairy godmother with brine in the blood and a wave in the heart—whose natures are dominated by the clarion music of the sea, this corner of the earth will make a special appeal, with the great breakers eternally surging and fretting against the rocks and rushing to one's feet "to perish in a mist of pearl." But however exquisite the scene may be in fine weather, with the pure turquoise of the heavens mirrored in the blue tranquillity below, it becomes almost more unforgettable and exhilarating upon rough and stormy days—when the sea gods let loose their fury and hurl the huge billows to crash and thunder in unrestrained rage upon the rocky barriers, crowned with their snowy coronals of spray; while oceanward, far as the sight can reach, "the sea-horses sweep magnificently, whirling white foam about their green flanks and tossing on high their manes of rainbow gold, dazzling white and multitudinous."

Immediately below lies a deep whirlpool almost enclosed by a girdle of sharp rocks, into which the breakers churn and foam incessantly—this is Chigogafuchi, or the Maiden's Pool, concerning which a legend of love and death is related in ancient books. Long, long ago, a priest of Kencho-ji, known as Jikiu, repaired to the sacred isle of Enoshima for the purpose of devoting one hundred days to prayer, worship, and the practice of austerities. As fate decreed, a *chigo,** or maiden acolyte, of another Kamakura temple made a similar pilgrimage at the same

*The Chinese characters for *chigo* can also be read as "page" lending a certain ambiguity to this tale.

time. Her name was Shiragiku, or White Chrysanthemum. They met: the maiden's beauty cast a fatal spell upon the susceptible divine, causing him to forget his priestly vows and to pursue his prey with amorous intent. She managed to elude his attentions for a time, but as his resolution showed no symptoms of abating, poor White Chrysanthemum solved the problems of love and life by casting herself into the cruel rocks of the whirlpool. On her last death journey she left a poem with the ferryman, to be delivered in case one should come in pursuit. One did come in pursuit. The too-persistent lover, on learning the doom of his hapless victim, determined to accompany her soul into the shades of those dim regions from whence no man returneth. Following in his beloved's footsteps, he also leaped into the seething waters. Hence the tragedy of Chigogafuchi, the Maiden's Pool.

A climb along the shelving rocks brings the wayfarer to another frail structure of wooden scaffolding, winding around a promontory of the cliff into the great cave, whose floor is almost level with the sea at high tide, and up whose dusky echoing aisles the waves rush with sonorous roar and clamor, breaking against their rocky confines in hissing drifts of spray. So frequently does this plank approach suffer damage, that recently a stairway has been cut in the cliff leading to a tunnel above in connection with the cavern, thus enabling the incessant stream of visitors and pilgrims to conduct their explorations unmolested, and in defiance of the menaces of the angry deep.

The entrance of the Dragon's Cave is said to be 30 feet in height, and pierces the heart of the rock to the depth of some 380 feet. According to ancient chronicles, at the time of the Kamakura period the cave of Enoshima was one of the seven holy places from whence it was customary to supplicate the gods for rain in times of drought. A visit to this cavern, so rich in legend, and the goal and destination of worshippers from time immemorial, is always a weird and mystifying experience. As one penetrates farther and farther into the gloom, gleams of soft light reveal an altar presided over by a shadowy priest with attendant silhouettes; from here candles are provided, by whose flicker the long black corridors are gropingly explored. Here and there the forms of dusky brine-encrusted gods are carved in the black walls of rock: "gray and solemn, buried in eternal darkness near the springs of things—feeling the earthquake rive its way to the light through the heart of the world, hearing the thud of breakers upon the outer wall of their island castle." Before their shrines burn with steady flame the candles deposited by the hand of faith—yellow points of fire illuminating the heavy gloom "like good deeds in a naughty world"—the whole effect conveying an indescribably mystic and unreal impression, as though the invader from the outer world were groping in "a mortuary pit, some subterranean burial place of dead gods." The labyrinth forks in the center; the lateral chambers being supposed to represent the wings of the dragon. Occasionally the rushing sound of hidden waters descending from above is heard with weird effect. Gradually the long passage narrows until it culminates in the last twist of the dragon's tail, wherein is another dark shrine tenanted by a dusky silhouetted image—the mysterious deity who is supposed to personify the ultimate reality of the universe, Dainichi Nyorai.

According to tradition the uttermost ends of this historic cavern are still veiled in mystery and are connected with the fiery heart of distant Mount Fuji. In fact a legend is extant concerning a man of ancient days named Nitan no Shiro, who entered a cave upon the western side of the mountain, pursuing his subterranean course until he finally emerged from the cave of Enoshima, but concerning details of this hazardous and ghostly journey—which must have borne a strong resemblance to the wanderings of disembodied spirits in the underworld—nothing remains and tradition is silent.

Alas, alas! that roses should have thorns and silver fountains mud; that clouds and eclipses should stain both moon and sun. In a world of imperfections every picture must have its reverse side, and a sad surprise awaits the pilgrim who climbs to Benten's rocky heights after an interim of years. The beautiful forest-shaded crest of Enoshima—in former times so remote, so fraught with the dim magic of the past and the mystic influences of the calm-eyed immortals as to seem part of more ethereal regions than the sordid elements of this commercial planet—has suffered change and melancholy desecration at the devastating hands of worshippers of that hideous and all-penetrating god, the Mammon of unrighteousness. Where formerly reigned peace, solitude, and hushed tranquillity, the ancient trees have been hewn down, the shadowy groves and ferny glades hacked away, and the rocks relentlessly cut and leveled by ruthless invaders to give place to an incredible array of restaurants, inns, shops, and emporiums wherein lie heaped formidable battalions of the island souvenirs—flanked by long, long rows of the all-pervading and unescapable picture-postcard! Verily hath it been said, "Where nature is most puissant to charm, there man is mightiest to destroy."

Farewell, beautiful Enoshima! As we recede and slowly wend our way across the frail bridge back to the busy world, the western mountains gradually assume their twilight vestment; from the sea creeps a faint blue haze, like a fairy veil of powdered turquoise, which clings to their flanks, rendering their purple heights immeasurably distant and remote. Suddenly the cloud gates of the west open, flooding the world with a radiance of splendor indescribable. Benten's magic isle, with her crown of sun-flamed foliage, is dyed in sunset gems of carmine, dazzling orange and molten amethyst. Her bases fretted by a foam of golden sparks, as a mirage she seems to hover between earth and heaven—like an enchanted boat, jewel-laden, and putting off to sea in an ocean of shimmering gold and liquid rose leaves. The glory of the cloud colors and mirrored in the pure snows of Mount Fuji, staining her white shroud with roseate tints that recall old cathedrals of the West; the death-rites of a perfect day are flaming in this feast of pageantry, which makes one wonder with old Isaac Newton, "Lord, what raptures hast thou provided for thy saints in heaven, when such joys are given to naughty men below!"

Farewell! farewell! Despite the havoc of the despoiler, to the heart of the faithful pilgrim this sacred isle will ever be the land of the gods, enshrined in beauty and loveliness immortal—oblivious to the inevitable lament, "Now all is changed—all save the changeless things: The mountains, and the waters, and the sky."

Index

Abutsuni, 181

Adachi Morinaga, 139

Akiba Jinja, 304

Amagoi-ike, 239, 249

Amanawa Jinja (Amanawa Shinmei-gu), 222

Amaterasu (Tensho Daijin, Sun Goddess) 49, 94, 222, 303

Amibiki Jizo, 183

Amida Buddha, Nyorai, 61

Ankokuron-ji, 287–88, 291

Antoku (emperor), 33

An'yo-in, 53

Anzan Jizo, 310

Aoto Fujitsuna, 64

Arai no Enmado (see also Enno-ji): 123

Ashikaga (family, dynasty, shoguns) 38

Ashikaga Ietoki, 56

Ashikaga Mochiuji, 58, 75, 165, 245

Ashikaga Motouji, 72, 74, 75

Ashikaga Nariuji, 75

Ashikaga Tadayoshi, 80

Ashikaga Takauji, 35, 79, 279

Ashikaga Ujimitsu, 74, 75, 165, 166

Ashikaga Yoshihisa, 58

Ashikaga Yoshikane, 60, 63

Ashikaga Yoshimasa, 225, 227

Ashikaga Yoshimochi, 139

Azuma (poetic term for eastern Japan), 182

Azuma Kagami, 47, 99, 222, 247, 318

Bato Kannon (Protectress of Horses), 53, 228

Benkei, 30, 105, 251

Benkei's stone, 251

Benten (sea goddess, see also Zeni-arai Benten) at Engaku-ji, 143, 144

Enoshima deity, 301, 316, 321, 323, 328
  at Gokuraku-ji, 242, 245
  at Hachiman Shrine, 96, 105
  at Hokai-ji, 280
  at Ryuko-ji, 254
  at Sugimoto-dera, 48, 50
  at Zuisen-ji, 72
Bishamon, 50
Bofuseki, 171
Bosatsu (*see also* Ryokan): 105, 243
Bukkoku Zenshi, 115
Bukko Zenji (Sogen), 133, 134, 162
Buppo-ji, 238
Bushido, 132
Butsunichi-an, 135

Chigogafuchi (Enoshima), 325–26
Chikaku (priest), 123
Chikuin (priest), 76
Chinwakei, 61, 138, 174, 275
Chisho (priest), 284
Chosei-in, 216
Chosho-ji, 287, 291–92
Chu Yuan (Chinese priest, Sogen), 133

Daibutsu (Great Buddha at Nara), 174
  Kamakura, 203–9, 210, 238
Daigaku Saburo (Hiki), 273–75
Daigaku Zenshi (Doryu), 108
Daigo (emperor), 44

Daijin-yama, 40, 62, 106
Daikaku-ike, 116
Daikoku, 225, 245
Daiko Shonin, 213, 215, 217, 220
Dainichi Nyorai, 327
Daito-no-miya, 72, 78, 82, 282
Dan Kazura, 99
Daruma (Dharma), 74, 129, 132
"Divorce temple" (Tokei-ji), 127
Doryu, 108, 114, 117–20, 121, 123, 165, 258, 140, 225
Dragon's Cave (Enoshima), 323, 324, 326

Ebisudo Bridge, 272, 277
Edo, 38, 77, 101, 179, 255, 300
Egaki Yagura, 177
Egara Tenjin, 43, 47, 72
Eian-ji, 58, 75
Eisai (priest), 132, 173, 177
Eisho (lady), 179
Eisho-ji, 179–80, 181
Endo Morito (*see also* Mongaku): 283, 284–85
Engaku-ji, 56, 60, 107, 119, 120, 128, 131–62, 163, 169
Enkan (priest), 279
Enma (god of the underworld) 52, 112, 120, 123–26, 144, 213
Enmado (at Yugyo-ji), 211, 215
Enmei-ji, 281, 282
En-Musubi no Kami, 170
Enno-ji (Arai no Enmado), 123–26

Enoshima, 143, 144, 236–37, 251, 253, 254, 263, 316–29
Eshin (priest), 50, 51, 113

Forty-seven Ronin, 282
Fuchibe (samurai), 80
Fu-Daishi (Chinese god), 302
Fudaraku-ji, 128, 283–86
Fudo, 63, 87, 117, 169, 170, 182, 186, 243, 284
Fudo temple (Imaizumi) 169
Fugen Bosatsu, 129, 174, 296
Fujigayatsu, 182
Fujisawa, 67, 210, 212, 218, 257
Fujiwara (family), 22, 181, 182
Fujiwara no Hidehira, 30
Fujiwara no Kamatari, 40, 62, 63, 106
Fujiwara no Tame-ie, 181
Fujiwara no Tamesuke, 70, 181–84
Fujiwara no Teika, 181
Fujiwara no Yoritsune, 274
Fukuishi (Enoshima), 322–23

Gamaishi (Enoshima), 322
Gangyo (sculptor), 87
Gekko Bosatsu, 83, 284
Genji-yama, 178, 180
Genno (priest), 190–202
Gensho (empress), 225, 230
Go-Daigo (emperor), 36, 66, 69, 127, 129, 187, 243, 247, 279
Go-Fukakusa (emperor), 191, 245
Go-Hanazono (emperor), 296

Go-Kogon (emperor), 135
Go-Komatsu (emperor), 211
Gokuraku-ji, 167, 182, 237, 238–46, 316
Gokuraku-ji Kiridoshi (pass), 236, 248
Gongoro Jinja, 234–35
Gongoro Kagemasa, 234–35
Goryo Jinja, *see* Gongoro Jinja
Go-Saga (emperor), 115, 162
Go-Shirakawa (emperor), 26, 105, 286
Go-Toba (emperor), 34
Go-Tsuchimikado (emperor), 227, 298, 305
Go-Uda (emperor), 44, 108, 243, 245, 298
Gyoki Bosatsu, 48, 51, 227, 228, 231, 237, 309, 310

Hachiman (god of war), 24, 27–28, 114, 133, 161, 303
Hachiman Shrine, 20, 33, 39, 91, 94–106, 124, 261, 288
Hachiman Taro, 95
Hachiman Temple, 47, 84, 177, 252
Hadaka Jizo, 281
Hakuroku-do, 136
Hanazono (emperor), 135
Hansobo, 90, 114, 116, 171
Harada Jizo, 116
Harakiri-yagura, 280
Harris, Townshend, 76–77
Hase, 208, 222, 225, 231, 262
Hase-dera (Shin Hase-dera), 225, 227, 232, 234

Hase Kannon, 53, 223, 225–33

Hatakeyama Shigetada, 192

Hatakeyama Shigeyasu, 151

Hatatate-yama, 180

Hattoku-ike, 215

Hayama, 238

Heso Yakushi (Kanazawa), 312

Hidehira, see Fujiwara Hidehira

Hideyori (Toyotomi Hideyori), 129, 299

Hideyoshi (Toyotomi Hideyoshi), 30, 47, 98, 105, 120, 129, 204, 269, 294, 299

Hikari-matsu, 254–55

Hiki (family), 272–74

Hikigayatsu, 272

Hiki no Ama, 272

Hiki Yoshikazu, 272–74

Hino Suketomo, 187

Hino Toshimoto, 187–89

Hiromoto, see Oe Hiromoto

Hirotsune (Taira no Hirotsune), 27

Hitaki Jizo, 85

Hoami (nun, see also Machi no Tsubone): 70

Hoitsu (artist Sakai Hoitsu), 323

Hojo (family, dynasty, regents), 34–36, 38, 64, 92, 273, 279–80, 318

Hojo Masamura, 275

Hojo Nagatoki, 164, 183, 240

Hojo Naritoki, 240

Hojo Sadatoki, 83, 87, 139, 143

Hojo Sanetoki, 311

Hojo Shigetoki, 240, 246

Hojo Takatoki, 35, 36, 187, 279, 280

Hojo Tokimasa, 22–25, 34, 36, 90, 92, 228, 240, 251, 273, 318

Hojo Tokimune
  and Amagoi-ike, 239
  and Doryu (priest), 121
  and Engaku-ji, 132–36, 143
  and Gokuraku-ji, 243, 244
  and Nichiren, 224, 264, 266
  and Ryokan (priest), 241
  consort of, 127, 128, 130
  father of, 164, 165
  Mongolian invasion, 35, 132, 251

Hojo Tokiyori
  and Gokuraku-ji, 245
  and Kencho-ji, 96, 107, 108, 112, 259
  and Komyo-ji, 293
  and Kosoku-ji, 223
  and Meigetsu-in, 163–65
  and Nichiren, 249, 259, 262
  retirement of, 183
  tomb of, 167, 169

Hojo Tokiyuki, 80

Hojo Tsunetoki, 293, 305

Hojo Ujinao, 43

Hojo Yasutoki, 237

Hojo Yoshitoki, 34, 82, 84, 102–4

Hokai-ji, 65, 279–80

Hoki Bosatsu, 230

Hokke sect, 121, 259, 265

Hokoku-ji, 55–63

Honen Shonin, 294, 295, 298

Hongaku-ji, 277–78, 279
Honkoku-ji, 289–90
Horikawa, 47
Hoshi no Ido, 236
Hosokawa (lord), 289
Hoyake Amida, 66, 70

Ichiman, 273–74
Ienari, *see* Tokugawa Ienari
Ietoki, *see* Ashikaga Ietoki
Ietsuna, *see* Tokugawa Ietsuna
Ieyasu, *see* Tokugawa Ieyasu
Iijima, 238
Ikegami Munenaka, 268, 269
Imagawa Noritada, 47
Imaizumi, 117, 169
Inamuragasaki, 33, 36, 239, 247, 248
Inari (fox god), 61, 63, 208
Inu no Kami, 84
Ippen Shonin, 67, 118
Ishikiri-yama, 178
Ita no Tsubone, 203, 206
Ito (prince), 226, 312
Ito Sukechika, 22, 23
Iwadono, 53
Izayoi Nikki, 182

Jakushi Myojin, 275
Japan-British Exhibition, 166
Jewel-Crowned Amida (Jokomyo-ji), 183
Jigen (priest), 279
Jigokugayatsu, 110
Jikaku Taishi, 51, 305, 309
Jinmu-ji, 309–10
Jingo (empress), 94, 97

Jishu sect, 210
Jizo, 50, 168, 174, 178, 237
    Black, 85
    Protector of Children, 126, 180
    Thousand, 86, 113, 244
Jochi-ji, 168
Jodo sect, 294, 298, 299, 305
Joen (maker of idols), 125
Jogyo Bosatsu, 250
Jokomyo-ji, 183
Joko Shonin, 204
Jomyo-ji, 60–65
Josen-ji, (Taya), 313, 314
Jufuku-ji, 138, 172–78, 180
Juhachi-mawari, 73
Juichimen Kannon, 53, 228–30
Juni Shinsho, 83, 201, 284
Juntoku (emperor), 68, 138, 274
Juroku-ido, 201

Kabanekura, 40
Kagechika, *see* Oba Kagechika
Kagetoki, *see* Kajiwara Kagetoki
Kageyoshi, *see* Oba Kageyoshi
Kago Shaka, 174
Kaiko-San (Shin Hase-dera), 232
Kaishun-an, 116
Kaizo-ji, 190–202
Kajiwara Kagetoki, 27, 108, 312
Kajiwara Segaki, 108
Kakuon-ji, 82–90, 117, 171
Kamakura Shrine, 46, 78–81
Kamatari, *see* Fujiwara no Kamatari

Kamegayatsu, 70
Kame no Ido, 166
Kame no Ike, 116
Kameyama (emperor), 105, 227
Kamimura (admiral), 272
Kami no To, 296
Kanazawa, 55, 66, 71, 72, 214,
    311–12
Kanazawa Bunko, 311
Kanazawa Hakkei, 311
Kane-arai-sawa, 324
Kannon (Kanzeon), 56
    Eleven-faced, 46, 50, 51
    Goddess of Mercy, 51–53,
    106, 113, 122, 174
    Hase, 225–33
    Hundred at Engaku-ji, 135
    at Kaizo-ji, 210
    Protector of Terute, 212
    Thousand-handed (*see also*
    Senju Kannon): 74
    at Tokei-ji, 128
Kano Tanshin, 298
Kano Tan'yu, 298
Kanto, 27, 29, 34, 165
Karaito (tsuchi no ro), 59
Kariyagasaki, 232
Kasho, 174
Kasuga Myojin, 231, 303
Katase, 223, 251–52, 263, 264,
    316, 317–21, 322
Kato Kiyomasa, 105, 120
Kazan (emperor), 51
Kencho-ji, 60, 90, 107–22, 123,
    165, 192, 259, 325
Kencho Kokoku Zen-ji, 108
Kesa Gozen, 284–85

Kublai Khan, 132, 251
Kinkisan (Enoshima), 323
Kinubari-yama, 55, 58
Kishu Zenji, 294, 298
Kiso (Chinese emperor), 73
Kiso Yoshinaka, 59, 252
Kiyomori (Taira no Kiyomori),
    20, 21, 22, 25, 28, 30, 31
Kobo Daishi
    Daikoku (god), 226
    eighty-eight resting places of,
    82
    and Gokuraku-ji, 240, 243–
    44, 246
    gomadan, 87
    Jizo, 303
    Juroku-ido, 201
    and Kakuon-ji, 82
    Kojin and Fudo, 63
    Munetate-ido, 86
    ryōbu shintō, 96
    Shingon, 240
    and Shoju-in, 237
Kojin (god), 62, 63
Kokuzo-do, 236
Komyo-ji, 282, 293–308
Kondake, 309
Konpira, 178
Koremori (Taira no Koremori),
    28
Koshigoe, 248, 251
Kosoku-ji (Juniso), 66–71
Kosoku-ji (Hase), 223–24
Kotsubo, 238, 303, 304
Kugyo, 102–4
Kumano Gongen, 67, 213, 214,
    218, 219, 221

Kumanosha, 64
Kuro Jizo, 84
Kusari Taishi, 89
Kusunoki Masashige, 36, 105
Kuzuharagaoka, 188
Kuzuharagaoka Jinja, 187–89

Machi no Tsubone, 68–70
Manpuku-ji, 251–52
Maruyama, 106
Masako
    daughter of Tokimasa, 23,
        228
    and Gokuraku-ji, 244
    and Komyo-ji, 308
    marriage to Yoritomo, 23–25
    retirement of, 63
    and Shizuka Gozen, 162
    Yoritomo's consort, 61, 99,
        100, 172–78, 203, 222, 272
    Yoritomo's widow, 92
Masamune (swordsmith), 277
Masamura, *see* Hojo Masamura
Masashige, *see* Kusunoki
    Masashige
Matsubagayatsu, 259, 276, 287
Matsugaoka, 96
Meigetsu-in, 90, 163–67, 168,
    169
Meiji (emperor) 78, 104, 189
Michizane, *see* Sugawara no
    Michizane
Minami no Kata, 289
Minamoto (family, shoguns),
    19, 20, 26, 33, 51, 95, 97,
    102, 273
Minamoto no Noriyori, 312

Minamoto no Sanetomo
    and Amanawa Jinja, 222
    assassination of, 33, 84, 102–
        4, 274
    and Engaku-ji, 137, 138
    and Enoshima, 318
    and Gokuraku-ji, 244
    and Jomyo-ji, 61, 62
    and Jufuku-ji, 172–74
    pardon of Shibukawa, 46
    and Unkei (sculptor) 68
Minamoto no Yoriie, 47, 99,
    102, 273, 274
Minamoto no Yoritomo
    and Amanawa Jinja, 222
    and the Daibutsu, 203
    death of, 63, 67
    and death of Noriyori, 312
    and death of Yoshitsune,
        251, 252
    early years of, 272
    and Egara Tenjin, 43, 47
    at Enoshima, 321
    founder of Kamakura, 19–
        33, 172, 208
    and Fudaraku-ji, 128, 283–86
    and Hase-dera, 226
    at Inamuragasaki, 247
    and Shizuka Gozen, 161
    and Sugimoto-dera, 50
    and Tsurugaoka Hachiman
        Shrine, 95–99, 104
    tomb of, 91–93
Minamoto no Yoriyoshi, 20, 95,
    105
Minamoto no Yoshiie, 19, 180,
    222, 234

Minamoto no Yoshitomo, 19, 20, 21, 22, 29, 172
Minamoto no Yoshitsune, 29–31, 101, 105, 108, 166, 251, 252, 274
Mino no Tsubone, 127
Miroku Bosatsu, 228
Misaki, 238
Mitsukuni, *see* Tokugawa Mitsukuni
Mitsunori (Saishin), 223
Miura (peninsula), 238
Mochihito (prince), 26
Mochiuji, *see* Ashikaga Mochiuji
Mongaku Shonin (*see also* Endo Morita): 283–86, 321
Mongolian invasion, 241
Monju Bosatsu, 119, 129, 142, 174, 245, 296
Mori (prince), 92
Morinaga (prince), 78, 79, 80, 81, 105, 289–91
Morito, *see* Endo Morito
Motouji, *see* Ashikaga Motouji
Munekiyo, 21
Munetaka (prince), 165
Munetate-ido, 86
Musashi (province), 268, 272
Muso Kokushi, 73–75
Mutsu-ura (south of Kanazawa), 71
Myoho-ji, 287, 288–91
Myohon, 274
Myohon-ji, 272–76, 277
Myojin, 254
Myoken Bosatsu, 254
Myoko-ike, 135

Myoryu-ji, 271–78

Nabe Kanmuri (*see also* Nisshin): 278
Nagatoki, *see* Hojo Nagatoki
Nagoe, 273
Naito (family), 299, 302
Naka-aki (Nakahara Naka-aki), 103–4
Naki Yakushi, 202
Nameri River, 55, 64, 272
Naritoki, *see* Hojo Naritoki
Nariuji, *see* Ashikaga Nariuji
Nichiei (*see also* Ryogon Shinno): 278, 289–90
Nichigaku (*see also* Daigaku Saburo): 275
Nichiren
    attempted execution of, 253–64, 316
    final days of, 268–69
    at Katase, 249–51, 316
    and Kencho-ji, 121
    and Kosoku-ji, 223, 224
    at Reisangasaki, 238
    temples and relics of, 287–92
    tomb of, 277
Nichiro, 223, 224, 289
Nikaido, 128
Nikko Bosatsu, 83, 284
Nintoku (emperor), 97
Nio (Deva Kings, Indra and Brahma), 48, 104, 174, 203, 272, 273
Nisondo, 300–3
Nisshin, 223, 277
Nisshutsu, 245

Nitan no Shiro, 327
Nitta Yoshisada, 36–37, 101, 237, 244, 247, 248, 279, 314
Nojimasaki (Kanazawa), 214
Noken-do (Kanazawa), 311
Norikata, *see* Uesugi Norikata
Noritada, *see* Imagawa Noritada
Noriyori, *see* Minamoto no Noriyori
Norizane, *see* Uesugi Norizane
Nozu (General Count) 109

Oba Kagechika, 27
Oba Kageyoshi, 100
Odate Muneuji, 244
Oe Hiromoto, 92
Ofuna, 39, 117, 127, 313
Ofuna high road, 131, 163, 168, 169
Ogigayatsu, 172
Oguri Hangan, 211–21
Ojin (emperor), 94–97, 308
Okajima Yasoemon, 282
Okazaki Yoshizane, 172
Okura, 47, 82, 172
Okura Inari, 61
Okurayama, 91
Onikage, 211–21
Ono Goroemon, 204
Ota Dokan, 179
Otahime, 303
Otonashi fall, 249

Reisangasaki, 237–39
Reizei Tamesuke, *see* Fujiwara no Tamesuke

Rencho (priest, *see also* Nichiren): 258, 259
Renge-ji, 293
Rinzai sect, 60, 72
Rissho Ankoku Ron, 262
Rokkaku-do, 97
Roku-Jizo, 86
Ryochu (priest), 294, 295, 297, 299, 302, 308
Ryogon Shinno (*see also* Nichie): 289
Ryokan (Ninsho), 237, 238, 240–46
Ryugu-Kutsu, 302–3
Ryuko-ji, 252, 253–57, 264, 316
Ryuoden, 113
Ryuto no Matsu, 303

Sadatoki, *see* Hojo Sadatoki
Sagami (province), 212, 219
Sagami Bay, 90, 216, 232, 238, 317
Sagami River, 32
Saimyo-ji, 163, 165
Sai no Kawara, 86, 125
Saké no Miya, 106
Sanetoki, *see* Hojo Sanetoki
Sanetomo, *see* Minamoto no Sanetomo
Sarubatake, 267
Sasukegayatsu, 208, 293
Sasuke Inari, 203, 208
Sato Shichizaemon, 313
Senju Kannon, 53, 114
Shaka, 74
Shaka Sanzon, 296
Shaku Soen, 128, 146, 227

Shariden, 136, 139, 140, 142
Shichimen-do, 257
Shichirigahama, 132, 248, 251, 256, 264, 317
Shigefusa, *see* Uesugi Shigefusa
Shigetada, *see* Hatakeyama Shigetada
Shigetoki, *see* Hojo Shigetoki
Shigeyasu, *see* Hatakeyama Shigeyasu
Shijo Kingo, 223, 261, 263
Shimazu (prince), 92
Shimazu Tadahisa, 92
Shingon sect (Shingonshu), 88, 240–41
Shinmei-gu, 303
Shinsho, *see* Juni Shinsho
Shinto, 40, 78, 97, 104, 321
Shioname Jizo, 70
Shiragiku (acolyte), 326
Shirahataoka, 106
Shirahata-no-miya, 97
Shi Tenno, 296
Shizuka Gozen, 101,102
Shojoken, 116–17
Shojoko-ji (Fujisawa), 210
Shoju-in, 237
Shoko Shonin, 294, 295, 308
Shomu (emperor), 236
Shomyo-ji (Kanazawa), 312
Shotoku Taishi, 112–13, 280, 298
Shozuka no Baba, 125
Shuku-ryu-chi, 140
Sode no Ura, 248
Sodezuka, 273

Sogen (Chinese priest, *see also* Bukko Zenji, Chu Yuan): 140, 161–62, 166
Sokonuke Well, 201
Sugawara no Michizane, 43–47, 230, 245, 308
Sugimoto Kannon, 53–54
Sugiyama Kengyo, 322–23
Suiko (empress), 112
Sukechika, *see* Ito Sukechika
Suketomo, *see* Fujiwara no Suketomo
Sumiyoshi, 105
Suzuri no Ike, 251

Tadahisa, *see* Shimazu Tadahisa
Tada Manju, 51
Tadayoshi, *see* Ashikaga Tadayoshi
Taiheiki, 35, 187, 244, 318
Tainei-ji (Kanazawa), 312
Taira (family), 20, 23, 25, 26, 100, 284
Takatoki, *see* Hojo Takatoki
Takauji, *see* Ashikaga Takauji
Take no Gosho, 273, 274
Takeshiuchi no Sukune, 97
Takuma (sculptor), 50, 56, 83, 174
Tamamo (lady), 190–91
Tame-ie, *see* Fujiwara no Tame-ie
Tanabe no Ike, 249, 256
Tatsunokuchi, 253, 256
Taura, 309, 311
Taya no Dokutsu, 313–15
Teika, *see* Fujiwara no Teika

Tenman-gu, 45–47, 245
Tendai sect, 309
Tengen-in, 114
Tengu, 304
Tengu no Koshikake Matsu, 310
Tenjin, *see* Tenman-gu
Tensho Daijin, *see* Amaterasu
Tenshozan (Komyo-ji), 296
Tenshu (lady), 129, 130
Terute Hime (lady), 211–21
Tokei-ji, 127–30, 131
Tokimasa, *see* Hojo Tokimasa
Tokimune, *see* Hojo Tokimune
Tokiwa Gozen, 29, 30
Tokiyori, *see* Hojo Tokiyori
Tokiyoshi, *see* Hojo Tokiyoshi
Tokiyuki, *see* Hojo Tokiyuki
Tokudo Shonin 228, 230–33
Tokugawa (family, dynasty,
    shoguns), 38, 47, 77, 124,
    128, 206, 299, 300
Tokugawa Ienari, 96
Tokugawa Ietsuna, 300
Tokugawa Ieyasu, 110, 134, 179,
    275, 294, 299
Tokugawa Mitsukuni, 73
Tokugawa Tsunayoshi, 166
Tokugawa Yorifusa, 179
Tokuso Gongen, 280
Tosa Mitsuoki, 70, 308
Toshimoto, *see* Fujiwara no
    Toshimoto
Tosho-ji, 279
Tsukikagegayatsu, 182
Tsumekiri no Mandala, 278
Tsunayoshi, *see* Tokugawa
    Tsunayoshi

Tsunetoki, *see* Hojo Tsunetoki
Tsurugaoka, *see* Hachiman

Uda (emperor) 44, 230
Udaijin, 104
Uenogahara (near Fujisawa),
    213, 218
Uesugi (family), 38, 165, 311
Uesugi Norikata, 165, 167
Uesugi Norizane, 311
Uesugi Shigefusa, 165
Ujimitsu, *see* Ashikaga Ujimitsu
Ujinao, *see* Hojo Ujinao
Unkei (sculptor), 50, 63, 68, 82,
    96, 105, 113, 124, 125, 128,
    168, 284, 298

Waka-miya, 97, 99, 106
Wakasa no Tsubone, 273–76
Warai-botoke, 302
Washi no Mine, 90
Wataru (samurai), 284–85

Yahata no Yashiro, 94
Yakushi Myojin, Nyorai, 76, 82–
    84, 201, 202, 245, 300, 310
Yakushi Sanzon, 284
Yakushi-dogayatsu, 82
Yamada Kengyo, 324
Yanagiwara, 99
Yasutoki, *see* Hojo Yasutoki
Yodo (princess), 127
Yogenin (lady), 134
Yogo no Matsu, 114
Yokoyama, 212–17
Yomei (emperor), 248
Yorifusa, *see* Tokugawa Yorifusa

Yoriie, *see* Minamoto no Yoriie

Yoritomo, *see* Minamoto no
    Yoritomo

Yoritsune, *see* Fujiwara no
    Yoritsune

Yoriyoshi, *see* Minamoto no
    Yoriyoshi

Yoshida Shoin, 76

Yoshihisa, *see* Ashikaga
    Yoshihisa

Yoshiie, *see* Minamoto no
    Yoshiie

Yoshikane, *see* Ashikaga
    Yoshikane

Yoshikazu, *see* Hiki Yoshikazu

Yoshimasa, *see* Ashikaga
    Yoshimasa

Yoshimochi, *see* Ashikaga
    Yoshimochi

Yoshinaka, *see* Kiso Yoshinaka

Yoshisada, *see* Nitta Yoshisada

Yoshitoki, *see* Hojo Yoshitoki

Yoshitomo, *see* Minamoto no
    Yoshitomo

Yoshitsune, *see* Minamoto no
    Yoshitsune

Yugyo-ji (Fujisawa), 67, 210–21

Yui, 40, 274

Yuigahama, 39, 98, 99, 116, 138,
    178, 235

Yui Matsubei, 300

Yui Shosetsu, 300

Yukiaibashi, 249

Yukiaigawa, 264

Yukinoshita, 137, 273

Zaimokuza, 128, 283, 291, 293,
    305

Zazen 132, 142, 164, 201

Zendo (Chinese priest), 295,
    300, 301

Zendozuka, 295

Zeni-arai Benten, 203, 208

Zenko-ji, 165

Zen sect, 131–32, 173, 192, 261

Zuirokuzan (Engaku-ji), 134

Zuisen-ji, 58, 72–77

Zushi 53, 238, 266, 303, 309

Born on May 5, 1867, in Oxford, England, Iso Mutsu was destined to become the only Englishwoman to bear the title of countess in Meiji-era Japan. This remarkable development was a result of her meeting, and falling in love with, the diplomat Hirokichi Mutsu (son of the great Munemitsu Mutsu). Against the objections of both their families, the couple continued a courtship that lasted seventeen years until the resistance to their union was overcome.

The international marriage took place in London in 1905, and lasted nearly twenty-five years; she and her husband lived in Japan as well as several foreign countries. In deference to protocol she adopted a Japanese first name, choosing Iso, meaning the seaside.

In 1910, she returned with her husband to Japan. They settled in the quiet, historical town of Kamakura, and spent the rest of their lives there.

The Kamakura of Iso Mutsu's day was renowned for its beauty and tranquillity, not yet disturbed by modern development. She made her many visits into the countryside, she wrote, "for the indescribable atmosphere of peace and mystic remoteness from the things of the earth that seem to envelop . . . so many of these Old-World shrines and temples." On the basis of her explorations she wrote *Kamakura: Fact and Legend,* spending years of effort on the massive project.

The author's funeral was held June 10, 1930, at a Methodist church near the Mutsu-inaugurated school. After the usual hymns and benediction, the pastor allowed a high priest from the Buddhist temple of Engaku-ji to mount the pulpit, where he delivered words of praise for Iso and recited a sutra for the departed soul.

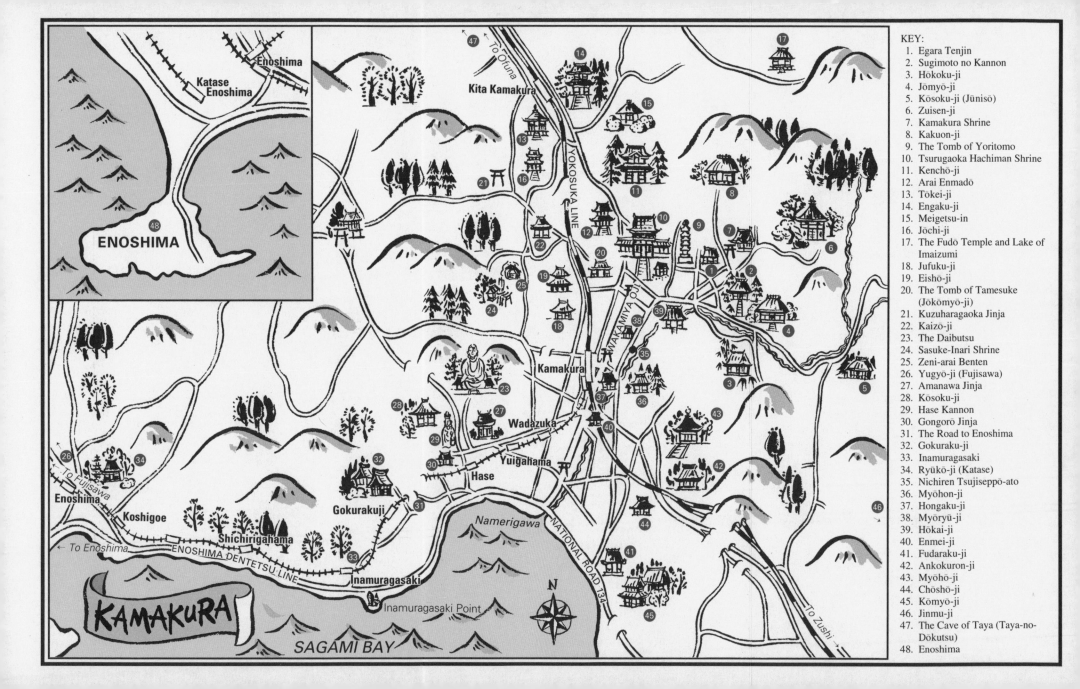

KAMAKURA

ENOSHIMA

Enoshima
Katase Enoshima

KEY:

1. Egara Tenjin
2. Sugimoto no Kannon
3. Hōkoku-ji
4. Jōmyō-ji
5. Kōsoku-ji (Jūnisō)
6. Zuisen-ji
7. Kamakura Shrine
8. Kakuon-ji
9. The Tomb of Yoritomo
10. Tsurugaoka Hachiman Shrine
11. Kenchō-ji
12. Arai Enmadō
13. Tōkei-ji
14. Engaku-ji
15. Meigetsu-in
16. Jōchi-ji
17. The Fudō Temple and Lake of Imaizumi
18. Jufuku-ji
19. Eishō-ji
20. The Tomb of Tamesuke (Jōkōmyō-ji)
21. Kuzuharagaoka Jinja
22. Kaizō-ji
23. The Daibutsu
24. Sasuke-Inari Shrine
25. Zeni-arai Benten
26. Yugyō-ji (Fujisawa)
27. Amanawa Jinja
28. Kōsoku-ji
29. Hase Kannon
30. Gongorō Jinja
31. The Road to Enoshima
32. Gokuraku-ji
33. Inamuragasaki
34. Ryūkō-ji (Katase)
35. Nichiren Tsujiseppō-ato
36. Myōhon-ji
37. Hongaku-ji
38. Myōryū-ji
39. Hōkai-ji
40. Enmei-ji
41. Fudaraku-ji
42. Ankokuron-ji
43. Myōhō-ji
44. Chōshō-ji
45. Kōmyō-ji
46. Jinmu-ji
47. The Cave of Taya (Taya-no-Dōkutsu)
48. Enoshima

To Ōfuna

Kita Kamakura

YOKOSUKA LINE

WAKAMIYA ŌJI

Kamakura

Wadazuka

Yuigahama

Hase

Gokurakuji

Shichirigahama

ENOSHIMA DENTETSU LINE

Inamuragasaki

Inamuragasaki Point

Koshigoe

← To Enoshima

Enoshima

To Fujisawa

Namerigawa

NATIONAL ROAD 134

To Zushi

N

SAGAMI BAY